A DISASTER OF OUR OWN MAKING

A DISASTER OF OUR OWN MAKING: HOW THE WEST LOST UKRAINE

BRANDON J. WEICHERT

Encounter
BOOKS

NEW YORK • LONDON

2024

First American edition published in 2024 by Encounter Books,
an activity of Encounter for Culture and Education, Inc.,
a nonprofit, tax-exempt corporation.
Encounter Books website address: www.encounterbooks.com

Manufactured in Canada and printed on acid-free paper.
The paper used in this publication meets the minimum requirements
of ANSI/NISO Z39.48–1992 (R 1997)
(Permanence of Paper).

FIRST AMERICAN EDITION

LIBRARY OF CONGRESS CATALOGING-IN-PUBLICATION DATA

Information for this title can be found at the
Library of Congress website under the following
ISBN 978-1-64177-409-3 and LCCN 2024032479.

For Angelo Codevilla,
who taught me how to really see the world.
You tragically left us when we most needed you.
Your wisdom is greatly missed.

TABLE OF CONTENTS:

BORNE BACK CEASELESSLY INTO THE PAST

by Curt Mills

"RUSSIA, RUSSIA, RUSSIA," the forty-fifth president of the United States once bemoaned, overtaxed from answering questions on the subject.

The gargantuan gangster's paradise that is Russia—famously a participant in nearly half the world's twenty-four time zones—has been the uninvited duet partner of American politics over the last decade. Though an engrossing and sibylline civilization, many Americans are simply exhausted from discussing it.

For Western uber-hawks, the recent months of war in Ukraine has failed to be much of a follow-up to the sugar rush of apparent vindication provided by Russia's botching of the first year of battle. For foreign policy restrainers, the stalemate (or something far worse) out East is another coming rhetorical and theoretical win—but also evidence of the distance they must march to acquire true power for their perspective.

For the once and future president, the libelous yet widespread belief he is in cahoots with the Kremlin continues to blot both his legacy and psyche. For left-liberal true believers, Vladimir Putin's seeming invincibility augurs the coming of a global Alt Right.

How did we get here?

Brandon J. Weichert is a cartographer of familiar, but dangerous terrain. Discussing the history of the elective, creeping expansion of the North Atlantic Treaty Organization (NATO) after the collapse of communism and the total victory of the West is to venture into a land where many deal falsely.

In his *jihad* against the forty-second president, the late provocateur Christopher Hitchens famously observed of Bill Clinton's "triangulations" that the Arkansan had "no one left to lie to" by the end of his reign. That diagnosis is generally applied to the last president of the twentieth century's domestic dealings, and his personal conduct.

But Weichert innovates by fleshing out the implications of Clinton's character on the world stage, singling out a forgotten episode for discussion. Weichert highlights the small matter of Kiev's nukes after the fall of the Iron Curtain. Clinton badgered the new Ukrainian state to disarm.

"The West, with its superior technological prowess, could have contributed to this Ukrainian push for alternative command-and-control capabilities that, over time, would have ensured that Ukraine had a reliable, robust nuclear deterrent," our author writes.

We are now in an era where previous, non-market participants such as the Kingdom of Saudi Arabia, and Japan, are sniffing around the worldwide nuclear bazaar. But Weichert urges us to consider a counter-history where balance of power realism was explored closer to its zenith. Says Weichert: "The Clinton administration saw only what was right in front of them. They pressured and cajoled Kiev into giving up what was probably the only thing that ultimately could have prevented the kind of conflict that now rages between Russia and Ukraine." And: "By 2023, Ukraine's sacrifice of their independent nuclear arsenal on the altar of global disarmament was obviously an awful decision."

Clinton is an easy target, but George W. Bush is easier still.

"At the start of Putin's rule [on the last day of 1999], he made Russian laws comport with European Union standards and ensured that Russia became a partner to NATO," Weichert reports. Even after the saber-rattling and mistrust of the 1990s—which included NATO intervention against Serbia, the historic Russian protectorate the defense of which set off World War I—a much-greener Putin was of an open (and perhaps sounder) mind.

"The real kicker during this time was the way Putin described Ukraine's potential accession into the NATO alliance as a 'positive development,'" Weichert spells out in bold. "What's more, while Putin was never one for liberal democracy of the kind the West practiced, there is little doubt that the Russian strongman began his journey as leader of Russia being at least friendly with the general concept of democracy."

Gone today is the *Tamagotchi* era of good feelings we experienced at the turn of the century. Colder realities reign. "The same way the Americans viewed Soviet missiles in Cuba or how U.S. officials would view a Mexico that joined a Russian military alliance today, is how the Putin government views a Ukraine that is in NATO's orbit."

But the big kahuna in this story is an item of arguable lore. Yet Weichert is a believer.

In lazy tellings, Washington and London are most often presented as lockstep *brat'ya po oruzhiyu*—brothers in arms. Like many marriages, it is unhappy in its own way. In his memoir, the forty-first president George H.W. Bush wrote that his counterpart, the British Prime Minister Margaret Thatcher, was "principled' but "very difficult" and "talks all the time."

Weichert would say that was true to form:

"Once the Berlin Wall fell in 1989, American and Western leaders began grappling with the prospect of fundamental geopolitical changes (and challenges) emanating from Eastern Europe. ... For her part, Prime Minister Thatcher aimed to keep 'the Warsaw Pact [as a] fig leaf for [Soviet leader Mikhail Gorbachev].'"

President Bush was not galvanized. He took matters into his own hands. Or at least, he entrusted the portfolio to his own *Sovietnik,* the iconic James Baker (then secretary of State).

At a summit in Ottawa, "Baker supposedly hatched what, in some circles, has become derisively known as the 'cocktail napkin agreement.' The basis of that informal agreement was James Baker's promise that, if Gorbachev pulled Red Army forces from East Germany, then NATO would not move eastward one inch."

We are reliant on perhaps Zapruder-tier evidence, but Weichert says alternative explanations enter the realm of fantasy.

"Baker is quoted at that meeting as assuring Gorbachev that, 'neither [President Bush] nor I intend to extract any unilateral advantages from the processes that are taking place' and that "Americans understood that 'not only for the Soviet Union but for other European countries as well it is important to have guarantees that if the United States keeps its presence in Germany within the framework of NATO, not an inch of NATO's present military jurisdiction will spread in an eastern direction.'"

What went wrong?

For many foreign policy realists, George H.W. Bush's administration remains the last, great example of American sobriety in decades. (Others see vindication now from the Trump years and a promise for the future.) The intervening twenty-four years, then, were a hijack job.

"These policy leaders, the neoconservative-neoliberal cabal, shared a universal disdain for Russia and a desire to effectively bust post-Cold War Russia apart into its constituent components. It wasn't enough to have deprived Moscow of its empire (which needed to happen). Instead, the neocon-neolib element abandoned all pretense of proportion and reason and embraced a maximalist approach that was designed to collapse Russia itself."

If such thinkers are ever called to account, Weichert would be more sparing and diplomatic in his judgment than many. Others would leave European security solely to the Europeans.

When Putin barged further into Ukraine in 2022, Weichert denounced the invasion in scalding terms and compared it to the folly of George W. Bush's invasion of Iraq. That this hawks-of-hawks cadre on the Ukraine war have now firmly isolated themselves from a writer as fair-minded as Weichert speaks to their escalating, dangerous isolation from reality.

What is to be done? Only conducting a reality check, says our author.

"Russia does not need to negotiate. They can just wait out the Ukrainians," he diagnoses starkly. The Kyiv forces "are already crumbling before the sustained pressure Russia is exerting on Kiev's forces on the frontlines. With American aid slowed, critical gaps in Ukraine's ailing defenses will be revealed, leaving Moscow's forces with a key moment of opportunity. That is, unless the Americans and the rest of NATO come rushing in to fight."

Total war, or perhaps, total collapse? These are the options the U.S. is staring down after thirty-five years of being on a primacist bender in Eurasia?

Weichert is clear about what America must *not* do: escalate over Crimea, specifically, which he says is a clear Russia "red line." If crossed, the Kremlin will contemplate using the bomb on the field. "And the Americans and their NATO allies keep ignoring Russia. ... They do not understand that Russia is prepared for any contingency."

Weichert sees a Prime Mover.

"NATO is now the vehicle of instability in Europe. It has expanded five times in thirty-three years, even after it had assured post-Soviet Russian leaders that it'd not do so. The war in Ukraine is entirely the result of NATO expansion."

Most commendable for a policy expert, Weichert is not allergic to real politics. "In fact, if [Donald] Trump is reelected, we may get lucky enough to either freeze the operations of NATO or disband the organization altogether—in favor of a defensive alliance that doesn't engender the kind of war it was supposed to be preventing."

CURT MILLS *is Executive Director of* The American Conservative *in Washington, D.C. He is a foreign policy and campaign writer. He has reported for* Politico, *the* National Interest, *and* The Spectator, *and is a former Robert Novak journalism fellow. He writes on X at @curtmills.*

INTRODUCTION

THE HUBRIS OF NATO

"THE GOD-KING has betrayed a fatal flaw: hubris." Those words were spoken by one of the Greek Spartan warriors when describing the Persian king, Xerxes, the villain in Zach Snyder's 2006 film, *300*. Hubris is an excellent word to keep in mind when speaking of human conflict. The word "hubris" is derived from the ancient Greek word *hybris* which means "excessive pride toward or defiance of the gods, leading to nemesis."

For a deeper understanding of the word "hubris," we should consider the meaning of the term, "nemesis." Those of us weaned on the unhealthy admixture of Hollywood films and cheap comic books think of the word "nemesis" means villain or, a bad guy. Darth Vader, Khan Noonien Singh, and Thanos are all examples that come to mind when Americans hear the word "nemesis." But that just shows our weak understanding of the word.

The true meaning of nemesis is simply, "the inescapable agent of someone or something's downfall." Interestingly, the Oxford online dictionary has an additional listing for "nemesis." According to Oxford, a term synonymous with "nemesis" is "retributive justice." By the way, a retributive justice system is one in which offenders are punished rather than rehabilitated.[1]

[1]

In other words, hubris leads to *punishment* for the person or group that has displayed hubris.

The current war between NATO-backed Ukraine and the Russian Federation today is chock full hubris. Wars, according to the father of the study of history, Thucydides, are generally fought for three reasons: fear, honor, and interest.[2] But who, or better yet, what, started the war in Ukraine? In between our exhortations of a global democracy and "human rights for all," we in the West believe that we know the answer. The reason Europe has been plunged into a major war in Ukraine is because the Russians and, specifically, the villainous Vladimir Putin, woke up one day, and wanted to slay Captain America and his fellow Avengers in Europe.[3]

Some version of this childlike morality play is the version of events playing in the background for most Americans and Europeans when they think of the war—if they think about it at all. And I can assure you that most of the leaders in the West would prefer their populations didn't think much about the ordeal tearing Ukraine apart.[4] One must wonder how that comports with their comic-book telling of events. After all, true heroes fight in the light while villains are the ones who prefer to skulk about in the darkness.

One can place hubris somewhere between Thucydides' understanding of fear and honor. It is a key element among the causes of warfare, both in Thucydides' time and in our own.[5] In fact, the theme of unchecked pride and ambition inspired the greatest of Greek writers, such as Aeschylus and Sophocles, and it was often a key element of classic Greek tragedies. Here again, the wisdom of the ancients surpasses our own understanding in the present.[6] In this conflict, however, the Americans and their NATO allies have been the ones most often displaying hubris. Since the fall of the Soviet Union and end of the Cold War in 1991, this hubris has been creating the conditions for the current war in Europe.[7]

Of course, the Russians have had a role to play as well. They are not innocent in this affair. Rarely in history are there clear "good guys" versus "bad guys" scenarios. This is another fictional worldview that American pop culture has inculcated in the masses. Still, some bear greater responsibility than others for the unfolding disaster in Ukraine such as those who possessed greater agency to impose their twisted visions for the future on the world. And in the aftermath of the Cold War, when Russia was laid low, there was little Moscow could do to implement any of its notions concerning imperial policy for the former Soviet states.

It must be understood that the Russia of today, for a variety of reasons *is not* the Soviet Union of yesteryear. My late colleague, Angelo Codevilla, put it best when he assessed that:

> *Russia is no more willing to conquer Europe than it is able. Willingness and ability had stemmed from the communist political apparatus that ruled the USSR and projected itself throughout the world. Sister communist parties and front groups made significant portions of foreign countries—especially European ones—positively eager for Soviet domination. The Soviet armed forces, already in control of Eastern and Central Europe, were well equipped to take, if not to hold, the rest. Now, the political infrastructure—the party that decided things in Moscow and the communist-friendly apparatus in Europe—is gone. Nobody in the West envies Russia. Russian influence in Europe now stems from Europe's reliance on Russian natural gas and from the opportunities for corruption that this entails.[8]*

SINCE THE END of the Cold War, Russia's population has contracted significantly. It has also become riven with ethno-religious tensions within its borders. From Russia's southern periphery, masses of Muslims have emigrated to Russia. Today there are so many Muslims living within Russia's borders that Moscow is now the European city with the largest Muslim population.[9] As a result, over the last 20 years—notably during Russia's conflict with Chechnya in the late 1990s and early 2000s—Islamic extremist violence has increased exponentially within the country. Meanwhile, in Russia's underpopulated (though resource-rich) Far East, waves of illegal Chinese immigrants have overwhelmed Russian territory.[10] This, too, is changing Russia fundamentally. Codevilla predicted that Moscow might expel the Muslim regions entirely from their federation or simply fence them off.[11] For my part, I have long speculated that Russia is set to lose its Far East to a resurgent China by the end of this century.

As for Russia's post-Cold War military, it had been a shambles until very recently. If anything, the Ukraine War has forced Russia to adapt quickly and implement much needed reforms to their sclerotic system in order to remain combat effective. My colleague Lee Slusher, a former intelligence analyst for the U.S. government with extensive experience handling the Russia portfolio, believes that Russia has fared far better than Western media sources are claiming in the ongoing Ukraine War. In fact, according to Slusher, Russia's military has outperformed the NATO-backed Ukrainians at every turn in the conflict—and will continue to do so, the longer that the horrible conflict rages.[12]

Regarding the modern Russian military, Codevilla believed that the force was "configured for area-denial rather than for projection of power. The Russian military establishment, unlike that of the tsars and of the Soviets, emphasizes technology to economize manpower that, for the first time, is scarce and precious in Russia. Russia's reliance on nuclear weapons recalls nothing so much as the 1950s Eisenhower doctrine of 'more bang for the buck.'"[13] Russia as a more defensive-minded power is, of course, something that the mainstream Western elite refuse to see. After all, Russia did invade Ukraine. But, as the February 2024 Tucker Carlson-Vladimir Putin interview showed: Russia viewed Ukraine (at least Eastern Ukraine and Crimea) as existing within its borders.[14] And as this work will demonstrate, Moscow was at least willing to accept Ukraine as an independent state, so long as it did not consider joining NATO. The deteriorating state of Russia's demography lends further credence to Codevilla's claims that Russia is defensive-minded by necessity rather than choice.

Sadly, it was NATO members—specifically the Americans and their British partners—who agitated for the current situation. There exists a group of mid-level, politically connected policymakers within the bureaucracy in Washington, D.C. who have been there from the end of the Cold War until the present. It was these elements in the U.S. government who set the current policies toward Russia in the wake of the Cold War. Former President Donald J. Trump derisively referred to this group as the "Deep State." Some have described this cabal as being part of the "Administrative State." Still others have called this group the "uniparty." Gary Dorrien named this relatively obscure element of powerful bureaucrats in our national security state the "Democratic-Globalists."[15] They are the neoconservative and neoliberal leaders who worked for both Republican and Democratic Party presidents following the Cold War and who share a maximalist vision of protecting U.S. interests abroad. This group also has undying enmity toward Russia.[16] And, as you'll read, they adhere to a quasi-religious commitment to NATO expansion.

This neoconservative-neoliberal cabal possesses one key attribute, what the Greeks in Zach Snyder's *300* called a "fatal flaw." They have a strong case of hubris. The people who belong to this group write lovingly of the need for an American empire (abandoning any pretense of America's republican founding). They speak dismissively of our allies. The democratic-globalists believe in a borderless world dominated by financial interests, with the United States sitting atop the system, always seeking out the next great threat, and preempting those threats, no matter how small or weak they are before those supposed threats can materialize.[17] Thus, threats such as Russia, which after the Cold War was a broken down, desiccated husk of a once-great country, becomes a de facto villain.

When the hammer-and-sickle came down for the final time over the Kremlin on December 25, 1991, no one could have imagined that a war between NATO and Russia would come *after* that momentous event. Peace, we were told, was at hand. The U.S. president during the final moments of the Soviet Union's existence, George H.W. Bush, assured uneasy Americans that the "rule of law" would replace "the law of the jungle" in some magnificent new world order.[18] The neoliberals predicted the "end of history" at the end of the Cold War. All major differences and conflicts would be subordinated to the economic and political realms. Warfare, as we understood it, was over because all major ideological questions had been resolved with the ultimate victory of liberal democratic capitalism over communism.

But hubris can turn heroes into villains overnight.

Instead of viewing the end of the Cold War as a chance for America to get back to being a country unpreoccupied with foreign affairs, as many Americans at the time wanted, the "democratic-global-ist" cabal—the permanent bipartisan fusion party, as my colleague Michael Walsh has described them—seized it as an opportunity to exploit Russia's weakness and amplify U.S. power. And while that all may sound good on paper (indeed, it was written down in a wild document that became known as "Rebuilding America's Defenses" by a now defunct think tank known as the Project for the New American Century), the reality was much more complex.[19]

In fact, a great debate raged at the dawn of the post-Cold War era. People like former Reagan administration UN ambassador, Jeanne Kirkpatrick and former Nixon administration speechwrit-er, Pat Buchanan, argued that the United States needed to become a "normal country in a normal time." The United States needed to pay much closer heed to the problems at home and distance itself from the rest of the world. Kirkpatrick argued that, "a good society is defined not by its foreign policy but by its internal qualities." As Kirkpatrick assessed, "foreign policy becomes a major aspect of a so-ciety only if its government is expansionist, imperialist, aggressive, or when it is threatened by aggression."[20]

On the other side of the debate were thinkers like the late Charles

Krauthammer and former George H.W. Bush administration official, Bill Kristol. Countering Kirkpatrick's astute arguments were
the impassioned calls from Krauthammer in the pages of *Foreign
Affairs* for Washington to exploit what he called America's "unipolar moment." Krauthammer supposed that by enhancing America's
relative power in the aftermath of the Cold War, the United States
could retain its dominant global status and prevent any new Soviet
Union-like threat from arising in the future.[21]

Rather than begin the process of looking inward to enhance
American life and ignore the siren song of excessive foreign en-
tanglements, Washington's policymakers heeded Krauthammer's
calls. For a while it seemed like the plan was working. An aggressive
policy of breaking down all global trade barriers was undertaken.
Meanwhile forceful democracy and human rights promotion became America's *sine qua non* in foreign policy in the post-Cold War
era. The elite who believed this claptrap also assumed that by liberalizing trade with China, they would bloodlessly cause China to
change its communist regime in favor of a democratic government
that supported capitalism. In fact, the only thing accomplished by
increasing trade with Beijing was enriching the Chinese—making
China, and *not* the United States, very wealthy and powerful.[22]

As for Russia, weakened and adrift after its defeat in the Cold War,
the Americans would ensure the old bear could never threaten its
neighbors again by encircling the defeated Russia and pressuring it
until it broke apart into smaller countries that could then be more
easily controlled. In fact, the greatest obstacle to the Western grand
strategy of breaking Russia apart forever (if one can even call what
we have pursued in Russia a "grand" strategy) has been Vladimir
Putin's regime. In 2022, writing at the blog for the *London School of
Economics*, Robert Wade describes his belief that NATO maneuvered
Russia into attacking Ukraine so as to have a pretext to implement
its long-standing fantasy of overthrowing the Putinist regime and
replacing it with something far more amenable.

Thus, the neoconservative-neoliberal obsession with regime change in every so-called autocratic state around the globe, the kind of plan that was instituted in Iraq in 2003, is very much still in effect with the much larger, nuclear-armed Russia today. Wade assessed that, "As the Afghanistan insurgency [during the Soviet-Afghan War in the 1980s] against the Soviet military helped to bring down the Soviet Union, the Western strategists hope that the Ukrainian insurgency against the bogged-down Russian military will help end the Putin regime."[23] Of course, at no point in these discussions has the neocon-neolib cabal questioned what happens if someone nastier than Putin replaces him?[24] What's more, if any nation in this fight is akin to the Soviet Union, it is, unfortunately, the United States which has painfully overextended itself in Ukraine and is now losing—with that likely defeat having immense implications far beyond the borders of tiny Ukraine.

U.S. power projection in Europe has been conducted via multilateral institutions, notably NATO (the European Union has also been a conduit for U.S. power). NATO, which had basically become the equivalent of a headless chicken the moment the Soviet Union was vanquished and the Cold War ended, was only more than happy to embrace the neocon-neolib cabal's ideas. It was entirely self-serving. After all, NATO had become a massive, multilateral bureaucracy in search of meaning. What would it do now that its favorite enemy, the Soviet Union, was no more? A rational person might have argued that it was time for NATO to disband, for European security to be left to the Europeans and the Russians, and for the Americans to go home. But that wasn't to be.

NATO, a true hero of the Cold War, has become the villain in the post-Cold War era. In searching for its new purpose, NATO settled on repurposing its old *raison d'être*. Sure, the Soviets were gone. Although, the Russians remained. The incorporation of many former Eastern European Soviet states ensured that a post-Cold War NATO would take on the preferences or, rather, the fears

and resentments of the nations that were at that point most recently oppressed and tortured by the Russians. Historical resentments
between Russia and Eastern European states run deep. It was not
only during the Cold War that these countries hated each other. Their dislike goes back centuries, as you will read in the second
chapter of this work.

To compound matters, as you will soon read in this book, NATO
had vowed not to expand beyond their 1991 borders. This was an
important development because the Red Army had famously and
unilaterally withdrawn its forces from Eastern Europe based large-
ly on informal guarantees made by American and Western leaders
vowing not to expand NATO closer to Russia's borders. In the post-
Cold War era, though, the cabal running Washington realized that
post-Soviet Russia was far too weak to do anything other than complain about NATO reneging on its promises to Moscow. Thus, this
cabal went about remaking the world (or trying to) as they saw fit.

After more than thirty years of this hubris, the results of their failures are seen and felt on every continent. These failures will reso-
nate throughout the age. Further, their stated goal of maximizing
American security by enhancing its global dominance has actually
done more to weaken the United States than anything Russia, China,
Iran, or al Qaeda could have done to America.[25] As I write in 2024,
we are at the precipice of these policies reaching the nadir of their
failure in the form of a likely nuclear third world war with Russia
over Ukraine. None of this was necessary and much of it could have
been avoided or, at least, mitigated if America and its NATO partners had simply lived up to the promises they made at the end of the
Cold War to ensure peace.

But hubris rarely adheres to reason. And, as the ancient Greeks
showed us repeatedly, it leads to the destruction of the one who displays hubris. Like ancient Athens, the United States has become an
aggressive democracy bent on domination. Internally, America is a
den of political and social instability. Externally, the United States

has spent the post-Cold War era forcing itself upon other nations that would have been better left alone.

Like ancient Athens with their Delian League, America spent the last thirty-three years compelling smaller states that were little more than vassals—notably in Europe—to stay inside the NATO and EU circle. Just as with the Delian League, NATO has become nothing more than a means to extend America's power far beyond its borders. And, as Athens did, America has pushed itself too far: It is overextended, and now faces the wrath of a coalition of rivals whose only common trait is a deep aversion to the world that the United States has been trying to build since the end of the Cold War—the world of the neocon-neolib cabal.

Ultimately, ancient Athens went too far. They angered the other Greek city-states that were not democratic, such as the powerful city-state of Sparta. Like Russia today, Sparta wanted the other city-states to leave it alone. They were an authoritarian culture, too. It was Athens' constant prodding along the periphery of what Sparta considered to be its territory, as well as Athens' incessant attacks against territories and peoples aligned with Sparta, that prompted Sparta to counterattack Athens. Sparta ultimately forged an alliance of fellow anti-Athenian, authoritarian city-states similarly threatened by Athens' totalitarian democracy.

The Peloponnesian War erupted, and the autocratic Spartans defeated Athens. The Athenians had been done in by their hubris. Their Delian League could not save them. Nor could Athens negotiate a settlement because Sparta and its allies had been so agitated by Athens they did not trust that democracy to behave even after a settlement was reached. Today, the matter of Ukraine's entrance into NATO serves as the spark for a wider conflict between militaristic, authoritarian Russia and the totalitarian democracy of the West. This conflict could see the end of NATO and the U.S.-led world order, unless a fundamentally different approach to Europe, Ukraine, Russia, and NATO expansion are embraced quickly by those in Washington.

Such an adjustment can only come with the rise of a new leadership that is totally divorced from the preferences and ideology of the cabal that has run Washington since the end of the Cold War.

Therefore, the 2024 presidential election in which former President Donald Trump and current Vice President Kamala Harris are facing each other is likely the most consequential U.S. presidential election in the last century. Harris, who swapped out with current President Joe Biden at the last minute will continue, and possibly worsen, the ongoing Ukraine War. Trump is rightly skeptical of NATO expansionism. What's more, Trump seeks to achieve that which Jeanne Kirkpatrick argued for in her 1990 essay, "A Normal Country in a Normal Time." Biden and his successor, Kamala Harris, on the other hand, are one hair-trigger away from starting a direct conflict with Russia over Ukraine's fate, and it could very well lead to a devastating nuclear world war.

As you will read in this book, Joe Biden and his family have been heavily involved in potentially elicit activities in Ukraine for years. Kamala Harris, meanwhile, has an ideological commitment to Ukraine that could see the United States pushed into a direct confrontation with Russia over Ukraine.

The hubris of America's elite is such that they would absolutely risk direct nuclear confrontation with Moscow over Ukraine rather than reassess their preferred policy and make radical changes to that program. Hubris, as always, kills the one who is engaged in such unacceptable behavior. In this case, sadly, it is America and NATO.

BRANDON J. WEICHERT
February 10, 2024
Naples, Florida

[A DISASTER OF OUR OWN MAKING

CHAPTER 1
FROM COLD WAR TO COLD PEACE

IN 1939, as World War II was just beginning, Winston Churchill was asked how the Soviet Union might respond to the threat of Hitler's Germany. Churchill's response was classic. "Russia," Churchill stated, "is a riddle wrapped in a mystery inside an enigma."[1] The West has long viewed Russia—whether it was the Russian Empire, the Soviet Union, or today's Russian Federation—with suspicion. A long history of hostility exists between the West and Russia that is hard to overcome. But if there was one moment in time when that tradition of hostility could have been replaced by a new era of amity between the West and Russia, it was in the aftermath of the Cold War.

In 1994, not even three years after the collapse of the USSR and the end of the Cold War, Russia's liberal president, Boris Yeltsin, exploded at his American counterpart, President Bill Clinton, at a security conference in Budapest. Yeltsin, who was known for having an exceptionally close friendship with Clinton and an affinity for Western democracy and capitalism, raged against what he saw as Washington's attempt to "split [Europe] again."[2] At issue was the expansion of NATO (as well as the EU) into the former Soviet republics of Eastern Europe. Clinton wanted a dual-track policy by which Washington would engage Moscow while also expanding NATO's reach and pull in Europe—right up to Russia's borders. Even for a pro-Western Russian leader, like Yeltsin, such Western actions were highly provocative.

At Budapest in 1994, Yeltsin explained how America's push to expand NATO into Eastern Europe was breaking the post-Cold War peace that he and others envisaged reigning in Europe. For Yeltsin, America's tireless quest for NATO to encompass all of Europe represented the gravest strategic threat imaginable. After all, Russia was not a member of NATO. In the post-Cold War era, NATO increasingly was viewed as little more than an extension of U.S. power in Europe. "No major country would live in isolation and any country would reject such a game itself," Yeltsin chided his Western audience at Budapest. To his friend and partner in peace, Clinton, the Russian leader inquired, "Why sow the seeds of mistrust?" Yeltsin then cautioned his ambivalent audience that, "Europe has not yet freed itself from the heritage of the Cold War [and] is in danger of plunging into a cold peace."[3]

The day after Yeltsin's fiery comments, a *New York Times* headline bleated in big, bold letters that, "YELTSIN SAYS NATO IS TRYING TO SPLIT THE CONTINENT AGAIN!"[4] A few days later, another *New York Times* headline read, "The World: Why Russia Still Bangs Its Shoe," a clear reference to the moment when Soviet Premier Nikita Khrushchev infamously stood before the United Nations General Assembly holding a shoe and vowed to "bury" the West, banging the shoe on the podium as he spoke.[5] If Yeltsin's comments were inflammatory, the Western press fanned the flames with their biased reporting. Specifically, the framing of Yeltsin's comments as harkening back to the heady days of the Cold War.

In fact, Yeltsin, while speaking frankly at a diplomatic conference—an act that the global elite automatically find offensive—was *not* threatening the West. He was trying to warn them about the way their actions were being viewed back in Russia. While NATO expansion may have been popular in the West, it was viewed with much concern by ordinary Russians and those who ran the country from the Kremlin at the time. Plus, Yeltsin was witnessing the rise of seri-ous political opposition from undemocratic elements.[6] The Russian nationalist-imperialist element threatened Yeltsin's proto-democra-cy. These forces wanted to break from the West, restore lost Russian greatness, and use force against both their foreign and domestic en-emies, if necessary. The perception of NATO as a growing threat to Russia helped to fuel these forces within Russia's polity.

Yeltsin was playing to domestic audiences with his speech. What's more, though, he was trying to send a message to Clinton. But Bill Clinton was not listening. No one in a position of leadership in the West really understood what Yeltsin was doing. They treated the Russian leader like a punchline simply because Yeltsin was a notori-ous alcoholic ruling a broken-down country. A sense of Hegelian de-terminism had also taken hold in the West as it related to NATO ex-pansion in Europe. The neoliberal and neoconservative triumphalists in Washington and Brussels could not fathom that the Russian leader was acting on his own agency. To these Western leaders, NATO ex-pansion would occur because it was a law of nature that NATO must expand. As Clinton himself had said at the Budapest conference, "No country will be allowed to veto [NATO] expansion."[7]

The Budapest conference was not a mere blip in an otherwise healthy relationship between post-Cold War Russia and the West—although, many Western leaders at the time did not see this. For his part, British Prime Minister John Major privately told advisers and reporters alike that Budapest was an isolated event, and that Russia was onboard with NATO expansion. President Clinton had long in-sisted that Yeltsin was in agreement with his plans to simultaneously expand NATO and engage with Russia.[8] None of these leaders took a moment to ask themselves why any foreign leader would welcome the expansion of a powerful military alliance to encompass lands along their exposed border.

Rather than listen to Yeltsin's concerns, after the conference, Clinton fumed to his aides about the incident. Bill Clinton was probably the greatest politician of his generation, certainly of his party. But this meant that he viewed everything through the prism of politics and the jockeying that occurs within that framework. So instead of understanding what happened as Yeltsin sincerely raising concerns that NATO expansion might be too provocative, as Yeltsin explicitly said it was, Clinton fretted to his advisers about how he was being "used" by Yeltsin. It turned out that President Clinton had not originally been scheduled to attend the conference and only did so because Yeltsin had pleaded with Clinton to come and signal his solidarity with the embattled Russian president. Clinton believed he had been set up by Yeltsin. The Russian leader needed to boost his flagging ratings at home and what better way to do that than by beating up on the U.S. president in public?

At no point, apparently, did Clinton believe that his administration's zealous commitment to NATO expansion could be a real source of concern for the Russian leadership. It was all political maneuvering for domestic purposes, all the time. But Yeltsin, in fact, *was* concerned about U.S. support for NATO expansion. Even before the contentious Budapest Conference in 1994, Bill Clinton and Boris Yeltsin exchanged a series of letters in which Yeltsin, in a more polite tone, expressed his concern and frustration over NATO expansion into territories bordering Russia. There was concern over the Clinton administration's rhetoric which called for cautious expansion as that rhetoric bumped up against the reality that was America's support for expedited NATO membership for former Soviet states. There was a growing fear among the Russians that "policy entrepreneurs" were "revving up the bureaucratic process for more rapid NATO enlargement than expected by either Moscow or the Pentagon."[9]

As you will read in the following chapters, there is a cabal of neoconservative and neoliberal ideologues in Washington, D.C., who have spent the post-Cold War era working feverishly to extend U.S. power and influence in Europe. These individuals form what my colleague at *The Pipeline*, Michael Walsh, has derisively dubbed the "Permanent Bipartisan Fusion Party."[10] These people are not well known to the public and have served in both Democratic and Republican administrations, ensuring the continuity of national security and foreign policy since the end of the Cold War. Their commitment to NATO expansion at all costs is due partly to their belief in a form of democratic globalism. But it is also born out of a hyper-commitment to American hegemony. The greatest irony, of course, is that in attempting to control every aspect of every part of the world—notably as it relates to nuclear-armed Russia—the loudest proponents of America's liberal hegemony appear likely to be the cause of the collapse of America's hegemony.[11]

These "policy entrepreneurs" in the Washington bureaucracy and think tank community, the Swamp, as President Donald J. Trump would later call it, are the reason why today the United States teeters on the brink of a nuclear world war with Russia over Ukraine. The warning signs that a conflict with Russia was coming, unless significant changes to the way the West operated in post-Cold War Europe were made, have been there for years. No one was listening, however. Increasingly, Russia believed that the continuous expansion of NATO was more than just a byproduct of Western inattentiveness. It was part of a purposeful plan to encircle and conquer a weakened post-Soviet Russia.[12] Yeltsin's standing in Russia diminished and paved the way for the rise of Vladimir Putin and his fellow nationalist-imperialists.[13]

The Russian View: America's Pattern of Aggression

A SERIES OF EVENTS occurred shortly after the Budapest Conference in 1994 that should have proven to Western policymakers the dangers of engaging in policy entrepreneurialism as it relates to the fundamental security of a nuclear power like Russia. The Balkan Wars dominated the discourse of the 1990s. As part of the breakup of the Soviet Union, several changes occurred to countries that once existed within the Soviet Union. The Balkans were one such place that had been held together by the brute force of a communist dictator, Jozip Broz Tito. Once the Iron Curtain fell, the ethno-religious rivalries of the Balkans erupted, and a multisided civil war resulted. A humanitarian crisis unlike anything seen since World War II soon followed.

There was a genuine desire on the part of the West to curb the humanitarian crisis. A working theory that became known as the "Responsibility to Protect" (R2P) came into fashion in Western elite circles during this time.[14] Essentially, humanitarian crises needed to be addressed by the militaries of the developed world rather than ignored as they were during the Cold War. There was, as the name suggests, a responsibility to protect the innocent people in a conflict zone, such as that of the Balkans. This view of using military force for humanitarian ends—to establish what Mary Kaldor once referred to as "human security" in the post-Cold War era—was highly controversial.[15] Even today, most Americans shudder at the thought of sending U.S. forces to engage in ambiguous humanitarian ends. The Balkans became the poster child for the kind of warfare that became prevalent in the 1990s. Basically, much of the warfare in the Balkans was predicated upon terrorizing the population whereas, traditionally, civilians are incidentally caught up in conflict.

The only problem facing the Western alliance was the fact that there were historical and cultural sensitivities that they needed to be mindful of in the Balkans. The region was overwhelmingly Slavic and had long been seen by Moscow as part of the international Slavic community which Moscow believed it had a responsibility to protect.[16] After all, the Balkans were the trigger point for World War I. Historically, it has been a powder keg of rival ethnicities and religions. Russia has long believed it has a duty to assist its Slavic cousins in times of crises. The idea that NATO would intervene militarily in the Balkans, a traditional Russian sphere of influence, without so much as consulting with Moscow, was an affront to Russian leadership.[17]

Because of the relative imbalances in power between the West and the Russians in the decade after the Cold War, Russia was careful not to separate too much from the West. But many Russian strategists believed that they could no longer count on the Americans and their partners to operate in a way that respected Russian concerns. The Americans were hellbent on a maximalist foreign policy that brought NATO to a weakened Russia's doorstep. Hence, the slow rise in tensions between Moscow and Washington began and Americans continued to downplay and ignore it for the sake of strategic convenience.

By 1999, when the United States and its NATO partners were again called upon to use force in the Balkans, this time against Serbian forces engaged in ethnic cleansing of the Muslim population of neighboring Kosovo, the Russians attempted to deploy a contingent of their troops to the Pristina Airport. This was an attempt by Moscow to lay claim to what most strategists assumed would be a key beachhead for NATO forces in their coming air campaign against Serbian forces. Russia did not want NATO to attack their fellow Slavs, the Serbs. A tense standoff ensued between NATO troops and Russian troops for control of the airport. Inevitably, the Russians stood down and NATO was able to deploy.[18] But it was a portent of things to come in the twenty-first century between the United States and Russia.

The Global War on Terror: A Missed Opportunity in Russo-American Relations

WHEN THE HORRIFIC SEPTEMBER 11, 2001, attacks occurred, President George W. Bush placed U.S. military forces on Defense Condition One (DefCon). This is the highest alert for the U.S. military. Since the Cold War, the Russians had closely monitored these alerts as they served as an indicator that the Americans might launch a nuclear attack. When Bush ordered DefCon One in response to the 9/11 attacks, it was Russian President Vladimir Putin who unilaterally ordered his forces to stand down, as he understood that the Americans were raising their defense condition in response to the terrorist attacks and not because they planned on attacking Russia.[19] The Russians had been dogged by Islamist violence for years, emanating from their hold on Chechnya.

The Russians behaved brutally toward the Chechen population in the 1990s. Western sympathies resided with the people of Chechnya, whom they viewed as a population being forced to remain within the borders of Russia against their will.[20] Yet, the Chechen resistance had turned to al Qaeda and other Islamist terrorists to assist in their war against Russia.[21] Part of the reason Vladimir Putin had assumed power in Russia was the Russian public's perception that Boris Yeltsin was incapable of handling the Chechnya issue. Putin resolved to fight the Chechen resistance with overwhelming force. The conflict was brutal. Many young Russians died. Even more innocent Chechen lives were lost.

Rumors spread that Putin had precipitated the war in Chechnya by launching what's known as a "false flag" operation. Some have speculated that Putin was itching for an excuse to reassert Russian authority over the quasi-breakaway republic of Chechnya. In order to do that, the theory goes, he had his intelligence service orchestrate an apartment bombing and blamed Chechen Islamists. This resulted in a massive war that ended in the destruction of the Islamist threat to Russia from Chechnya (as well as the threat that Chechnya might break away from Russia). Given the dark origins of Putin and his regime, though, this theory is a real possibility.[22]

So with the 9/11 attacks, Putin believed he saw a window of opportunity to bring the United States and the West into an anti-terrorism partnership. Shortly after 9/11, when it was determined that al Qaeda was responsible and operating in Taliban-controlled Afghanistan, the United States deployed CIA paramilitary officers and Special Forces units to Central Asia. This was a part of the world about which the Americans had little knowledge. The Russian government used its immense leverage over the Central Asian republics to help the Americans establish a military presence in the region.

Moscow did this in the hopes that the West and Russia might come to a greater understanding. Russian leaders hoped that by co-operating with Washington in the War on Terror, they would signal to the West that Russia did not intend harm either to Europe or the United States. With the newfound cooperation with the West on counterterrorism issues, Russian leaders believed they would curry favor with Western leaders and dissuade them from the aggressive NATO expansion to which they had been committed since the end of the Cold War.

Islamist terror would plague Russia throughout the early 2000s. The threat to Russia from Islamism—the same ideology that had at-tacked the United States on 9/11—could have been the point of unity that might have avoided the current disaster that now dogs Western, Ukrainian, and Russian leaders today. Sadly for those of us living in 2024, the arrogance of Western leaders and the inability of Russian leaders to move beyond the grand strategies of the previous centu-ry ensured that the Global War on Terror would become yet another point of division between post-Soviet Russia and NATO.

America's Follies in the Mideast and Russia

IN THE SIXTH CHAPTER of this work, the reader will learn about the damage that President George W. Bush's "Freedom Agenda" and the "Bush Doctrine" did to U.S. foreign policy in the twenty-first centu-ry. For now, however, it is enough to understand that the U.S. inva-sion of Iraq in 2003 was one of the straws that broke the proverbial camel's back of Russo-American relations. The Bush administration was convinced that Saddam Hussein's regime not only supported Islamist terrorist organizations but were also working overtime to build nuclear, biological, and chemical weapons of mass destruction. This was a deeply unpopular war in Europe, but the fear scenario in Washington following 9/11 was that Saddam might hand these WMDs over to al Qaeda, which, in turn, might use them on the United States in another major terrorist attack.

Since 2002, the Russian government increasingly had taken up the argument that the sovereignty of all nations should be respected and that, as a result, the world order which the Americans believed was a unipolar system (meaning one dominant power) was, in fact, a multipolar order.[23] Certainly, this worldview was a self-serving one. Compared to the United States, post-Cold War Russia was relatively weak. Feeling the geopolitical squeeze from an endlessly expanding NATO and being unable to stop that expansion, Moscow was striving to create the conditions at the diplomatic level that would prevent what Russian leaders perceived as an unacceptable encroachment on their borders by possibly hostile Western forces. Of course, it is unlikely that if the Soviet Union had won the Cold War rather than the United States, Russia would have countenanced respecting the rights and sovereignty of the defeated capitalist states. It's even less likely that a victorious Soviet Union would have accepted some international power-sharing agreement with those they defeated, as the Russian leadership of post-Soviet Russia wanted from the West.

Then again, however, the United States is different from most great powers in history. In the modern era, when the United States has gone to war and won, it has not taken foreign territory for itself. Whereas the victorious Allied powers in the World War I created an unfavorable peace with the defeated Germans—a peace that set up the conditions for World War II—the United States worked to rehabilitate Germany in the interwar period by giving them fair loans. After World War II, rather than hold territories that it had conquered throughout Europe, the Americans worked to rebuild the defeated lands of Germany (as well as the other Axis Power members) so that these countries could stand on their own and become productive members of the postwar order.

There were some attempts to provide aid to Russia in the aftermath of the Cold War. But what the Russians really wanted and needed was security assurances. Unfortunately, that was the one thing the West was unwilling to provide. Once Vladimir Putin ascended to power, he began to call for multipolarity in world affairs and claimed to be a staunch advocate of state sovereignty. In his view (and in the opinion of many other nations belonging to the Global South), the American threats against Saddam Hussein's regime were flagrant violations of international standards—the same standards that Washington routinely claimed it was protecting.[24]

George W. Bush predicated the 2003 invasion of Iraq upon the concept that Saddam Hussein was a rogue actor who was in defiance of international law by developing a WMD program in defiance of UN resolutions that were passed following Desert Storm. Because Saddam was said to be hiding these WMDs from the world and faulty U.S. intelligence showed Saddam partnering with al Qaeda, the use of force was declared justified. On top of these perceived threats and violations by Iraq, the Bush administration further argued that they were on a mission to democratize the authoritarian states of the Middle East.[25] It was that last part that galvanized Putin's regime against Bush's war in Iraq.

Putin started to believe that the Americans were not only attempting to encircle the weakened post-Soviet Russia, but that they were planning to overthrow his own regime.[26] Vladimir Putin feared that the American move against Saddam Hussein was merely a test run of an eventual U.S. mission to end Putin's reign in Russia and impose a weaker, pro-Western government there. Thus began Putin's total break from the United States. To try to prevent the war, Putin formed a troika with Germany and France—two of America's oldest allies in Europe—both of which opposed the American move against Iraq.[27] When that failed, Putin began marshaling his government for a long-term resistance to U.S. foreign policy and global democracy promotion.

In a forthcoming chapter, about the reader will discover how

American action in support of pro-Western elements in Ukraine as well as many former Soviet regions of Eastern Europe and the South Caucasus further prejudiced Putin's Russia against the West. American and European leaders routinely downplay the role that NATO's expansion along with America's overzealous commitment to democracy promotion along Russia's periphery—using economic, covert intelligence, and military means—played in turning Russia against the West. This is likely because Western elites are either lacking in self-awareness or simply in denial (or both).[28] It is entirely self-serving for Western elites to argue that NATO expansion had nothing at all to do with Russia's present opposition to the United States and the world order it purports to lead.[29] Nevertheless, Putin and his *siloviki* (security forces) are consistently clear that this is precisely why they have pivoted Russia away from the West.[30]

2007–08: The Wrath of Putin

AFTER YEARS OF SUCCESSIVE Soviet and Russian leaders (Gorbachev, Yeltsin, and Putin) telling Western leaders their opposition to NATO expansion, and successive U.S. governments not only ignoring these concerns but actively working against Russian interests, Moscow's autocratic government had had enough. Russia's economy is built upon the production of commodities, notably oil and natural gas. From 2006-08, the global price of oil was at historic highs. Russia benefited mightily from this situation. With the increased price of oil, Russia was able to turn quite a profit. Moscow reinvested much of that money into restoring their ailing post-Soviet war machine. The Americans and their allies in Europe had not listened to Moscow's concerns for twenty years. Now, Putin and his regime viewed the West as a growing threat to Russia's security.

The first signs of trouble—signs the West missed yet again—came in the form of President Putin's now infamous speech at the Munich Security Conference in 2007. Standing at a podium directly across from the U.S. Secretary of Defense Robert M. Gates, the late Arizona Republican, Senator John McCain, and a coterie of other Western leaders, Putin began his comments with the off-putting, "This conference's structure allows me to avoid excessive politeness and the need to speak in roundabout, pleasant but empty diplomatic rhetoric."[31] From that first sentence onward, Putin's comments were direct.

Putin began with a quote from U.S. President Franklin D. Roosevelt, a man who many credit with basically having built the international order during World War II. "When peace has broken anywhere, the peace of all countries everywhere is in danger."[32] The Russian strongman was attempting to hold an ideological mirror up to the West, to show them how the very principles of the world system they had worked so hard in the last century to create were being torn down—not by the tyrants of the world, but by the Western heirs of those who had built the liberal international order.

Putin railed against the inequality of a unipolar world as well as its inefficiency. He raged against what he viewed as America's "illegitimate actions" in Iraq (and elsewhere). In Putin's view, U.S. policies were not stabilizing the world as the U.S. government often excused its bloody interventions. American actions in the post-Cold War era were entirely destabilizing. Interestingly, Putin touched upon an issue that many critics of U.S. foreign policy, even within the United States, have noted: a lack of consistency and a complete lack of norms in the international arena. Putin asserted in his Munich speech that American actions—the unipolar world order—were actually compelling states to seek out WMDs as well as to create alternative power centers to the liberal international order.[33]

Several months after the Munich security conference, Putin ordered the invasion of the tiny South Caucasus nation of Georgia. For years, the Russian government accused Georgia of aiding-and-abetting Chechen terrorists.[34] In the run-up to the Russian invasion of Georgia, Moscow blamed Georgia for unprovoked attacks against the Russian-supported Georgian breakaway republic of South

Ossetia.[35] U.S. intelligence, however, had assessed that Russian forces quietly had been building up along their border with Georgia for months before any incident involving Georgia providing aid to suspected Chechen terrorists.[36] In Putin's mind, though, this invasion was a long time coming. If the Americans were not going to respect Russian security concerns and instead seek to encircle Russia—all while ignoring their professed beliefs in international law—then Putin was going to behave exactly as the Americans had been behaving and jealously pursue his own national interests.

The Arab Spring and Russia

AFTER THE RUSSO-GEORGIA WAR of 2008, President Barack Obama would attempt a reset in U.S.-Russian relations. Inevitably, as I will show in chapter eight, the reset ended in a predictable disaster. One of the reasons for the failed reset was the endlessly draining American foray into the Greater Middle East in the name of fighting terrorism. As the Putin regime saw it, though, the Obama administration was not interested in pursuing Islamists. They were invested in continuing the George W. Bush administration's so-called "Freedom Agenda" by using force, economic coercion, and covert action to undermine and overthrow Arab dictatorships and replace them with allegedly democratically elected governments that, in theory, would be more amenable to the United States and its Western allies.

Muammar Gaddafi in Libya and Bashar al-Assad in Syria were just two of the dictators who were targeted in Obama's covert war. These actions occurred within the wider framework of the Arab Spring (which, in fact, became an Islamist Winter). The Russian government was utterly bewildered by Washington's moves in the Middle East. This was partly because, in order to overthrow these dictatorships, America was often aligning with rebel factions that were affiliated with Islamist terror organizations, such as al Qaeda—the very same group that had attacked America on 9/11.[37]

More importantly, these *jihadi* groups were as much of a threat to Putin's Russia as they were to the West. Unlike the United States, the Russian Federation is home to one of the largest Muslim populations outside of the Middle East. Muslims living in Russia today have higher fertility rates than do native-born Russians.[38] Plus, Russia shares land routes between its territories and Muslim lands to the south. All these factors combined to give the Kremlin nightmares over what the Americans were doing in the Middle East. U.S. military actions were not only destabilizing the Middle East, but they were also radicalizing Muslim populations everywhere. The last thing the Russians wanted to contend with were millions of Muslims in their land heeding the call of *jihad* as the Americans destabilized the lands of Muhammad.

Further, in the cases of Gaddafi and Assad, these dictators were aligned with Russia. And, as I demonstrate in another chapter, Syria is of particular importance to Moscow's strategists because it houses one of Russia's few warm water ports. Everywhere Putin looked, he saw the perfidious hand of America and its Western allies picking apart Russian interests and slowly-but-surely encircling Russia. According to some reports, Putin watched in horror as Western media sources broadcast the final moments of the life of Libya's Muammar Gaddafi. Putin watched as Gaddafi was dragged by a rabid crowd out from where the deposed Libyan dictator was hiding—beneath a highway overpass in the Libyan desert—and was subsequently killed by the crowd. Putin had become convinced that Western intelligence services were plotting the same fate for him as that of Saddam Hussein and Gaddafi.[39]

The United States' quest for absolute security and its subsequent dedication to NATO expansion into Russia's periphery have created a tempest's brew in Moscow. At a time when Russians should have been solidifying their friendship with the West, Russians instead turned to very same kind of men who had spent the previous century brutalizing them. This was all because the agony of the post-Cold

War capitalist economy was too great for the Russian people to bear and because of the sense of insecurity that NATO expansion engendered among so many Russians. As you will read in the next chapter, the fear of encirclement and invasion has defined Russia's existence almost from its beginning. The West played into these negative historical stereotypes with their feckless policies, fueling Putin's rise, and creating an insurmountable crisis which has eventuated in the horrific Ukraine War today.

The Cold War ended and gave way to a cold peace. That cold peace has now devolved into a hot war. The only question that now remains is whether that hot war will become a great power conflict, pitting the U.S.-led West against the Russian Federation (and their Chinese, Iranian, and North Korean partners) over Ukraine.

CHAPTER 2

HOW DID WE GET HERE?

UKRAINE HAS been described by some historians as sitting at the "gates of Europe." A relatively flat land, the country possesses fruitful soil that produces an abundant bounty of foodstuffs—notably wheat—which has earned Ukraine another nickname: the breadbasket of Europe. It is also home to rich mineral deposits that make it an attractive target for neighboring powers such as Russia. Ukraine shares a large land border with Russia and its southern maritime borders include the Crimean Peninsula, which is a strategically vital port along the Black Sea—a body of water that allows Russia access to the warm waters of the Mediterranean Sea via the Bosporus Strait. The Black Sea is also a vital region for Turkey, which has a coastline along the southern portion of the sea.

There's much more to Ukraine, though, than food production and strategic positioning on the Black Sea. Many historians believe that the Russian civilization, known as the "Kievan Rus" originated in modern-day Ukraine. Of course, with Ukraine and Russia at war today, the Ukrainians dispute the particulars of this history. But for the longest time, it was safe to say that the origins of the modern Russian culture could be traced to modern day Kiev.

The Russians believe they are descended from the Vikings. Most historians think the specific origin tale Russians tell themselves is

inaccurate—but only slightly. Russians believe they are descended from an apocryphal figure known as Rurik. And while the existence of Rurik is questioned, the role of Scandinavian Vikings in
the Russian origin story is not in question. According to *The Russian
Primary Chronicle*, a history of Russia written by Russian monks in
the twelfth century, the people living in Novgorod, a city that today
exists in northwest Russia, had grown tired of division and strife
within their tribe. Unable to find a leader in their own ranks, the den-
izens of Novgorod reached out to the Vikings.

A minor Viking prince, Rurik, heeded the call and arrived on the
shores of Novgorod along with his two brothers, Oleg and Igor.
They brought with them a small army of servants to take power in
Novgorod. They assumed power in the year AD 862. In 879, however, Rurik is believed to have passed away. His brother, Oleg, succeeded him as ruler. A few years later, Oleg reportedly marched on
Smolensk and Kiev. At that point, Kiev, with its strategic position
on the Dnieper River, became the capital of Oleg's new empire—and
the inspiration for what many associate with Russian culture today.

Soon, Igor replaced Oleg as the ruler of the Kievan Rus dynasty
that had been established in what is today the capital of the independent nation of Ukraine. The Kievan Rus had become a trading
partner to the Byzantine Empire, which itself was once known as
the Eastern Roman Empire until Rome's collapse in AD 471. At that
point, the Eastern Roman Empire became the Byzantine Empire. It
was also the seat of the Eastern Orthodox Christian Church. Thanks
to this connection via trade and geographical proximity, the Kievan
Rus converted to Orthodox Christianity. At the time, the Kievan
Rus were considering joining the Islamic faith. But the leaders of
the Kievan Rus ultimately decided to join Orthodox Christianity because the Christians, unlike the Muslims, still permitted the use of
alcoholic beverages.[1]

These actions, though, formed the basis for modern Russian culture.

Sadly, the Kievan Rus would not last beyond AD 1237. An enemy greater than any other force the Western world had faced up until that point had blown west from the steppes of Asia: The Mongol Horde. Fiercely expansionistic and equally brutal, the Mongols rode fast and hard across the European plain from Asia and mercilessly conquered all who stood in their path. This included the glorious Kievan Rus. From the moment the Mongols captured Kiev and brought it under their reign, the evolution of the Russian people and culture was forever changed. Those we today call Russians were scattered from their beautiful redoubt along the Dnieper River and thrown into various nearby lands. Poland, Lithuania, and cities like Novgorod would become the new homes of those who hailed from the conquered Kievan Rus.

The Mongols had decimated, subjugated, and fundamentally changed the path of development for the Russian people. The Russian culture would have been lost under the brutal yoke of the Mongols had it not been for the fact that the Mongols believed in religious toleration. The Orthodox Christian community preserved the Russian traditions, language, and the culture among the dispersed populations who originally had called the Kievan Rus their home.

In the face Mongol oppression, many other cities, such as Novgorod and Rostov, struggled to replace the defeated Kievan Rus as the center of Russian culture. Despite the prosperity of these alternative seats of Russian power, it was the newer city of Muscovy (Moscow) that became the replacement for Kiev. Geography, as they say, is destiny. Moscow's geography was fortuitous for a nation that wanted to be at the hub of commerce and enjoy military dominance. Located at the place where the waters of the Volga, Oka, Don, and Dnieper rivers converge, Moscow was destined to be the new seat of Russian power. By the time the Russians were able to shake off the dominion of the Mongols and return to independence, Moscow was the new center of Russian power—as it has been since.

Men like Grand Duke Dmitrii of Vladimir and Moscow, who was

an early skilled Muscovite leader, stepped up to lead Muscovite forces in their final rebellion against what was then the waning rule of the Mongols. In 1380, Dmitrii found himself surrounded by superior Mongol forces. Rather than surrender, Dmitrii appealed to the shared Orthodox Christian faith of his troops.[2] The grand duke reached out to the Orthodox saint, Sergii of Radonezh who famously urged Dmitrii and his troops onward against the numerically superior Mongol forces by urging the Russians to, "Go forward and fear not [...] God will be on your side."[3] With this blessing in hand, Dmitrii led his forces to victory over the Mongols. This defiant example broke the Mongol's hold over the Russians and set them on the path to independence.

Because of this key role a leader of the Orthodox Christian faith played at the Battle of Kulikovo Field, many Russians came to believe that as long as Moscow and the Orthodox Christian Church were united in purpose, the "infidels" would be driven from Russian lands. What's more, once those infidels were evicted from the purported holy Russian lands, the Russian people would finally be reunited under Moscow's rule. That was how the center of power shifted from Kiev to Moscow in the Russian community.

Writing in *National Geographic*, Eve Conant observed that "Ukraine has repeatedly been carved up by competing powers."[4] Not only did the Mongols run roughshod over present day Ukraine during their Eurasian invasion, so too did the armies belonging to Poland and Lithuania in the sixteenth century. A century later, Russia went to war with the Polish-Lithuanian Commonwealth, resulting in Russia reacquiring much of present-day Ukraine. The Russian conquest of eastern Ukraine became known as the "Left Bank." The western portion of Ukraine—the "Right Bank"—became dominated by Poland.

Catherine the Great was the Russian leader who presided over the Russian conquest of Ukraine. Not only is Ukraine the gateway into southern Europe but, because of its presence along the Black Sea, it serves as the vital link between the otherwise landlocked Russia and the international waters of the Mediterranean Sea, which itself is a conduit to the Atlantic Ocean beyond.[5] Plus, at the time, the Muslim Ottoman Empire ruled from present-day Turkey and was a perennial challenger to the Russian Empire for dominance over southern Europe (where many of Russia's fellow Slavs lived).

The ethnic makeup of the entire region, ever since the Mongol invasion, has been a polyglot admixture of peoples who ordinarily would want nothing to do with each other. As mentioned earlier, the Scandinavian Vikings came down and intermixed with the Slavic populations. From there, Asian blood and culture was injected by the marauding Mongols.[6] Then came the Turks and their Islamic co-religionists. In southern Ukraine, there existed a large Muslim population known as the Tatars. The Muslim Tatars who lived on Ukraine's southern Crimean Peninsula were not part of the Ottoman Empire, although they did enjoy a strategic alliance with their co-religionists.[7] The Crimean Tatars essentially acted as an unconventional force augmenting the Ottoman Empire's influence into southern Europe.

The Crimean Tatars, thanks to their Islamic beliefs, were major practitioners of what today would be called human trafficking.[8] Much like the Islamic Barbary Coast Pirates of North Africa, who plagued shipping in the Mediterranean, the Crimean Tatars regularly raided their Slavic neighbors in Russia and Poland. They targeted women and children and took them as slaves to be sold at the open flesh markets in Turkey, where those Christian Slavs were purchased by the Muslims who populated those areas. The men and children were often put to work while the women were forced to become sexual slaves.[9]

Between Russia's geopolitical rivalry with the Ottoman Empire and its coping with the constant threat of Tatar raids from Crimea, Catherine the Great annexed the geostrategically vital Crimea.[10] After her conquest of Eastern Ukraine but before this annexation, Catherine conceived of a new scheme for the ancestral home of the Russian civilization. She called it "Novorossiya" ("New Russia").[11] It was a policy of blatant colonization. The Russian government encouraged daring Russian pioneers to settle Eastern Ukraine. The tsarina's regime wanted similar settlements to arise in Crimea, in order to out-populate the Crimean Tatar community there.[12]

At this point, Ukraine's identity as a separate entity from Russia was erased. It became part of the larger Russian Empire for more than a century. That is, until the end of the World War I when the Russian Empire collapsed and Vladimir Lenin and his Bolsheviks overthrew the Romanov dynasty that had ruled Russia for hundreds of years. The empire was replaced by the communist Union of Soviet Socialist Republics (USSR). As a result of this chaotic reorganization, in the 1920s, Ukraine briefly enjoyed independence (along with several other outlying Russian lands, such as Poland and Belarus), but then the Soviets ultimately reconquered these territories shortly after their supposed liberation.

Ukraine itself was too important, both strategically and economically, for Russia to let it go without a fight. To ensure Ukraine would remain in the Soviet fold, Josef Stalin, who succeeded Lenin as supreme leader of the USSR, completed Catherine the Great's conquest of Crimea by forcibly deporting all 200,000 Crimean Tatars to Siberia.[13] They were replaced by other populations from within Russia and the Slavic community.

After Stalin's reign of terror ended with his death in 1953, Nikita Khrushchev became leader of the Soviet Union, but not before triumphing in a massive power struggle between himself and Soviet Prime Minister Georgii Malenkov. Part of Khrushchev's impetus for ceding over Crimea to the control of the Soviet satellite government running Ukraine was to shore up political support for himself from Ukraine's powerful Communist Party in his struggle with Malenkov for ultimate control over the Soviet Union. Because most Soviet leaders viewed Russia and Ukraine were connected, in Khrushchev's words, by a "great and indissoluble friendship," it was nearly meaningless for Moscow to cede control of Crimea over to Kiev, since Ukraine itself was a satellite of Moscow.[14]

The preeminent international relations scholar, Dr. Paul Goble, famously described Stalin's decision to depopulate Crimea of its original Tatar population and then to repopulate it with ethnic Russians as a "poison pill."[15] Stalin, a devious and deeply strategic thinker (as well as a genocidal tyrant), assumed that if his empire ever did break up (which, of course, it did in 1991), having Russians living beyond whatever post-Soviet borders might arise would prevent the permanent dissolution of Stalin's empire. The urge for future, post-Soviet Russian leaders to protect their fellow Russians living in Crimea would be too great a desire to ignore and would, therefore, ensure that Russian power would always be present on the Black Sea.

And so it has been.

A wellspring of nationalist sentiment erupted in Russia following the collapse of the Soviet Union in 1991. Men like Vladimir Putin, who would go on to become the preeminent post-Cold War Russian leader—a strongman who ruled by the iron fist, like most other Russian rulers in history—became convinced that it was his mission to restore Russia's lost empire.[16] In the mythology that Russian nationalists crafted to justify their lust for power in the chaos that was post-Cold War Russia, Ukraine stood as the beating heart of the *siloviki*'s desire to restore Russian greatness.[17] And the Russian nationalists used Ukraine's long history as the birthplace of Russian culture and long-standing member of both the Russian Empire and, later, the Soviet Union, as justification for their plans.

It wasn't only nationalist politicians like Putin and his fellow *siloviki* who yearned for Ukraine to be placed under Russia's sphere of influence in the aftermath of the Cold War. Renowned Russian dissidents who challenged the might of the Soviet Union, such as Alexandr Solzhenitsyn, argued that Russia and Ukraine (along with Belarus and the ethnic Russian parts of Kazakhstan) needed to be under the same polity—led by Moscow.[18] In fact, Putin, an admirer of the anticommunist dissident who spent decades as a prisoner of conscience in the Soviet gulag, credits the now deceased

Solzhenitsyn as an inspiration for his quest to claim Ukraine as part of the new Russian co-prosperity sphere.[19]

So, it wasn't only militaristic nationalists with delusions of empire, such as Putin, who fundamentally believed in the mission to reabsorb Ukraine under Moscow's rule. Russian anticommunists were of the same mind. As you'll see, even the anti-Putin politician who Western intelligence services hoped would replace Putin, Alexei Navalny, was a staunch advocate of Putin's annexation of the Crimean Peninsula in 2014. After becoming an enemy of Putin and gaining the support of the West, Navalny was coy about whether he would cede Crimea back to Ukraine if he did, in fact, overthrow the Putinist regime in Moscow.[20]

There is, of course, another side to this twisted tale. The Western alliance after the Cold War reneged on what the Russian elite believed were the promises they had made to Soviet Premier Mikhail Gorbachev in order to get him to end the Cold War and remove Soviet troops from Eastern Europe.[21] As you'll read in a further on in another chapter, the United States and its NATO partners dropped the geopolitical ball in the decade after the Cold War. They turned a once-in-a-millennium dream to make Russia a truly Western state— creating a line of fellow capitalist democracies from Tokyo to New York to London to Warsaw and Vladivostok—into a nightmare. This nightmare caused the Russians to turn their backs on democracy and capitalism. Instead, the Russians ran back to their historical grievances against the West and into the waiting arms of vicious autocrats who wanted very badly to end the Russian experiment with democracy at the end of the Cold War.

CHAPTER 3

NATO: NOT ONE INCH EAST... JUST KIDDING!

THE END of the Cold War, contrary to how popular history may describe it, was anything but an orderly affair. No one in power, in either the West or in the USSR, fully understood how truly momentous was the breakdown of the Soviet Union. They were feeling their way through this epochal shift, the likes of which hadn't been experienced in most of the lives of those guiding policy at the time. Once leaders in the West began to realize that the Soviet Union was not just going through radical changes but was on its way to what former U.S. President Ronald Reagan had described as the "ash heap of history," a frantic movement of shuttle diplomacy between the United States, Europe, and the Soviet Union erupted.[1]

Conciliatory statements were made by the various leaders of the world at the time. Impassioned pleas to allow for the reunification of Germany erupted from the mouths of various leaders in Europe. Hope inside the oppressed nations of the Soviet bloc reigned supreme as, for the first time in generations, the people living there could see a world in which they were not living under the jackboots of the Red Army. For their part, Soviet leaders desperately tried to figure out how to thread the needle between liberalizing their sclerotic, failed system and avoiding a complete collapse of that totalitarian communist order.

As Catherine Belton assesses in her seminal work, *Putin's People: How the KGB Took Back Russian and Then Took on the West,* the top Soviet security officers knew as early as 1986 that the Soviet Union was in its final death agonies. These top KGB and military personnel, along with top Communist Party apparatchiks, began moving money and resources out of the coffers of the Soviet Union and to themselves, to "fund Communist-linked parties in the USSR's final decade of existence." Belton, an investigative reporter for *Reuters* with a long history of reporting on Russia, found that the "sums transferred by more surreptitious means, for more clandestine activities, remain unknown" today. Belton reported that Soviet officials conspired to move vast sums of Soviet wealth to the "crony companies at the heart of the vast system of black-market operations that kept the eastern bloc afloat." These included a "string of front companies" throughout East Germany, Austria, Switzerland, and Liechtenstein.[2]

All this activity represented a golden parachute for the Soviet elite who could see what was actually coming from Gorbachev's reforms (that it was leading to the collapse rather than the reform of the USSR). These would be the people who would rise to the prominence in the post-Soviet era, notably in the aftermath of the failure of Boris Yeltsin's pro-Western government. Most of the *siloviki* who populate Putin's regime were the beneficiaries of this, in the words of Yeltsin-era prosecutors, "vast criminal conspiracy."[3]

By November 14, 1989, two weeks after the fall of the Berlin Wall, President George H.W. Bush was already thinking about NATO expansion. According to international relations specialist, M.E. Sarotte, Bush cautioned his British counterpart, Prime Minister Margaret Thatcher, about excluding Soviet-occupied East Germany from any post-Cold War settlement. As Bush saw things, "What if East European countries want to leave [the] Warsaw Pact. NATO must stay."[4]

The Origins of NATO and the Warsaw Pact

THE WARSAW PACT was the Soviet answer to the North Atlantic Treaty Organization which was founded in the early days of the Cold War, at the close of the Berlin Blockade.[5] At that time, the Soviet Union attempted to blockade America's access to West Berlin (prompting the famous Berlin Air Lift), in violation of the post-World War II peace settlement signed between the victorious Allied powers. Realizing that the Soviet threat was real and would be pervasive in the post-World War II era—and convinced that communism marches on empty stomachs—the Americans endeavored to rebuild Europe as quickly as possible. Washington also desired to then take the newly rebuilt, free states of Western Europe and combine them into a defensive, collective security alliance.

This became NATO.

Like all Russian leaders, Stalin began to fear being encircled by rival powers to his West. NATO represented to the Russian elite the same kind of threat that the Polish-Lithuanian Commonwealth of the fourteenth-seventeenth centuries represented, or that Napoleon's France, or Hitler's Germany presented to previous Russian regimes. Stalin's goal, therefore, was to keep the European powers to his western flank disunited and weak while increasing Moscow's iron grip over Eastern Europe (to use it as a shield against the West). So, Stalin attempted to enhance his Eastern European shield by creating the Warsaw Pact.

Whereas NATO was a voluntary, defensive alliance based on mutual fear of Soviet expansionism, the Warsaw Pact was imposed and directed by Moscow. Western European states were viewed as equals with the more powerful United States in NATO during this time. Poland, Ukraine, and the other Eastern European Soviet satellite states were viewed as mere cannon fodder by Stalin. Hardly anyone living in Soviet occupied Eastern Europe truly wanted to be part of Stalin's anti-NATO alliance (other than the Soviet-installed puppets ruling those Eastern European states). If NATO in the Cold War was a voluntary, mutual defense pact of equals (with the United States being the first among those equals), then Stalin's Warsaw Pact was the opposite. It was an ideological response designed to enhance Moscow's iron grip over Eastern Europe and ensure that the imprisoned peoples of Eastern Europe were used as the buffer zone in any potential nuclear world war with the West.

The Warsaw Pact disbanded along with the Soviet Union at the end of the Cold War. As you read above, the United States and its allies chose to maintain NATO—even to expand it, after the Soviet threat was gone. Because of this decision, NATO in effect became what it had been in opposition to throughout the Cold War; it became the Warsaw Pact. America was no longer the first among equals in the NATO alliance. Instead, it was the dominant power and the other members were merely vassals, obsequiously furthering the maximalist agenda of the triumphal neoconservative-neoliberal elite who ruled the West following the Cold War. The Warsaw Pact was Stalin's attempt to solidify the gains he had made in Eastern Europe at the end of World War II and to use it as a cudgel against the West. At the end of the Cold War, America determined to solidify its gains in Eastern Europe and to use those recently liberated lands as cudgels in its new war against post-Soviet Russia.

The Cocktail Napkin Agreement

ONCE THE BERLIN WALL fell in 1989, American and Western leaders began grappling with the prospect of fundamental geopolitical changes (and challenges) emanating from Eastern Europe. Hence, Bush's comments to Thatcher. For her part, Prime Minister Thatcher aimed to keep "the Warsaw Pact [as a] fig leaf for [Soviet leader Mikhail Gorbachev]." As Sarotte assesses from her research on the subject, President Bush "was not convinced" by Thatcher's arguments.[6]

It was within this context of international desperation and hope in 1989-90 that then-U.S. Secretary of State James Baker, a close personal confidant of President George H.W. Bush, met with his Soviet counterpart, Eduard A. Shevardnadze, at the Ottawa Open Skies Conference on February 12, 1990. It was here, at the Ottawa meeting, that Baker supposedly hatched what, in some circles, has become derisively known as the "cocktail napkin agreement." The basis of that informal agreement was James Baker's promise that if Gorbachev pulled Red Army forces from East Germany, then NATO would not move eastward one inch. Of course, these claims are in dispute by Western powers today, as the Russo-Ukraine War initiated in February 2022 by Russia still rages.

Yet, there is ample archival evidence showing that such a "cocktail napkin" agreement was hatched by the Bush Administration and the Gorbachev-led Soviet government at the Ottawa Open Skies Conference.

For example, in a hastily handwritten note about his interaction with Baker, Shevardnadze scrawled, "And if U[nited] G[ermany] stays in NATO, we should take care about non-expansion of its jurisdiction to the east." Indeed, Baker "tried out the 'not one inch eastward' formula with Gorbachev" at the Ottawa meeting in 1990, according to participants at that forum. Specifically, Baker is quoted at that meeting as assuring Gorbachev that, "neither [President Bush] nor I intend to extract any unilateral advantages from the processes that are taking place" and that "Americans understood that 'not only for the Soviet Union but for other European countries as well it is important to have guarantees that if the United States keeps its presence in Germany within the framework of NATO, not an inch of NATO's present military jurisdiction will spread in an eastern direction.'"[7]

Soon, West German leaders, taking their cues from Baker, repeated similar assurances to Gorbachev and his representatives. Thus, decisions were made by Moscow that, had those assurances by NATO leaders not been made, would have turned out differently.

Were Western leaders lying? Certainly, the West German leaders who confirmed to their Soviet counterparts that the Bush administration was serious about its vow not to spread NATO power an inch eastward were being truthful. As for the Americans, their views on these Bush administration assurances were far more variegated. Still, it appears that Secretary Baker was speaking on behalf of his close friend, confidant, and boss, George H.W. Bush—and that both he and Bush were being sincere in their claims to disallow NATO to expand beyond its Western European jurisdiction.

Of course, reality presents opportunities. As mentioned earlier, few in the West (or in Moscow) truly believed that Gorbachev was presiding over the final days of the Soviet Union. The idea that the Red Army would vanish from Europe almost overnight or that the Soviet nuclear threat would evaporate or that communism would die shortly after the Ottawa meeting was almost farcical to world leaders at that time. Once the Soviet Union's total collapse did occur, however, the reality of that event set in, and Western leaders—notably in Washington and Brussels, where NATO is headquartered—began reacting to the new paradigm of a Soviet-less world.

Those who supported NATO expansion in the aftermath of the Soviet Union's demise, argue that the Baker-Shevardnadze talks at Ottawa in 1990 were informal. And, with the end of the Soviet regime, these pro-NATO expansion elements in the West insist that any such informal agreements, if they were made at all, were null-and-void when the Soviet government collapsed. Besides, NATO was a voluntary organization and not only did a unified Germany seek to gain NATO membership, but so too did the former Soviet bloc states. For these countries, Article V of the NATO Charter—an attack on one member is an attack on all—was reassuring. After decades of brutal oppression by the Soviets (and, even before the USSR, by the Romanov dynasty of the Russian Empire), Eastern European states believed that finally there was a force that could protect them from future Russian aggression.

All these calculations, though, came after the Bush administration made its assurances to the Soviets in 1990. For the post-Soviet Russian government, the promises made by Western leaders during the breakup of the Soviet Union were still good. First, Boris Yeltsin's liberal government, which presided over the weakest moment in Russian history since Lenin and his Bolsheviks took power between 1917 and 1918, relied heavily on the promises made by the Americans not to expand NATO in order to gain leverage over their more nationalistic political opponents in Russia. Second, the failure on the part of NATO to live up to the promises made by Western leaders in 1990 helped to ensure the rise of the Putinist regime and the inevitable evolution of Russia from a potential member of the Western establishment into the adversary it is today.

Of course, this would come well after Gorbachev ordered the Red Army to abandon its positions in Germany and the dismantling of the forward operating positions of the Red Army throughout the Warsaw Pact states. The Russians believe that NATO's expansion was part of some evil Western plot to destroy Russia forever and they might not be wrong. Sure, Western politics eschew long-term strategic frameworks in favor of short-term, slap-dash solutions that comport with the biennial and quadrennial election cycles. But the more one researchers the post-Cold War expansion of NATO, the more the same names and groups of policy intellectuals keep popping up across both Democratic and Republican administrations. Because these mid-level bureaucrats were able to ensure continuity between post-Cold War U.S. presidential administrations, overall U.S. foreign policy toward both Russia and NATO expansion into the former Soviet states of Eastern Europe became inexorable.

These policy leaders, the neoconservative-neoliberal cabal, shared a universal disdain for Russia and a desire to effectively bust post-Cold War Russia apart into its constituent components. It wasn't enough to have deprived Moscow of its empire (which needed to happen). Instead, the neoconservative-neoliberal element abandoned all pretense of proportion and reason and embraced a maximalist approach designed to collapse Russia itself. NATO expansion would be the weapon used to break apart Russia. And once Russia was swept aside into its smaller components, the democratic-globalists who rule the West would be able to exploit the bountiful natural resources of Eurasia.

Experience and wisdom have been in short supply in Washington, D.C. for many years.

With the expansion of NATO in the 1990s post-Cold War era, a time when Russia was at its weakest in generations, that ancient Russian fear of disunion and foreign domination came to the fore. This fear was most pronounced when Russia's experiment with Western democracy and capitalism proved to yield mixed results, at best, for that ancient nation. Many nationalists and holdovers from the Soviet days believed a nefarious Western plot was afoot to destroy post-Soviet Russia. These individuals ultimately rallied around Vladimir Putin and became known as the *siloviki*.[8] No matter how hard Western leaders denied that such a conspiracy was underway, the persistent actions of NATO to expand into areas, like Georgia and Ukraine, served only to further convince Russian leaders that the West could not be trusted.

Citing the infamous cocktail napkin agreement hatched between James Baker and his Soviet counterpart in the final days of the Cold War, Russian leaders began spinning a "stabbed-in-the-back" narrative that took hold in the minds of many Russians. The "stabbed-in-the-back" narrative became one of the ways that Vladimir Putin and his fellow *siloviki* rose to power, as they were the ones usually making this claim to the Russian people. Against a dark conspiracy to break apart Mother Russia, hatched by the same Western nations the Russians had counted on to help them recover from the decades of Communist misrule, Putin and his allies appeared to be the one bulwark standing in the way. People believed Putin would make Russia strong and great again.[9]

Not only had the Americans and their Western allies reneged on their "Not One Inch East" promise, but they had marched a thousand miles east since making that promise at the Ottawa Open Skies Conference. After completing that march, NATO consolidated its gains in the former Soviet bloc states by placing armies and weapons in those countries, threatening the territorial integrity of Russia itself. Indeed, these claims of the embattled Putin regime are unwittingly verified by the endless stream of breathless reports from various Western publications and leaders now insisting that Putin's government is on the brink of collapse (as of late 2023, Vladimir Putin's regime remains firmly in power in Russia).[10] This brings us to the open Western insistence today that there is immediate need to bring about the collapse of the Russian state and to ensure that it is broken down into its constituent parts.[11]

All these factors continue to influence Russian behavior toward its neighbors in the former Soviet bloc states. Leaving aside the question of whether the Soviet Union's collapse was imminent when Secretary of State Baker and other prominent Western leaders assured twitchy Soviet leaders that NATO would not expand an inch to the east, it is unlikely that Soviet forces—notably in East Germany— would have been withdrawn if Soviet leaders had known they'd be staring down a NATO army in Eastern Europe. It is likely that the Soviet acquiescence to pull back their forces from Europe sped up the demise of what Ronald Reagan called the "evil empire." In an alternate reality where the George H.W. Bush administration did not make a promise not to expand NATO an inch eastward, the the collapse of the USSR might have been far messier than it was, and Europe might have suffered greatly as a result.

But for the Bush administration's decision to promise no NATO expansion to the east to be meaningful, Washington would have had to be willing to stay committed to such promises. The failure of Bush's successors to do that, notably of Bill Clinton and his own son, George W. Bush, led to the current crisis in U.S.-Russian relations over Ukraine. This failure to uphold Western promises may yet lead to a nuclear world war with Russia or the collapse of NATO—and the subsequent humiliation and diminution of U.S. power at the hands of the Russian Federation.

The Denial of Western Elites

MICHAEL MCFAUL, who served as the Obama administration's ambassador to Russia and now works as an academic specializing in Russia at Stanford University, disagrees with this assessment. He, like so many in the Western establishment, has embraced the notion that NATO's expansion had absolutely nothing to do with the current breakdown in relations between the West and the Russian Federation. In McFaul's estimation, NATO expansion has merely been a "variable" rather than "a constant source of tension" between Moscow and Washington. McFaul goes so far as to say that "Moscow has in the past acknowledged Ukraine's right to join NATO." [12]

The former ambassador believes that the "Kremlin's complaints [about NATO expansion] spike in a clear pattern after democratic breakthroughs in the post-Soviet space." For McFaul and those who concur with his worldview, these attacks on NATO expansion by Vladimir Putin and the timing of them with advances made by pro-democratic forces in the post-Soviet space highlight the real threat to Putin: democracy. Therefore, McCaul believes that "taking [NATO expansion] off the table will not quell [Putin's sense of] insecurity [at home]." [13]

Ambassador McCaul is correct when he argues that Putin fears democracy. [14]

Yet, as has been noted throughout this work already, a succession of Russian governments made their concerns over NATO expansion crystal clear. Indeed, in the early years of Putin's reign, specifically 2002, the would-be tsar "radiated optimism about what he believed would be a Euro-centric, or even an Atlantic-centric, future for

Russia and some of its post-Soviet neighbors." At the start of Putin's rule, he made Russian laws comport with European Union standards and ensured that Russia became a partner to NATO. The real kicker during this time was the way that Putin described Ukraine's potential accession into the NATO alliance as a "positive development."[15]

What's more, while Putin was never one for liberal democracy of the kind that the West practiced, there is little doubt that the Russian strongman began his journey as leader of Russia being at least friendly to the general concept of democracy. Before becoming leader of Russia, Putin had insinuated himself amid the post-Cold War democrats who came to power in Russia under President Boris Yeltsin. Again, Putin was never in love with Western democracy. But he was not an overt opponent to it as he clearly is today.

At no point in McFaul's analysis of Putin's Russia does the former ambassador ask why Putin went from viewing Ukraine's entrance into NATO as not a big deal in 2002, to opposing it so vociferously 20 years later that invading the country at the mere thought of Ukraine becoming part of the Western alliance seemed like a good idea. It is probably because, at the start of his presidency, Putin believed that some new *modus vivendi* could be reached with the West and that the reason the West had mistreated Russia during the 1990s was because Moscow had been ruled by a drunkard, Boris Yeltsin. If a strong Russian who did not have Yeltsin's personal foibles were in charge, maybe that Russian strongman could get better deals with Western leaders and not allow for Russia, in its weakened state, to be pillaged by the democratic-globalist forces of the West. But, to the Anne Applebaums of the world, this is just more evidence of Russian disinformation having hijacked the foreign policy discourse on the American Right.

McFaul and his ilk should also inquire as to what prompted Vladimir Putin to move from being at peace with the concept of democracy in Russia and the former Soviet space to being a rabid anti-democrat.

The answer is not to be found in McFaul's deterministic, self-serving explanations, no matter how appealing they may be to the Western elites who have helped to craft the current mess with Russia. The real answer to these questions will not be discovered in the works of any member in good standing of the present Western political elite. Instead, it will be found in the works of the now deceased and disgraced former U.S. president, Richard M. Nixon.

In 1994, the thirty-seventh president went on a whirlwind tour promoting a new book, in which he made several foreign policy suggestions for the United States to embrace in the post-Cold War era. As things related to Russia, Nixon admonished Western leaders that, "communism had been defeated [in Russia], but the ideas of freedom are now on trial." Nixon cautioned his fellow Westerners that, if the ideas of Western-style democracy and capitalism did not work in Russia, then "there will be a reversion to not communism, which has failed, but what I call a 'new despotism' which would pose a mortal danger to the rest of the world because it will have been infected with the virus of Russian imperialism, which of course, has been a characteristic of Russian foreign policy for centuries."[16] In other words, NATO expansion did play a serious role in militating the Putinist regime against the West.

The only reason people like McFaul refuse to accept that explanation is because it would mean that their policies in the aftermath of the Cold War toward Russia failed and set up the very conditions Nixon was warning about in 1994.

Would America Accept a Russian-Backed Mexico or Cuba?

PUT ANOTHER WAY, how might the Americans view a Mexico or Cuba that opted to join a Russian-led military alliance? As we saw during the Cuban Missile Crisis in 1962, when the Soviets attempted to build intermediate range ballistic missiles (IRBM) in Communist

Cuba, President John F. Kennedy risked a world war with the Soviets to force them out. After a standoff, JFK negotiated for the pullout of the missiles in Cuba. But, had the negotiations failed, the United States likely would have resorted to military force to evict those Soviet missiles from Cuba.

The Putin government views a Ukraine in NATO's orbit the same way Americans viewed Soviet missiles in Cuba or how U.S. officials would view a Mexico that joined a Russian military alliance today. This is just basic international security calculus, no different from the calculations American leaders engage in routinely.

Western actions helped to break Russia's post-Cold War experiment with liberal democratic capitalism and the expansion of NATO to Russia's post-Cold War borders ensured that Russia would be a threat today. Everyone today must recognize this sad fact if we are to create viable policies designed to better protect the United States and avoid a devastating world war with Russia over Ukraine and the future of NATO. Just imagine if NATO not expanded eastward when Russia was on its knees. Or, if it had done so at a slower clip—or even if Putin's initial query for Russia to join NATO in 2000 would have been taken more seriously—just think about how much safer a world we'd be living in today. Some self-reflection on the part of Western leaders and their role in creating the present crisis would be nice.

CHAPTER 4

THE CABAL

THERE'S AN old debate in philosophy over the question of determinism versus free will. Determinists believe that events are
predetermined by things that came before them. One can find determinists in just about every field of study. In biology and sociolo-
gy, for example, determinists believe that people are merely the sum
of their genetics, and those genetics will influence the way people
react to situations and solve problems. Economic determinists are
Marxists at heart. Indeed, Marx himself created the entire concept
of economic determinism. According to Marx, all facets of society
and culture were created as a result of economic processes.

Whether they acknowledge it or not, there is a strain of determinism that dominates the thought process of the neoconservative-neoliberal cabal that runs our bureaucracy. After all, they're Trotskyists
at heart.[1] Further, this small group of individuals has been educated
at the same small collection of institutions. As a result, they move in
the same social circles—some are married to each other—and they
share a worldview that calls for a maximalist, aggressive U.S. foreign
policy in the service of the spread of global democracy, free trade, and
human rights. This group believes that Russia is the greatest threat
facing the United States. They are further convinced that Russia
is weak and can be broken apart through consistent application of

[51]

full-spectrum pressure through U.S. alliance systems.[2]

The cabal began applying its unique, hyper-aggressive worldview in the 1990s. Back then, they were upset that President George H.W. Bush did not send U.S. forces into Baghdad to topple Saddam Hussein's regime in Iraq after successfully liberating Kuwait in Desert Storm.[3] The cabal feared American leaders would be too short-sighted to seize the opportunities presented to the United States in the unipolar world. This group wanted to ensure that no threats would arise to challenge the United States in the post-Cold War era. Part of this strategy entailed using America's overwhelming military power to preempt perceived threats before they could materialize into full-on challenges to the United States.

All this sounds reasonable on paper—at least it does until one realizes just how far the cabal planned on taking this notion of preemptive attacks. Rogue states are a particular fixation of this group, as is the legitimate fear that these regimes might build nuclear weapons. But the real issue, of course, was preventing great state rivals from rising. Again, by itself this is a perfectly reasonable strategic aim—but the tradeoffs needed to be considered far more than they were.

The cabal rode high in the 1990s. They and their teammates got together and formed various inside-the-beltway publications, like *The Weekly Standard*. They met up at places like the American Enterprise Institute (AEI). The cabal got Grover Norquist to share his insights about ensuring the top 1% wage earners kept getting their big, juicy tax cuts. Frank Luntz would be brought in to smooth the whole thing over with the focus groups of plebes they'd routinely trot out to see if their policies were resonating with the common folks in Flyover Country. They signed onto documents penned by the officiously named "Project for the New American Century" (PNAC) which effectively called for the United States to do that which John Quincy Adams begged his fellow countrymen never to do: go abroad in search of monsters to destroy. Doing so, Adams feared, would make the United States the "dictatress of the world."

Well, what'd he know anyway? Those who formed the democrat-ic-globalist cabal knew better than those old rustics, like the found-ers, what with their quaint ideas about liberty and non-interven-tionist foreign policy. The cabal's members were sure they were the smartest people in the room. At least that what they told themselves. Yes, the 1990s were finger-lickin' good for the cabal. They got to act as a shadow government with no real power—just a lot of loose donor money, little oversight, and much ambition (as well as that all-important factor of hubris).

As the years passed, the cabal worked to build a case against Saddam Hussein's Iraq. They even got their great political rival, President Bill Clinton, to sign the Iraqi Liberation Act in 1998.[4] Saddam figured heavily in their plans. When 9/11 occurred, the old bugaboo about Saddam Hussein was brought to the fore. Looking for a chance to apply theories first formulated in the PNAC "Rebuilding America's Defenses" document (many of the PNAC members found jobs in the George W. Bush administration), Iraq seemed like an excellent place to test their concept of regime change through preemptive warfare.

The argument for invading Iraq in 2003 was simple. In the after-math of the surprise terrorist attacks on 9/11, the cabal began warn-ing the public that Saddam Hussein had been surreptitiously building nuclear weapons and was working with al Qaeda. The Bush adminis-tration feared that those nukes could be used by al Qaeda in another round of terrorist attacks against the United States. The neoconser-vatives were operating on very poor intelligence. But they ignored the people raising necessary questions about the reliability of the intelli-gence they were using to build a case for the war they wanted anyway. According to the cabal, the Iraq War would be a cakewalk, so none of the objections would matter.[5] And, they hoped, there would be a new fear of America instilled in the minds of anyone who would ever again threaten the United States, as did al Qaeda on 9/11.

The essential element to understand is the concept of preemp-tive strikes or aiming to hit an enemy early in the process of them becoming a threat to the United States rather than waiting for that threat to materialize. Like so much of what the cabal believed, it was a deterministic view of the world. Certain countries, usually autocracies, are inherently designed to become threats to the United States. Better to kill the baby in crib rather than wait for it to mature into a real menace in the future. But there was no real or verifiable evidence that Saddam had either been working on a nuclear weapons arsenal contrary to UN resolutions or that Iraq was planning to again attack the United States. There was even less indication that the secular Ba'athist dictator, Saddam Hussein, had somehow made common cause with the Islamists of al Qaeda.

The United States went to war in 2003 on the basis of this faulty intelligence. It was all to prove a theory about the need for America to dominate the world using preemptive warfare. The entire concept was like something from a Philip K. Dick dystopian science fiction story. In fact, the way the neocons viewed the world was eerily similar to the plotline from the 2002 Steven Spielberg film, *Minority Report* (which was based on a Philip K. Dick short story). That story depicts a United States in the mid-twenty-first century that has people who can see the future working for the police force. These "precogs" (short for "precognition") can anticipate when a crime is about to happen—and can provide actionable intelligence allowing authorities not only to stop the criminal but to prevent the crime from happening entirely.

Minority Report presents a dystopic world because those who have been accused by the precogs have no recourse. The precogs' visions of the future are recorded and stored on computer files. The police arrest the future criminals and punish them by sticking them in tubes where they are mentally reprogrammed to not commit crimes again.

Sadly for the characters in that story, it turns out that the precogs, like anything human, are imperfect. They do not account for free will. Just because someone is considering killing a cheating spouse and her lover, does not mean that that person will, in fact, act. By relying on a fixed vision of the future that is far from certain (because the future is *always* uncertain), innocent people suffer. The entire program, therefore, is an abuse by the state against the people.

The neocons of the West are a lot like the characters in *Minority Report*. By acting on overhyped threats under the rationale that they were preventing a greater threat forming in the future, the cabal was creating the very conditions for destroying American power. It was true with Iraq in 2003. It was true of U.S. policies toward the greater Middle East during the so-called "Arab Spring." What's more, it is true of U.S. policies toward Russia in the post-Cold War era.

Ultimately, the cabal's policies will not result in a world made more secure for the United States. It will merely create a world gone mad. This policy, if continued, will eventuate in a great power war with Russia. Russian power is unlikely to be broken. Even if it is, any victory the United States enjoys under such conditions would be a Pyrrhic one at best.

The cabal did not believe that countries, such as Iraq or Russia, could ever be capable of taking different actions to make themselves less threatening. Of course, as T.E. Lawrence is depicted saying in *Lawrence of Arabia*, "Nothing is written!" Libya was viewed similarly to Saddam's Iraq. Yet, in 2003, Libya's strongman, Muammar Gaddafi, changed tactics, and became a useful ally for the United States in fighting Islamist extremism throughout North Africa. Sadly, the cabal, as one may recall, couldn't leave well-enough alone and decided to topple Gaddafi's regime in 2011—replacing it with chaos and Islamist mania.

The arrogance of the cabal, though, is much like that of the Bourbons of old: They have learned nothing and forgotten nothing. As such, the cabal blunders on with American citizens paying the price for their hubris and ignorance.

The cabal's obsession with a future Russian threat became so prevalent at some point that it prevented more reasonable policies with Moscow from being explored. NATO would be used by the United

States to stunt the potential for a Russian threat from materializing by expanding its reach into Eastern Europe and, quite possibly, the Southern Caucasus region. The cabal believed it was preserving American interests and enhancing America's security by preventing a renewed Russian threat from rising. In fact, Washington was making the United States weaker by overcommitting to multiple conflicts divorced from the national interest, and instead dedicated to ambiguous concepts of human rights and democracy promotion. These awful behavioral patterns and belief systems led the United States down the pathway to what seems likely to be a highly destructive war with Russia over ancillary issues like Ukraine's status as an independent nation.

Russia was never going to have the kind of relationship with America that Great Britain or Canada enjoys. Few countries have such unique relationships. But did Russia have to be the enemy that it is today? It did not. The cabal ruling Washington and the other Western powers insisted upon it because of their fear that, one day, Russia *might* evolve into a threat we cannot manage. To their way of thinking it has been better to make it evolve more quickly into precisely the threat we fear, thereby ensuring conflict between the West and Russia. The whole thing is a mess.

The neoconservatives' deterministic worldview is utterly unnecessary. They created the very dangers we are forced to live with today. No one other than this group was as committed to NATO growing beyond where it was in 1991. They wanted to grow NATO, even though they understood that Russia would view such actions as an existential threat. Yet it wasn't only the militaristic neocons who were destabilizing America's hard-won victory in the Cold War. It was the neoliberals as well.

There are many points of contention between modern neoliberals and neoconservatives. For example, neocons understand that untrammeled free markets can negatively impact social bonds where those free markets are created (or, in the case of neoliberals, imposed). Neoliberals are far less skeptical about the impact of free markets on societies. And this is key because after the Cold War ended, in keeping with Francis Fukuyama's thesis that America's ultimate victory in the Cold War represented the "end of history," neoliberals developed an almost evangelical fervor about expanding the sphere of free markets. In the wake of the USSR's collapse, Russia, with its vast mineral wealth and lack of central governing authority, became a prime target for the rabid, freewheeling neoliberal theories of the 1990s to be applied.[6]

Thus, the neocon-neoliberal cabal found that whatever their differences, they had much more in common. By the time the Ukraine War was in full swing, the expansionist policies of the cabal had been in full swing for over 30 years. These policies have led American power to a dangerous place. Overcommitted and strained, Washington's War Party cannot simply continue to plug away at the policies that created our present crisis in the first place and expect a different result. Until we resolve to fundamental rethinking of U.S. foreign policy and America's role in the world, we will continue to be led to the slaughter.

[A DISASTER OF OUR OWN MAKING

CHAPTER 5

BILL CLINTON'S EMPTY PROMISES TO UKRAINE

O N JANUARY 10, 1994, an extraordinary event in the annals of nuclear disarmament occurred. After two years of painstaking negotiations, the post-Cold War government of Ukraine announced that it had finalized a deal with both the United States and the Russian Federation to dismantle its nuclear weapons arsenal. Ukraine possessed the third-largest nuclear weapons arsenal in the world. The collapse of the Soviet Union had occurred so rapidly that the Red Army was forced to rapidly abandon its positions in the Soviet bloc states. Ukraine was an integral member of the Soviet bloc and had long been the location of a massive Soviet nuclear weapons arsenal. That arsenal was left behind by the evacuating Red Army. In all, 175 long-range missiles and 1,800 warheads were left in Ukraine.[1]

Experts argued that the nuclear weapons arsenal Ukraine inherited was antiquated and poorly maintained. According to the Defense Threat Reduction Agency (DTRA), which was the main U.S. government entity charged with securing Soviet weapons of mass destruction in the aftermath of the Cold War, while the Ukrainians possessed the nuclear arsenal left behind by the Red Army, the launch codes for the weapons remained in Moscow.[2] As Eric Gomez of the libertarian CATO Institute, postulated, "Russia retained effective command and control over the nuclear weapons on Ukrainian territory. Ukraine could not launch the missiles or use the warheads, and therefore the arsenal could not be used as a deterrent." Gomez concluded that, "even if Ukraine did obtain command and control, it did not have the infrastructure to safely maintain these weapons."[3]

Trying to wrest control of the launch codes from Russia would have been difficult, but possible, given how desperate the position of Russia was in the immediate aftermath of the collapse of the USSR. The West could have negotiated for this. If that was too far out of reach, then the West could have used its superior technological capabilities to deconstruct the weapons, with the intention of repurposing the nuclear materials. After all, this is basically what ended up happening when the decision was made to dismantle them. Of course, many experts say this would have been too difficult. But, given how vulnerable the removal of the nuclear arsenal made Ukraine to future Russian aggression, such a move would have been far more conducive to international peace than the utopian dream of total nuclear disarmament.[4]

Besides, Ukraine inherited more than nuclear missiles and tactical nuclear warheads from the former USSR. The Soviets left behind nuclear-capable Tupolev Tu-60 "Blackjack" bombers loaded with nuclear weapons. While the nuclear missiles the Red Army left behind required launch codes, the bomber-based nukes did not. The Ukrainian president at the time, Leonid Kravchuk, alluded to this during the pressure campaign Kiev was subjected to by both Washington and Moscow regarding their possession of the Soviet era nukes. Not only could Ukraine have deployed nuclear bombers, but the country also possessed SS-24 nuclear missiles that could have been fired by Kiev rather than Moscow. Lastly, reports from that time indicated that, "Kiev [was] developing a command and control system of its own that could be used to launch [the nuclear weapons] without Moscow's permission."[5]

The West, with its superior technological prowess, could have contributed to this Ukrainian push for alternative command-and-control capabilities that, over time, would have ensured Ukraine had a reliable, robust nuclear deterrent. Had the West done this rather than spend its time and diplomatic capital bullying Ukraine into sending its nukes back to Russia, history might have turned out differently. As John Mearsheimer argued at the time, "Ukrainian nuclear weapons would be an effective deterrent against a Russian conventional attack or nuclear blackmail."[6]

The possession of the third-largest nuclear weapons arsenal in the world *would have* served as the ultimate check against any Russian leader seeking to reabsorb Ukraine into the Russian sphere. Alas, the Clinton administration saw only what was right in front of them. They pressured and cajoled Kiev into giving up what was probably the only thing that could have prevented the kind of conflict that now rages between Russia and Ukraine. Clinton effectively did the bidding of the Russians, who were terrified at the prospect of Ukraine possessing a nuclear deterrent but lacked the power or the clout at the time to force Ukraine to return those weapons.

The Budapest Memorandum

THE UKRAINIANS extracted a promise from the Clinton administration that proved to be key in getting them to abandon their massive, though older, nuclear weapons arsenal. The Americans vowed to militarily defend Ukraine if Russia ever threatened them again.[7] For their part, the Russian government recognized Ukraine as an independent nation-state.[8]

Despite the era of good feelings between the signatories of the Budapest Memorandum, there was much disagreement between the Russians, Americans, and Ukrainians. These disagreements were only compounded by the fact that words like "assurances" in English were translated into Russian and Ukrainian as "guarantees," leading to all manner of confusion when interpreting the treaty today. As is typical of diplomats, they were committed to getting a deal done at all costs, even though there were serious—insurmountable, even—disagreements between the parties involved. So, the diplomats papered over these fundamental disagreements and pushed ahead with a very flimsy, contradictory, and even dangerous document.[9]

Aside from the bad translations of key words and phrases, another critical element was glossed over by these eager diplomats. That was the Russian requirement for Ukraine to remain neutral. While not explicitly in the Budapest Memorandum, Russian diplomats, as with the infamous "cocktail napkin" agreement between James Baker and Eduard Shevardnadze in 1990, trusted that their concerns about a militarized Ukraine on their southwestern border would be accounted for by their partners in the West and in Ukraine. So long as Russian worries over a potentially hostile Ukraine were respected, Ukrainian sovereignty would be assured. But short of a universal enforcement mechanism, international law and norms come down to the ability of powerful state actors to adhere to such agreements as well as their desire to respect them in the long run. The ability and desire to respect international agreements by powerful states is always changing.

Besides, the signatories to the Budapest Memorandum—notably the United States and Russia—could not even agree as to whether the document was a binding treaty or merely a political document.

Yet, in the West, most view it as a legally binding treaty. That is why so many today who support Ukraine's cause in the face of Russian aggression are incensed by Russia's actions: Moscow had agreed with Washington and the international community to respect Ukraine's right to exist. These individuals, such as Frederick W. Kagan, argue that even if Ukrainian neutrality was enshrined in the Budapest Memorandum, Putin's government was always prepared to find a reason to strike at Ukraine.[10]

Indeed, when Putin announced his invasion of Ukraine in February 2022, he listed a multitude of other grievances. Although,

Kagan is cherry-picking the timeline to suit his argument that Russia never could have been at peace with an independent, though neutral Ukraine, it was only after years of what Putin believed were Western provocations directed at Russia that Putin ultimately decided to invade his neighbor. Further, in the early 2000s, Putin was on record not only accepting Ukrainian independence but also being at peace with Ukrainian integration into the European Union—and possibly even eventually becoming part of NATO.

Kagan and the other neoconservatives who believe that Russia has no legitimate qualms with the West over Ukraine should be asking is themselves what, precisely, caused Putin to change his mind?

In any event, Kagan's assertions are tedious, unhelpful, and often self-serving (not only is Kagan a notorious hawk but his sister-in-law is Victoria Nuland, a State Department official known for her long-time hostility to Russia).[11] Why would Kagan say anything contrary to the Ukrainian position when he and his family have been so intimately involved with Washington's aggressive foreign policy choices of the last quarter of a century? Kagan comes from a long line of rabid hawks. His father, Donald, was a major foreign policy player for decades and imbued a militancy onto his two sons, Frederick and Donald Kagan, that has shaped their worldviews from the beginning of their careers as influential defense intellectuals. Just as they helped push America into war with Iraq in 2003, the Kagan clan has had an outsized role in shaping the conflict with Russia over Ukraine.

Something very few people who point to the Budapest Memorandum appear to understand is that the Russians had always maintained a strict caveat in their embrace of Ukraine as its own state: Kiev had to uphold the concept of neutrality. Thus, in order for Russia to view Ukraine as not being a potential threat along its border, Kiev had to avoid joining NATO. Once the Budapest Memorandum became part of the international legal regime, it looked as though Ukraine might avoid an unfortunate run-in with their Russian neighbors so long as they adhered to the terms.

Indeed, the initial governments of Ukraine ranged from ambivalent about both the West and Russia to being far friendlier with Moscow than the West. This situation persisted until 2014, when pro-Western forces launched a coup which overthrew the pro-Russian president of Ukraine, Viktor Yanukovych, in what's become known as the Maidan Revolution of that year. Before that, Russia made no indication that it intended to reconquer Ukraine. It sought to meddle, for sure. But it seemed to stay its hand from an outright reconquest.

Lost in Translation

IN 1994, with the passage of the Budapest Memorandum, it appeared that Kiev's decision to use the massive nuclear weapons arsenal inherited from the Red Army as a bargaining chip to extract geopolitical concessions from both the Americans and Russians was paying dividends. By 2023, Ukraine's sacrifice this independent nuclear arsenal on the altar of global disarmament was shown to be an obviously terrible decision. But the Ukrainians should have known that the promises the Clinton administration made to them were next to worthless. As the late Henry Kissinger once said, "It may be dangerous to be America's enemy, but to be America's friend is fatal."[12]

What American leader would commit the lives of U.S. servicemen and women to war with nuclear-armed Russia over Ukraine? And as President Joe Biden today continues to insinuate that U.S. forces could be deployed to stop a Russian reconquest of Ukraine if Ukrainian defenses collapse, the other question that should have been asked back in 1994 suggests itself: How long will any U.S. president who does such a thing last in office?

The agreement was also made while all sides appeared to be wearing blinders. Everyone who signed it seemed to believe that the geopolitical system that existed in 1994, when the memorandum was signed, would persist in perpetuity. The Americans assumed the Russians would be forever weak. The Russians under Yeltsin believed the Americans could be taken at their word. The Ukrainians, too, thought the Americans were reliable partners. Further, at that time, the Ukrainian government wasn't yet insane enough to move itself too close to NATO.

This isn't to excuse Russia from any wrongdoing in contributing to the current crisis. A future chapter will address Russia's culpability in the current Ukraine situation. Although, we cannot simply ignore all the missed opportunities and broken promises from the West in the lead up to this current impasse. As was stated earlier, reality is constantly changing. Thus, new opportunities for states to exploit the international system are always arising. The West likely did not set out to expand NATO or to incorporate Ukraine into the growing NATO alliance. But, the reality of a weakened Russia in the 1990s and the fears of the liberated Eastern European states that the Russian bear might once more return to threaten them—to say nothing of the American need for absolute security—all presented Western policymakers with what they viewed as an historic opportunity.[13] Over time, NATO expansion became the *sine qua non* of U.S. policy toward Europe. And, as you will read in the following chapter, the George W. Bush Administration pushed NATO expansion so far that Moscow could not help but to view it as a growing threat to Russia's sovereignty and security.

These calculations, as you will read, were dangerously misguided. Instead of enhancing our national security and expanding the sphere of liberty, NATO's expansion eastward coupled with the Western craze of incorporating Ukraine into that alliance has degraded our security and risked diminishing the sphere of liberty.[14] There is no greater proof of this failure than the sight of Russian forces marching against their democratic neighbors. By December 2023, Western leaders who mindlessly cheered the West into courting nuclear war with Russia over Ukraine were finally admitting what this author had been writing about for two years in the pages of the *Asia Times*: Russia is poised to win the Ukraine War and come out stronger.[15]

Meanwhile, the Western alliance is set to walk away from the conflict bruised, bloodied, and defeated.[16]

If Western leaders believe that appearing before the raging Russian bear in a bloodied and defeated form is going to deter further aggression from Moscow, then they do not understand the Russian mindset.

The Budapest Memorandum is another American promise made more than two decades ago that helped set the stage for what is now becoming one of the bloodiest wars in Europe since World War II. Moreover, this is a conflict that threatens to pull America and its NATO partners into a direct conflict with nuclear-armed Russia over an issue that country considers to be paramount to its territorial and national security. Mearsheimer's predictions in 1993 were correct. A nuclear-armed Ukraine, while it would have presented its own set of problems for Western policymakers, also would have deterred Russia from invading as it ultimately did in February of 2022. And the world would have avoided the prospect of a nuclear third world war.

Here again, the echoes of World War I can be heard today. It was a series of expansive, interlocking, complex diplomatic agreements that were entirely unmanageable from the start, the great powers of the day managed to turn a tiny, regional conflict in the Balkans into the Great War. Today, it seems, enmeshing diplomatic concordances may be pushing the world toward a similar reckoning.

CHAPTER 6

GEORGE W. BUSH GOES FOR BROKE ON UKRAINE

AMERICA'S FORTY-THIRD president, George Walker Bush, is likely one of the most controversial U.S. presidents in history. A man remembered for rising to power in the aftermath of a contentious legal battle in 2000 with his Democratic Party opponent, former Vice-President Al Gore, Bush quickly was thrust into the pantheon of American wartime presidents after the terrorist attacks on September 11, 2001.[1] Following those attacks, Bush momentarily enjoyed one of the highest approval ratings of any American president in history.[2] But Bush wasted all the goodwill he engendered for his no-nonsense leadership in the aftermath of 9/11 when he leveraged that political and diplomatic capital to push the United States into the unpopular Iraq War in March 2003.[3]

Bush's legacy is forever tied to 9/11 and the subsequent failed wars in the Middle East. Few remember that George W. Bush was powered by his ideological adherence to the notion that democracy must be spread to every corner on the globe.[4] Indeed, the so-called "Bush Doctrine," enacted after 9/11, became synonymous with the neoconservative vision of using preventive military force to spread democracy and overthrow autocratic regimes.[5] The Bush Doctrine

[67]

would become the basis of President Bush's even more expansive foreign policy vision known as the "Freedom Agenda."[6] The forty-third president's forceful engagements in the Mideast, notably in Afghanistan and Iraq, were his most visceral demonstrations of the "Freedom Agenda."[7] Yet, Bush's "Freedom Agenda" was intended not only for the Middle East, but everywhere. It was a truly global policy. Ukraine and the former Soviet states factored heavily into these ideological machinations.[8]

George W. Bush was ushered into office carried by the notion that he was the anti-Bill Clinton candidate in the 2000 presidential election. Americans were tired of Clinton's playboy routine, and they were generally dissatisfied with Clinton's foreign policy.[9] In one famous debate with Al Gore, Bush vowed to not let the U.S. military get bogged down in the multilateral humanitarian operations that had defined the Clinton years. Yet, unbeknownst to the public, once 9/11 occurred, Bush would define his foreign policy through expansive military commitments. Unlike Clinton, who favored working alongside allies, Bush preferred to "go-it-alone."[10] He embraced what the preeminent Yale Cold War historian, John Lewis Gaddis, defined in 2004 as a policy of, "unilateralism, preemption, and hegemony."[11]

It had been eight years since the Republican Party held the White House by the time George W. Bush was sworn in. That's an eternity in U.S. national politics. By January 2001, the geopolitical situation had irrevocably changed from what it had been when George H.W. Bush had handed over the White House keys to Bill Clinton in January 1993. Terrorism, rogue states, and neoliberal economics had replaced the Cold War era thinking. But the GOP, as always, was slow on the uptake. George W. Bush had staffed his administration with Cold War-era policy hawks, like Donald Rumsfeld, who was named as Bush's secretary of defense.[12] Rather than talk terrorism, the primary national security agenda at the outset of the Bush administration was national missile defense.[13]

This was a key criticism of former White House Counterterrorism

Czar, Richard Clarke, one of the few holdovers from the Clinton administration.[14] Even after the terrorist attacks on 9/11, the Bush administration did not drop their Cold War era fixation on missile defense.[15] In fact, they used the continued threat of global terrorism and the nuclear-arming of rogue states, such as Iran or North Korea, as an excuse to push their missile defense agenda forward.

Missile Defense, NATO Expansion, and Ukraine

RONALD REAGAN had envisioned creating a space-based missile defense system—dubbed "Star Wars" by his critics. The Washington bureaucracy, ever fearful that the Hollywood cowboy would upset their perfectly designed game of "Mutual Assured Destruction" (MAD) and détente with the Soviet Union had fought this idea from the start. Despite their resistance, the concept continued to work its way through the defense establishment, taking many different forms, across many different alphabet soup government agencies and defense contractors.

The missile defense concept the Republican Party and the Washington defense establishment came to favor was a less space-aged solution than the one Reagan desired. By placing ground-based missile interceptors not only along America's borders but also in countries bordering the Russian Federation, preexisting technology was being deployed in new ways rather than having to go through the difficulty of creating entirely new systems to support space-based missile defense. Of course, there were plenty of reasons to prefer the space-based missile defense concept to the ground-based interceptors Washington and the GOP favored in the post-Reagan era.

A space-based system would already be in orbit, where a nuclear missile crosses on its way to its intended target on Earth's surface below. A second-stage launch—when it crosses into space—is when a nuclear weapon is most vulnerable to interception. What's more, knocking a nuclear weapon off its course in orbit significantly

[69]

reduces the risk of radioactive fallout on the ground below. Since most space-based missile defense concepts called for the deployment of powerful lasers to instantly zap incoming nuclear missiles off their course in space, the prospect of creating dangerous debris fields in orbit was significantly reduced as well. And placing such systems in orbit, high above the nations of Earth would mitigate the headaches of having to constantly negotiate with various countries to use their territories for missile defense purposes.

As United States Air Force Captain Joshua Daviscourt wrote in 2021, "[Ground-based missile defense] is an antiquated, $70 billion answer for long-range ballistic missile attacks, as well as being prohibitively expensive. Each interceptor rocket has a probability of effectiveness at only 58 percent." Daviscourt goes on to conclude that space-based missile defenses are the only viable course for reliable missile defense.[16]

In fact, Edward Teller, one of the greatest American scientific minds of the twentieth century and the father of the hydrogen bomb, favored the space-based missile concept over any other form of missile defense shield.[17]

A ground-based interceptor system, however, is a very complex system. It's also far riskier than the space-based model. Think of it as trying to shoot a bullet with a bullet. Plus, the ground-based interceptor is having to launch a rocket from the ground—pushing against gravity—while a nuclear weapon, in its final stage of deployment, uses the Earth's gravity to boost its accuracy. Not only is the ground-based interceptor working against gravity, it is also waging nuclear war in the atmosphere. Even if a nuclear missile is successfully intercepted by a ground-based system, the chance of spreading radioactive fallout over cities below is great. Proponents of the ground-based system point to the success of Israel's Iron Dome missile defense system. Indeed, this is a highly successful missile shield. Although, Iron Dome is designed to shoot down incoming conventional missiles. It is not necessarily designed—or tested—to intercept nukes.

The George W. Bush administration began the process of placing missile defense shield components in NATO countries, notably nations closest to Russian territory, such as Poland.[18] But NATO lacked key members, like Ukraine, to Russia's south. Thus, Ukraine became an attractive potential member for NATO so that Washington could place its interceptors there, creating a network of ground-based missile interceptors all along Russia's border. Moscow viewed this as a threat to its nuclear deterrent. Once 9/11 occurred and the Bush administration enacted its Freedom Agenda, the American quest for missile defense fused with the messianic push to spread democracy everywhere oppression existed, rapidly destabilizing the Russo-American relationship—placing Ukraine in an untenable position between these two nuclear-armed juggernauts.

President Bush did not just envision incorporating Ukraine into NATO. Like much of his foreign policy, he had a far more expansive idea of where things should go for the former Soviet Union. Georgia, the birthplace of Stalin, a nation far removed from the North Atlantic or even Europe, was another country that the Bush administration wanted to include in a new round of NATO expansion. Located in the South Caucasus, Georgia was a tiny nation nestled beneath Russia, beside the Caspian Sea, and atop of Iran, Azerbaijan, and Armenia. Bush wanted both Ukraine and Georgia in NATO. Naturally, Russia opposed this.[19] So did Germany and France, two key NATO members.[20] The rest of NATO had mixed opinions on this Bush agenda of expanding into Ukraine and Georgia.

The damage was done, however. The Russian government did not believe that NATO expansion was a result of mindless naiveté or post-Cold War euphoria that could be stopped with careful diplomacy and increased military and economic cooperation with the West. The hyper-paranoid Vladimir Putin and his *siloviki* believed that, despite America's rhetoric about democracy, its real goal was to encircle Russia.[21] As noted above, there was a plan to place missile defenses throughout the NATO states bordering Russia. But that was an initiative of the Bush administration and not one that was necessarily shared by previous American leaders of the post-Cold War era. In fact, there'd been several attempts by European leaders to reshape NATO into a counterterrorism and humanitarian aid force in the post-Cold War era.

In its post-9/11 paranoia and imperiousness, however, the Bush administration was committed to a maximalist foreign policy. They had taken the inertia of the relatively open field that existed in Europe following the collapse of the USSR as a sign that they could push America's defensive perimeter from the Atlantic to deep inside of Europe, near Russia's reduced post-Cold War borders. The Bush administration claimed the goal of the missile defenses in former Soviet bloc states was to shoot down potential Iranian nuclear missiles. Moscow did not buy this explanation. In fact, Putin believed his regime was the intended target.

The Russian nuclear weapons arsenal, after all, has long been perceived by Soviet and, later, Russian leaders as the only check against another Western force attempting to encircle, invade, and dismember Russia. A nuclear missile defense shield placed in European nations nearest to Russia's borders, no matter how rudimentary, would significantly stunt the efficacy and reliability of Russia's nuclear deterrent. What's more, the existence of a growing web of American-built ground-based missile interceptors in nations once controlled by Moscow was a continual reminder to Putin and his *siloviki* of just how weak—and vulnerable—that Russia had become following the collapse of the USSR.

Putin could never allow such a situation to arise.

"They Lied to Me. I'll Never Trust Them Again!"

NOVEMBER 22, 2004, was a particularly formative moment in Vladimir Putin's journey from being amenable to the West to becoming an ardent adversary to it. On that day, Putin watched in horror as protesters took to the streets of Kiev to contest the results of a contentious, run-off presidential election between Viktor Yanukovych and Viktor Yushchenko. It was determined that during the second round of voting pro-Russian elements engaged in blatant election rigging. Given this fact, over a million Ukrainians turned out to protest the results. Ultimately, the third round ended up being cleaner than the second and Yushchenko and his pro-Western allies ended up in power.[22]

The Russians were certainly invested in making Yanukovych their man-in-Kiev. A silent, shadow war had raged between the West and Russia over the outcome of the Ukrainian presidential election. For Moscow, they needed Ukraine to remain neutral—if not somewhat tilted toward Russia. For Washington, fully engaged in pursuing Bush's "Freedom Agenda" at the time, the only obstacle to their plans for converting Ukraine into a full-fledged member of NATO (as well as the EU) and eventually placing ground-based missile defense interceptors there, was the government in Kiev. A strict policy in Ukraine of either neutrality or being pro-Russia was unacceptable to permanent Washington, as such a Ukraine would deprive the cabal of its ability to achieve its objectives in Europe.

Ukraine is a major gateway into southern Europe. Further, Ukraine's history of being at one time or another dominated and divided amongst its more powerful neighbors (Russia, Poland, and the Ottoman Empire) has made the country's population—and its history—truly unique. Recall Catherine the Great's conquest of Ukraine. Russian colonists landed first in Eastern Ukraine and then in Crimea. These are the two regions of Ukraine that are populated mostly by Russian-speakers and have the most affinity for Russia.

The western side of Ukraine, however, has long been culturally more similar to the West. This east-west regional divide plays out in Ukrainian electoral politics. It has defined the nation's domestic political scene since Ukraine first became an independent nation-state at the end of the Cold War. Thus, the candidates who ran for the

2004 election—Viktor Yanukovych and Viktor Yushchenko both represented the two sides of this divide.

Yanukovych belonged to the pro-Russian Party of Regions. He had previously served as the governor of the Donetsk Oblast. If that sounds familiar, it is because Donetsk is currently one of the Russian-speaking breakaway provinces in Eastern Ukraine over which the Russians and Ukrainians are currently warring.

Viktor Yushchenko, meanwhile, represented the pro-Western portion of the Ukrainian electorate. The presidents who preceded these two candidates in 2004 were either firmly neutral toward the West and Russia or, as was proven by Ukrainian President Leonid Kuchma during the Cassette Scandal in 2000, they were violently pro-Russian. At that time, Kuchma, who had run Ukraine as a proxy of Russia for about a decade, was accused of orchestrating the murder of Georgy Gongadze, a journalist investigating claims of widespread corruption within the Kuchma regime. Of course, there was widespread corruption. For his trouble, Gongadze was murdered and his badly beaten body—and severed head—were found in a shallow grave. It would later turn out that a disgruntled bodyguard of President Kuchma's had secretly recorded the Ukrainian strongman asking political allies to dispense with the pesky Gongadze. The caustic recordings of Kuchma scheming to have his political rivals whacked were given to the press in Ukraine, causing a national scandal.[23]

Kuchma and Russia began looking for replacements to succeed Kuchma as the pro-Russian voice in Kiev's government. Ukraine was, after all, far too important for Russia to simply let it slip into the orbit of the West. But the corruption that aggravated so many in Ukraine would not be tolerated for much longer. When the next presidential election occurred the Ukrainian people were not going to be as passive about Russian-backed manipulations of their political system.

Both Moscow and Washington viewed the 2004 presidential election in Ukraine as a fulcrum point for the country; a time in which the country's fate of either becoming part of the Western alliance or staying in Russia's shadow, would be decided. During the tough election in 2004, things between the pro-Russian Yanukovych campaign and the pro-Western Yushchenko campaign were so bad that someone attempted to assassinate the pro-Western candidate. Using a poison called dioxin, Yushchenko was dosed with the lethal chemical surreptitiously while at a campaign stop.[24] It nearly killed him. The dioxin was so severe that it disfigured Yushchenko's face for many years thereafter.

According to my colleague at the *Asia Times*, David P. Goldman, Putin watched the Ukraine election results on live television from his posh *dacha* outside of Moscow. Those who were with Putin that evening describe the Russian strongman as having a progressively irate reaction to the images displayed on his television. "They lied to me," said Putin of the United States (I suspect Putin was referring, specifically, George W. Bush, who had developed a bizarre public affinity for the Russian dictator that Putin appeared to reciprocate). "I'll never trust them again," Putin concluded bitterly.[25]

From that point on, the race for dominance in Ukraine between the U.S.-led Western alliance and Russia was afoot. It would only intensify from there.

The Role of Poison in Russian Intelligence Operations

POISON IS A PREFERRED method Russian intelligence uses to dispose of political opponents.[26] In 2007, for example, longtime Putin critic (and a former Russian intelligence officer himself), Alexander Litvinenko, was poisoned by polonium-210, a rare radioactive isotope that, "when ingested, is lethal." The British intelligence services, along with Litvinenko as he lay dying in a British hospital from the poison, determined that the polonium-210 was surreptitiously administered to him by a Russian assassin at the posh Millennium Hotel in London. Litvinenko had left the Russian intelligence service in 2000 and had become what *The Guardian* described as an "ebullient and needling critic" of Vladimir Putin while living in exile in London. Because of his criticism of his former Russian intelligence colleague-turned-president, Vladimir Putin, Litvinenko died a painful, public death.[27]

Other critics of Putin's regime have faced similar threats. Again in 2018, in Salisbury, England, Russian expatriate, Sergei Skripal and his daughter, Yulia, were poisoned with the nerve agent known as novichok by two assassins from Russia's military intelligence service, the GRU. Sergei Skripal himself originally served in the Russian military GRU. Skripal had become a double-agent for British intelligence, was discovered, arrested, thrown in a Russian prison, and ultimately sent to Britain as part of a prisoner swap between the Russian and British governments in 2010. He became a British citizen thereafter and is presumed to have continued working for British intelligence.[28]

The assassination attempt on the Skripals was part of a longer string of Russian poisonings against suspected threats going back to Yushchenko in 2004. Like the Yushchenko poisoning, though, the Russian assassins botched the operation. The Skripals survived their ordeal. Unfortunately, though, several innocent British civilians were exposed to the nerve agent and did not survive—including an innocent mother of three. Several other first responders have had to deal with long-term medical complications from having been exposed to the novichok nerve agent as well.

Thanks to the investigative reporting of Bellingcat, a private intelligence firm many suspect to be part of the Western intelligence machine, the British authorities were able to identify the two would-be Russian assassins of the Skripals. Although, Eliot Higgins, the founder of Bellingcat, categorically denies these claims of an association with Western intelligence, many of their scoops have panned out.[29] Thanks to Bellingcat's investigative work using open-source intelligence methods, the British authorities were able to issue arrest warrants for the would-be assassins of the Skripals. The British government was able to pressure Moscow through diplomatic channels to atone for their violations of the Chemical Weapons Act.

What Was Ukraine Worth to Washington?

RUSSIAN INTELLIGENCE SERVICES were highly active in Ukraine during the tense 2004 presidential election. They were using every means, much as the U.S.-led coalition was, to sway that election in their favor. The issue comes down one of strategic prioritization.

Was it a greater strategic priority for the West to prevent Moscow from ensuring its proxies control Ukraine, thereby keeping Ukraine as a neutral nation separating Russia from Europe? Or was it more important for America to give Russia a wide strategic berth in Ukraine so as to ensure Moscow remained cooperative in more important pursuits, such as containing Iranian nuclear ambitions or keeping them on friendly terms with NATO?

Evoking Spengler's 2008 criticism of Western elites:

> *"America's idea of winning a strategic game is to accumulate the most chips on the board: bases in Uzbekistan and Kyrgyzstan, a pipeline in Georgia, a 'moderate Muslim' government with a big North Atlantic Treaty Organization base in Kosovo, missile installations in Poland and the Czech Republic, and so forth. But this is not strategy; it is only a game score."*[30]

LIKE SO MUCH ELSE that President George W. Bush touched, America's so-called strategy in Ukraine and the former Soviet space ended up backfiring on America and its partners. It also solidified the perception in Russia that the United States was trying to destroy Russia in its post-Cold War weakness.[31] Russia can be a geopolitical doorway into Eurasia, or it can be wall blocking Western influence across the Eurasian landmass—where much of the world's natural resources and population exist; a region that is home to America's greatest strategic challenger, the People's Republic of China.

After the Cold War, there was a chance for the doorway to be opened and held ajar, but that was always a tenuous prospect. By the time of the George W. Bush presidency, the door was closed, and the wall was being erected. President Bush went for broke in Ukraine. Now, we're broke.

CHAPTER 7

IT'S ALL ABOUT CRIMEA (AND SEVASTOPOL)

O NE OF the most potent myths about Russia comes from Tsar Peter the Great's final moments on Earth. A man who had lived in Britain as a student and fallen in love the with globetrotting British Royal Navy, when he returned to the Russian Empire to ascend to the crown, Peter envisioned replicating Britain's maritime dominance. Until that point, thanks to its geography, Russia had been a continental power; possessed of a strong army and a meager navy.

From the British, Peter the Great also came to understand the value of trade. Specifically, maritime-based trade.

Nations become wealthy and powerful through their ability to conduct trade across vast distances and to project power across similar distances. Britain would never have enjoyed the wealth and prestige it had for hundreds of years had it not been for the acquisition of their vast overseas empire, conquered thanks to the potent Royal Navy. Similarly, the United States, with its continent-encompassing borders, surrounded by two major oceans (the Atlantic and Pacific) as well as the Gulf of Mexico, created a dominant position for itself atop the international system by building a navy that could go wherever it pleased, whenever it pleased.

Compare that to Russia. Landlocked and iced in, Russia has about three zones from which it can project power and enhance its global trading position: the Pacific Ocean, the Baltic Sea, and the Black Sea.[1] Russia must possess warm water ports to maintain a lucrative trading presence as well as a powerful naval position. In the Pacific, Russia controls Vladivostok. Along the Baltic Sea, Russia has only the Kaliningrad enclave that it took from Germany in World War II. At the Black Sea, Russia has Sevastopol in Ukraine's Crimean Peninsula. Thanks to their alliance with the Assad regime of Syria, the Russians have enjoyed access to a warm water port along the Eastern Mediterranean known as Tartus since the 1970s.

Since the fall of the Soviet Union, with the exception of Vladivostok, control of each one of these warm water ports has remained a dubious prospect for Moscow. Until the last few years, when Moscow opted to move in large amounts of tactical nuclear weapons, Kaliningrad, nestled in between Poland and Germany, was always a bizarre throwback to a bygone era. Russian leaders feared it could be cut off from Russia by its European neighbors. The Syrian Civil War that erupted in the midst of the Arab Spring in 2010 placed Russia's access to the Eastern Mediterranean via Tartus in jeopardy, too. In the aftermath of the Cold War, Sevastopol was in a foreign land—Ukraine—subject to a lease renewal every decade. If Moscow lost Sevastopol, it lost the Black Sea. Russia would be sent back in time in terms of its maritime strategy, locked up in the vast, frozen expanses of Eurasia, as it had been centuries ago.

The notion of Russia acquiring warm water ports has become so ingrained in the Russian psyche, thanks to Peter the Great, the tsar who ruled from 1682-1725 and moved Russia's capital from Moscow to St. Petersburg (named after himself, of course). More than that, though, Peter believed that the West was culturally and technologically superior (and therefore militarily more powerful and wealthier) than Russia. St. Petersburg, a beautiful waterfront city that looked more European than Russian, was the symbol of Peter the Great breaking from the Russian traditions of his predecessors. Yet, one element of Peter the Great's predecessors remained: the will to dominate Russia's surrounding regions and to expand Russia beyond its present borders.

Sadly for Peter, he was afflicted with a "malignant disease of prostate, or bladder, or urinary stone disease."[2] The unspecified illness killed him slowly and painfully, and his death was officially recorded on February 8, 1725, after 42 years of reigning as tsar of the Russian Empire.

Unable to accomplish all that he had dreamed of doing, a feverish and agonized Peter purportedly issued his final command as the tsar of the great Russian Empire as he was dying. According to legend, the great man outlined a vision of his successors taking over large swathes of Eurasia—from Constantinople to India—in the name of their holy Motherland.[3] As the great writer, Peter Hopkirk claimed in his magisterial history of the "Great Game" between the British Empire and Russian Empire for control over Central Asia, Tsar Peter the Great commanded all his successors to "Go forth and conquer the world."[4]

In 1878, an article in the *Atlantic* outlined how Russian tsars were operating according to a secretive archive created by Peter the Great in which his grand plans for Russia's global domination were outlined. So concerning was the Russian threat to Europe that, upon his death in exile on the balmy rock of St. Helena, Napoleon supposedly quipped that, "In fifty years, Europe would either be republican or Cossack."[5] The iron grip of the Cossacks never fell upon Europe in the nineteenth century, as Napoleon had feared. Yet, the rumors of Peter's deathbed command and the stories of his secret trove of complex plans for dominating Europe, were the stuff of many nightmares among European leaders—notably Britain's weary imperial strategists, who fretted over the loss of India to an expanding Russia and who disliked Russia's despotism.[6]

These horrible nightmares of a despotic Russia sweeping across

Europe (and then the world) defined the West's overall view of the country and colored each interaction with Russia from then on. It has not helped the Russian cause that a succession of tsars, then Soviet rulers, and now Vladimir Putin have operated in ways that suggest they do, indeed, aspire to live up to Peter the Great's apocryphal last wishes. There is almost no chance that Peter the Great's last will and testament is anything but a myth. Nevertheless, Russia's behaviors, notably toward Ukraine's Crimean Peninsula, are the stuff of classical great power geopolitics.

Catherine the Great Fulfills Peter the Great's Warm Water Vision

TSARINA CATHERINE THE GREAT, who originally hailed from Prussia, brought her Enlightenment ideas with her when she married Tsar Peter III. After her first husband, a reputed drunkard and womanizer, died under mysterious circumstances, Catherine defied Russian traditions and ascended the throne herself. The tsarina then tried to impose democratic and Enlightenment reforms onto Russia's feudalistic, despotic regime. She even invited the European philosopher, Voltaire, to help craft a new constitution for a more European Russia. It ended in failure, led to a rebellion, and forced the tsarina to use the very despotic means she sought to extirpate from Russia. The result, however, was an even stronger and more expansionistic Russian state.

Out of that jarring experience came Catherine's invasion of Ukraine. Because Russia was a frigid, mostly landlocked empire, Catharine needed to acquire warm water ports outside of Russia to project Russian power abroad and fulfill Peter the Great's calling. Hence, the interest in the Black Sea port city of Sevastopol in Ukraine's Crimean Peninsula.

Since Catherine the Great's time, the Russian Black Sea Fleet has served as one of the key elements of Russia's maritime power.

The conquest of Crimea and the establishment of the Russian Black Sea Fleet based in Sevastopol fundamentally transformed both the region and Russian grand strategy. Throughout the Cold War, Sevastopol was a strategically vital location from which the Soviet Red Navy could project its power. After the Cold War ended and Russia found itself shorn of many of its imperial holdings, Moscow jealously clung onto its few remaining warm water ports out of fear that it would find itself locked inside of Eurasia, as it had been before Catherine the Great's conquest of Crimea.

Both for historical and geographical reasons, Moscow aimed to maintain its presence in the great port city. With its position in Crimea, the Russian Navy could "send reinforcements and supplies for its power projects outside of the Black Sea."[7] What's more, it was from Sevastopol where Russia's "first military intervention outside of Europe since the Soviet collapse" took place.[8] Thus, the Russians will not abandon Crimea without a fight. Indeed, this was precisely why, as the Ukraine War has intensified, Russian leaders, such as Prime Minister Dmitri Medvedev, have openly declared Russia's willingness to use nuclear weapons in defense of their position in Crimea.

Sevastopol: Catherine the Great's "White Gorge"

THE CITY OF SEVASTOPOL itself, originally named Akhtiar (meaning "White Gorge"), was built by the Russians who annexed southern Ukraine from the Crimean Tatars in 1783. It has been described as a "great bay with several harbors set in a 'natural amphitheater' of rocky hills."[9] When Sevastopol was built, it was a "mere two or three days from Constantinople [Istanbul] by steamship."[10] In other words, it is a position that allows for decisive power projection, unlocking the Black Sea and the regions beyond Russia.

Sevastopol was entirely a Russian creation. From the outset it was built to serve Russian interests. It also was designed to provide a considerable amount of strategic defense for Russia if they were threatened from their southwest. Whether we in the West like it or not, this is the reality. No amount of caterwauling or scheming from the West will change the Russian position that they will fight to the death to preserve their hold on this critical area. Basic geopolitics means that Russia must remain ensconced within the "White Gorge" if it is to continue as a serious player on the world stage today.

Ending Russia's Role in the Black Sea

MUCH LIKE THE George W. Bush fantasy of bringing Ukraine into NATO and using it as place to base ground-based missile defenses, the notion that Sevastopol can be bloodlessly taken from Russian control is a psychotic delusion. It's extreme and impractical. Like most of what has been done since the USSR collapsed, Western policies ostensibly aimed at enhancing NATO's strength and reach are actually diminishing both.

There was a moment in 2010, when Moscow came to view its continued presence in Sevastopol as threatened by the West. One of the campaign promises of the pro-Western 2004 Ukrainian presidential candidate, Viktor Yushchenko, was that his government would not renew the Russian Navy's $90 million a year lease of the base at Sevastopol. According to Yushchenko, the navy's presence weakened Ukraine's sovereignty. In the years following the 2004 Orange Revolution, it looked as though the pro-Western side was going to have its way. But in 2010 there was another shift in Ukraine's political winds. The pro-Russian Viktor Yanukovych was back from the political dead and was made president in that year's election.

Overnight, Ukrainian policy on Russia's presence in Sevastopol shifted. The attempt to terminate Russia's lease of Sevastopol was foiled. The Russians would remain ensconced at Sevastopol until at least 2042.[11] Not only did NATO have egg on its face, but the Russians were now alerted to the West's greater strategic designs.

The Russian obsession with acquiring warm water ports going

back to Peter the Great could not be undone with some coy political maneuvers by pro-Western elements within Ukraine. And with the failed move by the West to try to dislodge Sevastopol from Russian control, a new crisis was set to unfold: one that would forever mar the legacy of U.S. President Barack Obama and set Russia and Ukraine on the terrible path to the bloody war they are presently fighting.

Realizing the uncertainty of Ukraine's domestic politics, Russia was prepared to use military force to reconquer the Crimean Peninsula if it ever again appeared as though their hold on Sevastopol was weakening.

CHAPTER 8

OBAMA'S BLUNDER

BARACK OBAMA was just 47 years old when he became the first African-American to be elected to the U.S. presidency. Amidst reassuring calls of "hope" and "change," Obama was viewed by most voters—even some Republicans—as a necessary break with the crisis-laden presidents who had come before him (particularly George W. Bush).[1] Obama was the youngest man to assume the presidency since John F. Kennedy was elected in the tight 1960 presidential election.[2] Obama, representing the state of Illinois, had only been in the United States Senate a few years before he defied the Democratic Party's leadership and ran against the DNC's preferred candidate in 2008, Hillary Rodham Clinton.[3] Overcoming both the Clinton machine and, later, the grizzled Vietnam War hero and 2008 Republican Party presidential nominee, Senator John McCain of Arizona, it looked to some like Obama might be the wunderkind who would save an America in deep crisis.

As a result of his relative youth, Obama was perceived as being more dynamic than either Hillary Clinton or John McCain. In addition, he had an impressive academic pedigree. Others believed Obama was one of the best orators to have ever served in the Oval Office.[4] When sworn into office on January 20, 2009, Obama inherited an economic crisis at home and the failed Mideast wars of his predecessor. Add to that a growing crisis with nuclear-armed Russia, which had invaded Georgia in August 2008, and it looked like Obama inherited a world on the brink of total calamity. Obama's uniqueness as an educated, young, African-American man—"No Drama Obama" as he was nicknamed by staffers—made many think that he would be able to craft new solutions to persistent problems.[5] For many Americans tired of war and worried about the future of America's economy, it looked like America had elected just the right kind of dynamic leader to overcome the compounding crises and push America forward into the new century.

As is often the case, however, appearances are deceiving.

The qualities many Americans believed marked Obama out as a hopeful candidate who could break from the failed policies of his predecessors, the world's dictators saw as indicative of a naïf to be pushed around. In fact, then Vice President Joe Biden, had declared that America's enemies were going to spend Obama's first year in office challenging the United States as never before to "test the mettle" of the young and inexperienced Barack Obama.[6] Notably, Russian leadership was poised to seek heavy concessions from Obama regarding NATO expansion as Vladimir Putin and his *siloviki* viewed Obama as a weak and immature American president, specifically when compared to former President George W. Bush.

Obama, a postmodern man, had no clue as to the kind of premodern man Vladimir Putin is.[7] In a ridiculous maneuver that no one truly believed, Putin had stepped down as president of Russia because term limits in the democratic constitution created in the immediate aftermath of the USSR's collapse imposed them upon the Russian president. Rather than simply pack up and go home after his two terms in office, though, Putin decided to handpick a successor, Dmitri Medvedev, and then name himself as the new Russian prime minister. To be clear: it was a superficial swap designed to lull Western elites into a false sense of security.

Apparently, the newly elected President Obama had fallen for

Putin's ruse. Two days before Obama was slated to have his first in-person meeting with Putin, Obama decided to criticize the new Russian prime minister by basically calling him an old man stuck in the Cold War past. Obama encouraged Putin's presidential successor, Medvedev, to "move forward in a direction" with Obama.[8] It was a strange and, frankly, silly strategy by the forty-fourth U.S. president and it was doomed to fail. Throughout Obama's first term, he attempted to play Putin and Putin's handpicked successor against each other.

What Obama did not seem to comprehend was that Dmitri Medvedev was little more than an outgrowth of Putin (otherwise Putin would never have left the Kremlin). Nevertheless, Obama persisted in this delusion that Medvedev could be divorced from Putin for years.[9] This wishful thinking as grand strategy has become a hallmark of America's foreign policy elite—especially as it relates to post-Cold War Russia and Ukraine.

Putin was already looking to humiliate the new American president. After Obama's dismissive comments of Putin, the cagey old KGB hand was going to make Obama eat his words.

Putin Humiliates Obama

THE FIRST MEETING between President Obama and Vladimir Putin occurred at Putin's *dacha* just outside Moscow. This was the same place where Putin watched the events of the Orange Revolution unfold on the streets of Kiev in 2004 and in which he vowed to "never trust [the Americans] again!" Putin had been smarting about the West in Ukraine since at least 2004. Now, a year after his successful military operation against the pro-Western government of Georgia and faced with a truly green new American president, Putin wanted to flex on America; the Russian leader wanted to demonstrate to the world that he was the dominant world leader (and therefore Russia was more powerful than the United States).

Obama, because of both his naiveté and his ideological preferences, inadvertently played into Putin's hand. William J. Burns,[10] who had served as the George W. Bush administration's last ambassador to the Russian Federation (later, he was made the undersecretary of state for political affairs by Obama, and President Joe Biden would make Burns his CIA director) recounted of the fateful first meeting between Obama and Putin that, "President Obama's initial question [to Putin], about ten seconds, led to a 45-minute monologue by Putin."[11] In fact, the body language of the respective parties in the video from that July 2009 meeting is very telling. Obama sits, beaming from ear-to-ear, in an ornate chair beside Putin. Like some addled schoolboy, Obama is leaning on the left arm of the chair, as if hanging on Putin's every word, looking at Putin as though Putin were the wiser, senior leader. Obama is almost ebullient at the start of the meeting whereas Putin is curt and condescending.

The dynamic established at this meeting could not be more harmful to the United States.

Obama's demeanor can be explained not only by his ignorance about Putin, but also his strong ego. Most men elected to the presidency have very large egos. Barack Obama, though, was known to many as having an extremely outsized ego and a very high estimate of his own abilities. In this case, it was obvious that Obama was still flying high from his electoral victory, and believed his mere presence might cow the brusque Putin. Up against a former KGB counterintelligence agent-turned-Russian-strongman, though, Obama was brought down to Earth by Putin in short order. And, as Putin spoke down to the young American president, it was evident that Obama had been bested by the wily Putin.

For his part, Putin, sat throughout the meeting in a somewhat slouched position. His demeanor was dour. Putin's legs were spread apart, and the Russian strongman barely looked over at the American president. When he did glance over at Obama, it was done in a dismissive way. For the most part, Putin stared coolly into the cameras arrayed before the two world leaders. Everything about

Putin's behavior in that meeting was messaging to his people that Putin was the alpha male, and the forty-fourth American president was basically Putin's new pet poodle.

After the meeting, Obama's critics back home dutifully piled on. Many were reminded of another previous young Democratic president, JFK, who was upstaged in his first meeting with the Soviet Premier Nikita Khrushchev.[12] Dejected, Obama returned to the United States and did what he often did: He handed unwanted policy portfolios to his vice-president, Joe Biden. The vice-president became the point man not only for Russia but, inevitably, Ukraine.

The "No Drama" Obama No-Show

THIS IS WHERE the nightmare saga of the failed Obama administration foreign policy fuses with the sordid tale of the Biden family's alleged corrupt dealings in Ukraine. Biden was given a free hand by Obama. Obama's ego prevented him from thinking about the public shellacking Putin had given him. Rather than roll up his sleeves and behave like the statesman he was elected to be, Obama shirked his presidential duties, deferred to his older vice-president, and focused his attention elsewhere. (It was a hallmark of the Obama years, even respecting issues where Obama was focused—such as the debt ceiling talks with Republicans—that Obama was incapable of negotiating effectively). What was needed was a persistent president, not a sly handoff to the vice president.

Obama's handoff was yet another example of his inexperience.

Joe Biden had been cast in the 2008 campaign as the senior statesman. As one friend of mine who had worked on the Obama-Biden 2008 campaign in Florida described the relationship between Obama and Biden, "Biden was the Obi-Wan to Obama's Luke Skywalker." Of course, Biden was far from a wiseman guiding the Obama administration's foreign policy. After all, Biden's entire career in politics proved that he was wrong on almost every major foreign policy issue that he was ever involved with when he served as the longtime chairman of the prestigious Senate Foreign Relations Committee.[13]

Nevertheless, it was easier for Obama to place the difficult policy portfolio in Biden's lap and then blame him if the whole thing went upside-down. Of course, the whole situation was destined to go badly *because* Obama entrusted a man like Joe Biden to be his point man. The forty-fourth could live up to his nickname of "No Drama" Obama only because he was so colossally disengaged from the most difficult policies (this was a common complaint among even some of Obama's staunchest supporters). This was especially true of Obama's handling of Russia and, eventually, Ukraine.[14]

Obama's Reset: Lost in Translation

OUT OF THE DISASTROUS first meeting with Putin and then Obama's inclination to hand off the Russian and, eventually, Ukrainian portfolios to Joe Biden, came the Obama administration's much ballyhooed "reset" with Russia. The opening salvo in the Obama administration's push for renewed relations with Russia began with a small, but telling, embarrassing flap. Secretary of State Hillary Clinton met with her Russian counterpart, Sergei Lavrov, and handed him a giant, circular, red plastic button. She thought the Russian word for "reset" was written in white ink across the button. In fact, her staff mistranslated the Russian word for "reset" and instead had printed the Russian word for "overcharged."[15]

In a sense, this isn't wrong. The Americans were overcharged about the prospects of expanding democracy and human rights via NATO into the former Soviet states of Eastern Europe. Obama was foolish enough to think that, somehow, he could divide Putin and Medvedev and get Medvedev to work with Obama while isolating Putin. The Russians, meanwhile, were overcharged about preventing NATO expansion from happening at all costs. At the same time, Obama was so desperate for the appearance of better diplomatic relations with Russia that the Putinist regime was able to overcharge the Obama administration by extracting onerous concessions from Washington without being made by Obama to reciprocate.

As the *New York Times* reporter and Russian expert, Peter Baker, chided the Obama administration in the second term, "the story of the administration's 'reset' policy toward Russia is a case study in how the heady idealism of Mr. Obama's first term has given way to the disillusionment of his second."[16] Baker's assessment is strikingly apt. This gets us back to the question of how Obama's naiveté, inexperience, and idealism combined into one self-destructive policy: his administration's Russia (and Ukraine) policy.

Obama did a funny thing when he became president. He clearly wanted to negotiate with Russia to create a reset in relations. Yet he hired many of the same people—or individuals who were trained by many of the same people—who had created America's failed policies toward post-Soviet Russia to begin with. He was drawn to the neoconservative and neoliberal-types who refused to acknowledge basic geopolitical realities and instead clung, with an almost religious belief, to the idea of spreading democracy globally. Specifically, this cabal of defense policy intellectuals believed that NATO must expand into the former Soviet regions, no matter what. These individuals further refused to accept that post-Soviet Russia was going to be with us for some time, just as pre-Soviet Russia was with the world for over a millennium. The Obama administration was staffed with people whose names should by now be familiar to most readers Individuals such as Victoria Nuland at the State Department as well as Michael McFaul, to name just two.[17]

Like many inexperienced idealists, President Obama's Russia policy in his first term was wildly different from that of his second term. In the first term, as Peter Baker assessed, Obama's overriding belief was that he alone, by his mere presence on the world stage, could fundamentally change the nature of the Russian state and culture. When that idealistic policy failed to produce the desired result, Obama then came into his second term turning heavily to the Russia hawks.[18] The hawks not only exacerbated the crisis with Moscow, they may have been directly responsible for the horrific war that has killed as many as half a million Ukrainians and destabilized the region.[19]

The Obama administration had a series of issues it needed Russia's cooperation with when President Obama took power in 2009. Notably, it needed help from Moscow to maintain the tenuous supply lines into Afghanistan, where NATO forces had been engaged in a war since October 2001, fighting Taliban and al Qaeda insurgent groups that were responsible for the 9/11 terrorist attacks. Obama was obsessed with nuclear disarmament and believed that playing-nice with Russia would lead to a massive disarmament between the two powers. One of the first substantive actions Obama had taken as president was removing the components for President George W. Bush's rudimentary missile defense shield in Poland. Obama then effectively abandoned the Georgians to their fate in the wake of the 2008 Russian invasion. This was done after the Americans had spent years goading the Georgians into risking war with Russia, making Tbilisi's leaders think that NATO would come to their aid if war did come (Georgia would be proven wrong in this assumption and Kiev should've been paying close attention to Georgia's fate because it is basically the fate that now awaits Ukraine).

Yet, the one issue Russia cared most about—and that the West, after two decades of experience, should have understood was crucial to post-Soviet Russia—was Ukraine and its status as a neutral country along Russia's southern border. The Obama administration would not address this concern because they, like the rest of the Western establishment, were committed to integration of Ukraine into the NATO alliance. Rather than stay focused with laser-like intensity on the Ukrainian question, Obama's team drifted all over the place. They enacted a nuclear arms reduction treaty with Moscow in 2010, the New START Treaty limiting the size of America's nuclear arsenal but allowing Russia to both modernize its existing nuclear weapons arsenal and even to expand its non-strategic nuclear (otherwise known as tactical nuclear) arsenals.

Instead of shifting the focus of America's missile defense program to space (where it should have been from the start), the Obama administration favored a cockamamie alternative to both the space-based missile defense plan that Reagan wanted as well as the ground-based interceptors that George W. Bush favored: sea-based missile defense. The Obama administration got next to nothing substantive from Russia in return for all these concessions. And neither side would budge on the issue of Ukraine's entry into NATO which meant that all the concessions made by Obama to Russia empowered the Russians militarily while weakening the United States.

The reason problems with Russia persisted after Obama's reset was that there was only one issue Moscow cared about and Obama did not address it. To be fair, it's the one issue that no one in the West dares to address, because most still harbor fantasies about driving Russia out of Sevastopol, depriving her of access to the Black Sea, and isolating Russia deep inside Eurasia. Further, so much of the corruption that is tearing apart Ukrainian society is being encouraged by Western elites because they are its beneficiaries. (As I will demonstrate in another chapter, Hunter Biden, to give just one example, is a key recipient of this lucrative international corruption in Ukraine). Putin understands this. Obama could have left nuclear armament talks off the table and probably even have kept the ground-based interceptors in Europe if he had given a guarantee of America respecting Ukrainian neutrality and affirming that Ukraine *would never* be made part of NATO.

Obama never touched it. The whole thing was a waste of time from his point of view. Obama's relationship with Russia ended in 2016 exactly where it had begun: in the doldrums, with Russia willing to risk war. The Ukraine question, however, would remain the lesion festering on the Russo-American relationship. So long as Putin believed America and its Western allies were committed to expanding NATO by incorporating Ukraine, Moscow would never lower its guard.

CHAPTER 9

VIKTOR YANUKOVYCH COMES IN FROM THE COLD, GETS KICKED TO THE CURB

THE STORY of Viktor Yanukovych, the pro-Russian Ukrainian leader who was prevented from taking office in 2004 during the Western-backed Orange Revolution, did not end in 2004. As with so many politicians, even those living in notoriously corrupt and violent countries like Ukraine, Yanukovych's electoral failure was not final. After having lost the painfully corrupt 2004 presidential election, Yanukovych spent the next six years rehabilitating himself in public. While still a member of the pro-Russian Party of Regions, Yanukovych had done a decent job of distancing himself from Moscow (without alienating his benefactors in the Kremlin). In fact, by the time he ran again for the presidency in 2010, Yanukovych was dubbed "the most trusted man in Ukraine" because of his efforts to rehabilitate his image with the wider public.[1]

What's more, when the 2010 presidential election took place in Ukraine, the West found itself in a pickle: the two candidates running for the Ukrainian presidency, Yanukovych and Ukraine's prime minister at the time, Yulia Tymoshenko, were both considered pro-Russia. So, the U.S. State Department made an assessment, based on inputs from several leading Ukrainian politicians—including the former Ukrainian President Leonid Kuchma—that Yanukovych was a better option than his opponent.[2]

Yanukovych won the presidency in 2010.

Remember, however, that Ukraine is a land torn between two worlds: the Russian orthodox world to the east and the liberal world to the west. Ukraine is neither a great power like Russia nor a super-power like the United States. And, unfortunately for Ukrainian leaders, their government is not the only group navigating Ukraine's future on the world stage. Good Ukrainian leaders must balance their national interests (as well as their personal political preferences) with the concerns of their larger neighbors to the west and the east. This is the plight of all middle powers. Yanukovych, despite clearly being pro-Russian, made a good attempt to thread the geopolitical needle between the hulking Russian bear to his east and the insatiable eagle of the west. Essentially, Yanukovych was trying to make a strong stand in the middle of Ukrainian politics.[3] He was destined to get slammed by both sides. In fact, that is precisely what happened to him in 2014.

Ukraine, like Russia and much of the rest of the former Soviet bloc, has been dominated by rapacious oligarchs.[4] These mostly corrupt elites took over lucrative state assets, such as Ukraine's massive natural gas conglomerate, and privatized them—ensuring windfall profits for themselves, rather than the Ukrainian people. Most of these elites were financially tethered to the West. Yanukovych needed their support for his public rehabilitation.[5] These oligarchs chose to support him because, in 2010, his rival was deemed to be far worse than him. As it is with so many politicians, Yanukovych had to keep his donors happy. And the bulk of his oligarch supporters never would have supported him if he had retained his overt pro-Russian sentiments.[6]

For a period of time, Yanukovych kept Ukraine neutral and secure—just as the original post-Cold War agreements between the United States, its allies, and Russia had called upon him to do. Yes, Yanukovych still paid fealty to Moscow. That was likely for political expedience. At the same time, Yanukovych moved Ukraine closer to Europe and the United States during his time in office while still eschewing demands for Ukraine to become a full-fledged member of the Western bloc.

If the West had really been interested in keeping with the post-Cold War agreements it made with the Russians, that should have been enough. Obviously, however, they were not and this is why so many outside the West view Westerners as double-dealers who cannot be trusted and who must, at all times, be resisted.

The end of the Cold War clearly not the end of hostilities for the West, and sadly it became a time of exploitation. There was a deeply flawed conceit among the neoconservative-neoliberal elites in Washington that, no matter what, Russia would one day return to being a rival. Rather than wait for that day to arise, these elites attempted to put the United States in the most advantageous position possible so as to avoid what they feared would be another cold war with Russia. By placing Western influence in the former Soviet states ringing Russia's borders, Western elites assumed they could contain any growing Russian threat and prevent any new round of hostilities from erupting into a decades-long global cold war.

But the neoconservative and neoliberal elite in America and Europe failed to comprehend that the embrace of bloc mentality *after* the Cold War precipitated the very conflict we were all supposed to avoid! They had created for the West a self-fulfilling prophecy. Contrary to what these elites believed, Russia's return as Europe's phantom menace was not a predetermined outcome. Western actions designed to preempt the resurgence of Russian threat after the Cold War, in fact, had created a renewed Russian threat.

Yanukovych's Rise Was Legitimate

There was an added complication for the West: the Russophilic Ukrainian President Viktor Yanukovych's election in 2010 was declared by independent, international election observers to have been a "free and fair election" that was an "impressive display" of democracy for the rest of the world to follow. Thus, once in power, and after he again started playing geopolitical footsie with Moscow, it was would prove very difficult for the enraged Western alliance to castigate Yanukovych as an illegitimate leader as they had done to him in 2004. For his part, Yanukovych was not some mindless puppet of Moscow with no agency of his own. Still, there were serious realities that he, as Ukraine's legitimately elected leader, had to contend with.

For example, when Yanukovych took power, Ukraine was heavily dependent on cheap natural gas provided by neighboring Russia. Meanwhile, a plurality of Ukrainians (not a majority, mind you) favored greater European integration. At the same time, the Russian-speaking eastern part of Ukraine—where Yanukovych's political base resided—favored improved relations with Russia. What's more, the oligarchs responsible for Yanukovych's successful rise to power were almost all pro-Western (they preferred doing business with and housing their ill-gotten fortunes in the West). So, Yanukovych was in an unenviable bind. Yanukovych "pleased his base with symbolic and cultural measures, like talk of unity or cooperation with Moscow in key industries—even if it went nowhere—along with more serious steps like making Russia an official language, rejecting NATO membership, and reversing his pro-Western predecessor's move to glorify Nazi collaborators as national heroes in school curricula."[7]

Much to the chagrin of the dubious Western elites, Yanukovych authorized the renewal of the Russian Navy's lease of the Sevastopol base in the Russian-speaking enclave of Crimea along the Black Sea. That was likely the point of no return for Yanukovych in the eyes of those aforementioned Western elites, who were committed to covertly rolling back Russian presence in the Black Sea and elsewhere. Still, Yanukovych did not fully embrace Putin's Russia. He declined Putin's offer to join the Eurasian Economic Union (EEU), which was Russia's attempt at creating a mini-EU-style customs union in

Central Asia and Eastern Europe out of the former Soviet states.

The EEU was viewed with suspicion in the West but what few in the West understood at that time was that Putin was more worried about the rise of China's Belt-and-Road Initiative into Central Asia. The EEU was his attempt to increase Russia's power relative to that of China's in Eurasia (although, had the EEU performed as Putin hoped it would have, it also would have been used as a counterweight against unwanted Western influence into greater Eurasia). For the EEU to have any geopolitical teeth, though, Moscow needed Ukraine to be part of that customs union rather than the EU/NATO alliance to the West. Ukraine had vast amounts of natural resources, was traditionally viewed as the breadbasket of Russia by Moscow, and had a large industrial base in the Russian-speaking parts of Eastern Ukraine.[8] Yanukovych understood that the main impetus for Putin's support of his presidency in Ukraine was to eventually get Yanukovych's government to abandon any desire to join the Western EU/NATO alliance and, instead, join the Moscow-led EEU.

Yanukovych said "Нет, спасибо," ("no, thanks") to Putin. This effectively neutralized the EEU. Even after Putin offered Kiev a sweetheart deal on even cheaper Russian-produced natural gas, Yanukovych avoided sending Ukraine into the waiting arms of Putin's EEU. But the Western alliance was still dissatisfied with Yanukovych for not explicitly joining them in an obvious bloc directed against Russia. As George W. Bush had once put it shrilly, "You're either with us or with the terrorists."[9] And as hated by the Western elites as George W. Bush was, his Manichean worldview was readily embraced by them—especially when it came to viewing post-Soviet Russia as an inherent enemy of the West (which, at least for some time after the Cold War, it was not).

Yanukovych went further in separating both himself and his nation from Russia: he refused to heed Putin's demand to merge Ukraine's energy sector with that of Russia's. Such a move essentially would have made Ukraine a vassal state of Putin's Russia in all but name. Putin retaliated by refusing to renegotiate what most viewed as a lopsided natural gas agreement between Russia and Ukraine favoring Moscow. Because of Yanukovych's intransigence regarding Putin's obvious imperial dreams for Ukraine, Ukrainians suffered. At no point, however, did these moves by Yanukovych endear him to the implacable Western alliance. They hated and distrusted Yanukovych because he would not be their puppet—just as he would not allow himself to be completely run by Moscow.

Yanukovych went on to further ingratiate himself to the hostile West: He insisted he would continue moving Ukraine toward entry into the European Union. He also created a free trade agreement with Europe. He then adhered to Western demands and took a much-needed loan from the International Monetary Fund (IMF). Unfortunately for Yanukovych, the IMF loan came with the typical Western inducements that rarely create successful or stable countries and often that ensure the countries who take those loans are broken down states oriented toward the West rather than financially stable and independent countries.

As per the dictates of the IMF loan, Yanukovych had to eliminate tariffs that were designed to protect Ukraine's domestic industries, to freeze all wages and pensions of already impoverished Ukrainians, to embrace excessive austerity, and to end the energy subsidies that his state-owned natural gas firms paid to ordinary Ukrainians. To secure a loan from the West, Yanukovych basically had to further impoverish his own people and make his ailing country perennially dependent on the West. It is strange that the West cannot understand why so many developing countries resent the West—especially when its loans, which are supposedly designed out of sympathy for the plight of these countries, do so much damage to those countries that take them.

Something to consider here are the works of former Goldman Sachs analyst and prominent economist, D'Ambisa Moyo. She has long criticized the practice of Western aid to foreign countries.

According to her stellar research, Western loans, such as the ones Yanukovych took from the IMF, do little to foster successful, independent nations. Instead, they often create pathways of dependence that permanently destroy a country's ability to survive and thrive in our hyper-competitive world. Instead, Moyo argues that Western nations should encourage "trade, not aid" for these developing nations. It's akin to the old saw, "Give a hungry man a fish and he'll eat for the day. Teach that hungry man to fish and he'll eat for life." Westerners should not be handing out aid with destructive strings attached. They should be identifying those in these countries with which they can trade and, in turn, helping those countries build their own economic capacities and stand on their own.[10]

Nevertheless, Yanukovych did what the West wanted him to do. In return, organs of the Western, neoliberal-neoconservative elite, such as the Brookings Institution, began changing their tune—albeit temporarily—about Yanukovych. Basically overnight, most Western outlets went from painting Yanukovych as a Russian stooge to portraying him as a complex man implementing a "more nuanced" foreign policy than they had previously considered. All it takes to buy good press in the West is to do their bidding—even at the expense of your own country, it seems.

Not that Russia was much better for Ukraine. Or for Viktor Yanukovych.

It is important to understand that, despite his long-running effort to restore his image following the events of the 2004 Orange Revolution, Yanukovych was corrupt. He abused his position once he obtained power. But that was no different than his Western-backed predecessor (or even his predecessor's predecessors). Ukraine is one of the most corrupt countries in the world and has been for decades. So, abusing one's political office for personal gain is the equivalent of breathing in that system, regardless of whether any given politician is pro-Western or pro-Russian.

Sensing foul play over the issue of Yanukovych's sudden westward turn, Vladimir Putin huffed-and-puffed at Yanukovych to try to intimidate the Ukrainian president into serving Russia's ends once more. As Branko Marcetic described in a 2022 *Jacobin* piece, "Putin performed a one-man good-cop,-bad-cop routine, offering Yanukovych a no-strings attached loan the same size as the IMF's, while squeezing him with what amounted to a mini-trade blockade." The European Union refused to counter Putin's offer. Without Russian trade, and with the EU refusing to offer anything to replace Ukraine's trade with Russia, Yanukovych was about to preside over the total collapse of post-Cold War Ukraine. Seeing where the geopolitical winds were blowing, Yanukovych accepted Putin's offer and ultimately declined the Western loan.

The moment Yanukovych did that, however, his fate was sealed. Shortly after his deal with Russia and his abandonment of the tentative EU deal, the protests against his continued reign erupted in Kiev. Yanukovych's days as Ukraine's president were numbered.

2013-2014: Euromaidan and the Birth of a New, More Divided Ukraine

WHEN UKRAINE'S EUROMAIDAN REVOLUTION occurred, most Western media sources portrayed the event as a necessary expression of democracy against the brutal reign of an awful tyrant, Viktor Yanukovych. Preceding the outburst of protests against Yanukovych's presidency, there were several pro-democracy non-governmental organizations (NGO) that had popped up in Ukraine. These NGOs were almost universally supported, either directly or indirectly, by the United States government and various other Western governments. In fact, various prominent U.S. State Department officials, such as Victoria Nuland, were pictured mingling among pro-Western Euromaidan protesters in the streets of Kiev.

At the time, Nuland was serving as the assistant secretary of state. She appeared amongst the anti-Yanukovych protesters who had assembled in Kiev's Independence Square one day after her then-boss, Secretary of State John Kerry had expressed his "disgust with the decision of Ukrainian authorities to meet the peaceful [Euromaidan] protest ... with riot police, bulldozers, and batons, rather than respect for democratic rights and human dignity." Secretary Kerry urged "utmost restraint" by President Yanukovych's security services and declared that the United States stood "with the people of Ukraine." Kerry then added the kicker by saying, "They deserve better."[II]

Nuland's visit was described by Western media sources in the most innocuous way. Walking alongside her was the head of the European Union's foreign policy, Catherine Ashton. The two were seen handing out food to the protesters and shaking hands with members of the Ukrainian security services who were visibly on edge as the protests grew in number and lasted longer than many had assumed they would. Ukrainian opposition leader, Arseny Yatsenyuk, described the ordeal as a "great victory" for his anti-Yanukovych forces. Nuland and Ashton continued behaving as though they were merely doing the routine jobs that diplomats do under such circumstances, then met with President Yanukovych for a high-level discussion on how to end the crisis. Nuland planned on delivering a speech about her meeting with Yanukovych from outside Ukraine's Presidential Administrative Building.

But Nuland's visit was anything but routine. For starters, she was not the U.S. ambassador to Ukraine. She was one of the highest-ranking officials from the State Department other than the secretary himself, John Kerry (who had the night before made a stark declaration against Yanukovych's continued reign). The fact that she and the EU's top foreign policy leader were meeting with groups joining the protesting of what was, by definition, an internal Ukrainian matter, further indicated to outside audiences how radical a move this was by top Obama administration officials.

The meetings in which Nuland participated were strange not only in appearance but because they made it obvious that Ukraine was being used as a proxy battlefield between Washington and Moscow in a shadow war that would determine the fate of Ukraine in the twenty-first century. Not long after the Euromaidan protests, WikiLeaks, a controversial international whistleblowing organization, obtained a covert recording of a phone call between Nuland and U.S. ambassador to Ukraine at the time, Geoffrey Pratt. The recording became a lightning rod, not only in U.S.-Russian relations, but also in U.S.-EU relations since the assistant secretary of state, in her frustration, had blurted out "F-ck the EU!" in the middle of the recorded conversation. Moscow had a field day using that part of the recording in an attempt to undermine U.S.-EU solidarity throughout the 2014 crisis in Ukraine.[12]

Beyond the salacious bits of the conversation, what the recording shows is just how deeply enmeshed in coordinating the opposition to Yanukovych the neoconservative element of the Obama administration was. For them, this was all about rolling back what they viewed as unwanted Russian influence. In fact, given how quickly the American side rallied their armies of "pro-democracy" NGOs and got all their representatives in Washington and Europe on the same page, it is very likely that the Obama administration was merely seeking a trigger event, such as Yanukovych reneging on his EU trade deal, to initiate the anti-Yanukovych protests. There was nothing organic about the 2014 revolution in Kiev. It was all coordinated covertly by the United States.

In the explosive recording, Nuland is directing which opposition leaders should be elevated in a post-Yanukovych government. She sounds much more like a ringleader in a coup than a concerned third party engaged in an effort to help a developing nation navigate a geopolitical crisis. The two senior American diplomats then discuss strategies for pressuring an apparently recalcitrant European Union into supporting the regime change operation that the neoconservatives within the Obama administration were orchestrating in Kiev. As the recording suggests, the EU was not as sanguine about the intense covert American efforts to kick Yanukovych to the curb in exchange for a more pro-European Ukrainian leader because the Europeans rightly feared provoking Russia.

As Jonathan Marcus of *The BBC* assessed in 2014, "[The EU] certainly cannot win a short-term battle for Ukraine's affections with Moscow—it just does not have the cash inducements available. The EU has sought to play a longer game; banking on its attractiveness over time. *But the US clearly is determined to take a much more activist role* [emphasis added]."[13]

The Europeans were likely far more apt at making a realistic assessment of the situation and the longevity of the American plan for Ukraine than was the Obama administration. Of course, the power disparity between the United States and Europe ensured that Washington would have its way. Yet, by having its way, Washington was ensuring that Ukraine's fate would be an unhappy one. As a succession of Russian leaders have made clear since the end of the Cold War, Ukraine's membership in NATO and, to a lesser extent, the EU, would be viewed as a direct territorial threat to the Russian Federation. The neoconservatives in Washington had outmaneuvered the Russians in their covert war for control over Kiev. For a matter as critical to Russia's direct national security (as Russian policymakers viewed it), though, the Kremlin would risk a war to secure what it perceived as Russia's interests in Ukraine.

Again, Yanukovych's role in this affair was hardly above-board. When the Euromaidan protests erupted in Kiev in November 2013, he quickly sent in the fearsome Berkut, Ukraine's secret police based on the Soviet model, to break them up. He then passed legislation severely limiting freedom of speech for his people as the crisis mounted. Yet, the more that Yanukovych attempted to tighten his grip on power, the weaker that grip became—and the more the protests spread. By January 2014, the protests had expanded beyond Kiev to multiple other Ukrainian cities.

A Bloodbath in the Streets, a Coup Behind-the-Scenes

FEBRUARY 20, 2014, is a date that will live in infamy for the people of Ukraine. That was the day the Euromaidan protests, which had been relatively peaceful until then, turned bloody. Snipers began shooting into a crowd of anti-Yanukovych protesters. High-powered rifles were used and 50 people were murdered in the crowd. The protesters and the anti-Yanukovych political opposition within Ukraine insisted Ukrainian troops deployed to disperse the crowd fired on the protesters. The Yanukovych regime denied these accusations. The more they denied, the angrier the people in Ukraine became, and the more resistant to Yanukovych's continued authority they became.[14]

Throughout the three-month-long protest against his nominal ally, Viktor Yanukovych, Vladimir Putin urged the embattled Ukrainian president to use force against his protesting people. To his credit, Yanukovych had resisted these calls from Moscow. By February, though, it looked as though Yanukovych had changed his mind and decided to blast away fifty innocent people in the growing crowd of his citizens who opposed his presidency. Yet, the timing of these events should raise eyebrows. After all, the massacre occurred less than a week after the Victoria Nuland recording was disseminated via WikiLeaks. That leak was highly damaging both to the Obama administration and the question of regime change in Ukraine.

Ever since that awful day, rumors have persisted that the crowd was fired upon by right-wing extremists who were leading opponents of Yanukovych. As this theory goes, the Ukrainian opposition to Yanukovych, which had a strong right-wing bent, was annoyed that the protests were not leading to an overthrow of Yanukovych. The peaceful nature of the protests was a problem for those parties interested in taking direct action against the Yanukovych government. To encourage more outright opposition that might lead to the overthrow of the Yanukovych, these elements sought to gin up those protesters and create chaos in the streets. What better way to do that than by having paramilitaries take up strategic positions near where the protesters had encamped, and then use military style sniper rifles to shoot into the crowd?

The moment that this occurred, of course, Yanukovych's reign was over. Had it never occurred, Viktor Yanukovych likely would have survived as president of Ukraine. History today would be fundamentally different, too. Instead, the moment the fifty protesters were murdered and the rest of the Euromaidan protesters were galvanized against the regime, Yanukovych fled Kiev, and then to Russia. His presidency was over. Ukraine was now an open field for the West. Thus, Putin had little time to craft any other kind of response than the ham-fisted one he ultimately embraced.

CHAPTER 10
LITTLE GREEN MEN LAND IN CRIMEA

V ERY SHORTLY after Yanukovych fled Kiev for Russia, while protesters in Ukraine's Independence Square were celebrating their victory, about 500 miles to the southeast of Kiev, in Simferopol, the regional capital of Crimea, pro-Russian protesters gathered outside of the regional government's parliament building. Clearly, if pro-NATO elements were going to take western Ukraine, then pro-Russian elements would take eastern Ukraine and Crimea.[1] This is precisely what occurred. As pro-Russian Crimean protesters were storming the regional parliament building in Simferopol, Russian military vehicles rallied on the highways in Crimea that stretched from Sevastopol in the south (where the Russians have a large naval base) to the northern portion of the Crimean Peninsula. Soon, scores of heavily armed, green-clad, masked soldiers bearing no identifying insignia began appearing on the streets of Crimea.

It was as though they simply teleported there from another universe.

There were Western reporters on-scene as the mysterious invaders began taking over the streets. When asked who they were representing, the soldiers would reply in broken English (with thick Russian accents), "No comment." Quickly, Western governments began accusing the invaders of being part of the Russian military. The Kremlin immediately denied these claims. Obviously, if the Russians had sent a traditional invading army to rip Crimea away from Ukraine it might have precipitated a larger conflict with the West. It certainly would have galvanized a response from Ukraine's military.

But the lack of any identifying marks on the soldiers, and the fact that the invaders were coming from within the Crimean Peninsula— along with the reality that few in the West were itching for a direct confrontation with nuclear-armed Russia over Crimea—meant that the Putinist regime got away with annexing Crimea. The Russians believed that NATO had used covert means to overthrow their preferred Ukrainian leader. Therefore, Moscow would respond in-kind. This is to say nothing of the fact that most of the people living in Crimea were Russian-speakers who preferred to remain closely aligned with Russia rather than the West.

Due to their mysterious and sudden appearance in Crimea, the invaders became nicknamed the "Little Green Men" because their only identifying marks were the green camouflage uniforms. The name also perfectly captured the mysterious menace they posed to the wider region. Many began to worry that if the Russians could just basically walk into part of Ukraine and annex it without so much as waving their national flag, they might engage in such unconventional tactics in other places as well? After all, there are many other nations in Europe that have large Russian-speaking minorities. Should Moscow be offended by the way those Russian-speaking minorities are treated by their home governments, would Russia deploy its Crimean strategies in those places?

For example, there are Russian minorities in places like Abkhazia and South Ossetia in Georgia, not to mention places like Estonia, Moldova, and other former Soviet bloc states. Moscow has long adhered to the belief that they are the flagship nation representing the Slavic people, and should any force threaten Russian-speaking minorities, no matter where they may be located, Russia has always maintained that it has the right to intervene on behalf of its fellow

Russian-speakers. This is, of course, absurd. Nevertheless, this is what Russian leaders have long believed going back to the days of the tsars. Good luck trying to change their minds about that notion.

Three months after the Little Green Men seized Crimea, a plebiscite was held in April of 2014. According to the results of that vote, a majority of Crimeans voted to officially leave Ukraine and join the Russian Federation.[2] That same month, the Russian-speaking eastern portion of Ukraine created breakaway republics in the east and asked that they be recognized by Moscow as independent from the pro-NATO government that had replaced the Yanukovych regime in Kiev. Once the breakaway republics began forming, the Ukrainian military was called into action to stop the separatism in the east. According to *Vox*, "That feeling of disenfranchisement among eastern Ukrainians [after their preferred leader, Yanukovych was overthrown] is real, and the rebels likely do have some organic, local support."[3]

As fighting between Ukrainian and Russian-backed separatist forces in eastern Ukraine intensified, several knock-on events occurred that brought the world closer to a serious regional war that could have gone global at any point. During this time, on July 17, 2014, the Malaysian Airlines Flight 17 was shot down. All 298 souls aboard that airplane were killed. It is believed that the twitchy eastern Ukraine separatist forces manning the Russian-provided air defense systems protecting eastern Ukraine from air attack mistook the Malaysian airliner for a bomber and mistakenly shot it down.[4]

A month later, in August 2014, the pro-Russian separatists in the east were losing decisively to the Ukrainian military. Just when it looked as though the separatists were about to be defeated, however, the Kremlin intervened yet again. This time, it was by sending a large Russian force into eastern Ukraine to stop the Ukrainian military from conquering the pro-Russian breakaway republics that had cropped up following Russia's successful annexation of Crimea.[5]

From that point onward, Ukraine's status as a sovereign

nation-state was in question as its territorial integrity was picked over by the West and Russia.

The Minsk Agreement:
Peace in Our Time or Merely a Strategic Pause?

"THE 2014 MINSK AGREEMENT was an attempt to buy time to rearm Ukraine." Former German Chancellor Angela Merkel infamously revealed to the German newspaper *Die Zeit* in 2022, as the full Russian invasion of Ukraine was underway that year. "It also used this time to become stronger, as you can see today," the once powerful and highly popular German leader added.[6]

These comments in 2022 ran counter to the official narrative the West had crafted about the controversial (and ultimately ineffective) Minsk protocols. According to the Western narrative, the Europeans and their American allies, along with Ukraine's post-Yanukovych government, had negotiated with Vladimir Putin's regime in good faith for a peaceful resolution to the Ukraine conflict. In the Western interpretation of events, it was Putin who had thuggishly undermined that agreement at every turn and strove to negate it so that his forces could conquer Ukraine—with minimal resistance from a blinkered and well-meaning West.

Merkel's admission shows that this narrative is wrong. There was a quiet consensus among the Western alliance that it needed to buy time for Ukraine to arm and equip its ailing forces following the successful overthrow of Viktor Yanukovych. Ukraine needed a long-term lull in the fighting with Russia in the east to enhance its forces while preparing to forcibly remove the Russians from Crimea. Without the intervention of NATO to buy Ukraine time, the Ukrainian military would lose to the Russian Army, which had intervened on behalf of the flailing pro-Russian separatist forces in Eastern Ukraine in August 2014.

The first Minsk Agreement was an isolated affair. The

post-Yanukovych Ukrainian government met in Minsk, Belarus, with the leadership of the pro-Russian separatist forces from Eastern Ukraine. They reached a tentative, twelve-point deal to end their conflict. The delivery of humanitarian aid, prisoner exchanges, and the withdrawal of heavy weapons were key elements of the Minsk I ceasefire. The deal was too weak and far too ambiguous, allowing for violations of the ceasefire by both sides. Minsk I broke down relatively quickly and the fighting in Ukraine continued.[7]

Minsk II was a different matter.

Unlike the first Minsk accords, which were limited to the two warring sides in the conflict, the region's great powers midwifed the Minsk II Agreement. The Organization for Security Cooperation in Europe (OSCE), led by the French and German governments, met with representatives from Russia and Ukraine in Minsk. A thirteen-point plan was agreed upon by all sides. It was comprehensive. Yet, like Minsk I, there was difficulty in getting the deal finalized. While Washington made a show of supporting Berlin and Paris in their efforts to stabilize the Ukraine crisis with both Kiev and Moscow, the fact of the matter was that U.S. representatives were not present at the negotiations. And the lack of American diplomats during the Minsk II negotiations ensured that the Russian side would not take the agreement seriously.

Of course, the Ukraine crisis is a strange affair. On the one hand it is the definition of a peripheral, parochial matter in southern Europe. Yet, the fact that the Ukraine crisis has erupted within the context of the greater issue of post-Cold War NATO expansion, meant that NATO's most important founding member, the United States, needed to be at the table. Because American representatives did not show up to stand side-by-side with Germany and France, the Ukrainians didn't take calls for a ceasefire seriously nor did the Russians.[8]

Putin, of course, claims that he followed the Minsk I and II agreements to the letter, only to have the American-led NATO alliance betray him and undermine the tenuous agreements at every turn.

As Merkel's comments suggest, the West was not serious about following the agreements. Yet, Putin was no saint in this affair. He, too, sought to undermine the agreement.[9] For example, his overt support for the separatist movements in Eastern Ukraine were a clear violation of the Minsk agreement. Meanwhile, the agreements themselves—Minsk I was originally crafted in 2014 and Minsk II superseded that agreement a year later—were poorly written. Both the Russian and Ukraine sides misinterpreted elements of that poorly written agreement. The Russians believed that the separatists of Eastern Ukraine should have been incorporated into the national assembly in Kiev, thereby giving Moscow a vote in how Ukraine is governed.

A key point of contention that existed even after Russia agreed to the Minsk II protocols was that the agreement called for the removal of all foreign forces in Ukraine. Everyone knew that the Russian military had positioned itself throughout the pro-Russian breakaway provinces of Eastern Ukraine. Yet, Moscow refused to comply with this point in the Minsk II deal because the Kremlin never admitted that it did, in fact, have forces deployed within Ukraine.

NATO Expansion: Reviving the Ghosts of a Horrible European Past

ALL THIS, THOUGH, was beside the point. Putin did not believe that the West—notably the Obama administration—was serious about ending the conflict peacefully. The specter of NATO expansion had become an all-consuming obsession on the part of most Russian leaders. Russia would not operate in good faith if it did not think the Americans were serious about doing the same. The issue of Ukraine's neutrality was simply too important for the Russian leadership.

More importantly, when Putin finally decided to initiate his full-blown invasion of Ukraine in February 2022, one of the primary reasons cited was the failure of the U.S. and its Western partners to "provide security guarantees" Moscow had requested from the West in December 2021.[10] What do you believe Putin's number one point of contention was with Washington? It wasn't Ukraine's government banning the speaking of Russian in their school system. Nor was it the alleged shoddy treatment of Ukraine's Russian-speaking population. Of course, these were complaints Putin had made. Yet the primary issue was getting the West to sit down and negotiate limits to NATO enlargement. So, again, despite what the Western elites tell themselves, the Russians have been very clear regarding their red lines ... and no one in the West cared to listen.[11]

The reason why Putin took on such an aggressive posture in December 2021 was because he believed the U.S. president at that time, Joe Biden, was a weak man who would fold under the first bit of pressure. The other reason Putin behaved this way was because, as covered in this book, for decades Russian leaders have tried broaching the subject of NATO expansion (diplomatically)—especially in Ukraine—and they were ignored. The West kept moving into what Russia viewed as its defensive perimeter while the Russians' concerns were never once ameliorated or considered by the Western alliance. With Biden in office, and with the Americans having never taken Minsk II seriously, Putin believed he had a rare window-of-opportunity to change the strategic situation in his favor.

While imperfect, the Minsk II Agreement was the best chance the world had to avert the disaster we are living through today in Ukraine today. Germany was the most powerful nation on continental Europe. France was the most potent military there (it even possesses a sizable, advanced nuclear weapons arsenal). Together these two European states are foundational members of both the European Union and NATO. Both Paris and Berlin have been consistently skeptical about NATO expansion in the post-Cold War era, specifically as it relates both to Georgia and Ukraine—the two countries that Moscow viewed as their red lines. Their concerns about pushing NATO expansion too quickly and too far into Russia's surrounding environs were routinely downplayed by policy planners in Washington. But their concerns should have been heeded. And had the Americans taken their concerns more seriously, it is possible, we would have also taken the Minsk II Agreement more seriously. Which, in turn, Moscow would have as well.

Writing in the pages of *American Affairs Journal,* the Russia scholar, Hal Gardener, assessed that:

> *A general settlement between the United States, European countries, Ukraine, and Russia is crucial to prevent the further destabilization of eastern Europe that could, in turn, further antagonize western Europe. Such a destabilization would deepen the divisions between pro-NATO and pro-EU sociopolitical movements and anti-NATO and anti-EU movements on both the right and the left. In general, both left-wing and right-wing political parties in states closest to Russia (Poland, Finland, Sweden, and the Baltic states) tend to take a strong anti-Russian position, no matter whether they are for or against NATO or EU membership. But left-wing and right-wing parties in both France and Germany—the two countries that now form the core of the European Union after the UK's exit from the EU (Brexit)—tend to oppose both EU and NATO membership.*[12]

THE RUSSIANS have demonstrated to the West, first in Georgia and then in Ukraine, that they will use all their means to prevent those countries with deep historical ties (and cultural significance) to Russia—to say nothing of their geopolitical importance—from officially joining the Western bloc. At first, the Russians were amenable to coming to a diplomatic understanding with NATO and the EU over the fate of these former Soviet countries. As demonstrated earlier, though, by 1994 the Russians became suspicious of Western intentions. By the time Putin was in charge, after years of trying to find some common ground with the West, the Russian autocrat decided resistance was his only option.

Evoking Gardener again, "A resolution [to the Ukraine crisis] can take place only once the uncoordinated enlargements of the

NATO and EU are restrained and redesigned."[13] After his four post-Cold War predecessors ignited the current crisis with rapid, endless NATO and EU "double expansion" into regions that are geopolitically sensitive to Russia, former President Donald J. Trump attempted to thread this needle by attempting to get the mother of all geopolitical deals with Moscow and prevent what the forty-fifth president feared might become a potential nuclear world war with Russia over Ukraine and NATO enlargement. But the toxic domestic American politics of the Trump era, the unfounded (and entirely false) belief among Trump's many detractors that he was some kind of Russian agent, prevented Trump from realizing that policy. What's more, elements of Trump's own administration undermined him because they disagreed with his stance that NATO was an anachronism from the Cold War that ended long ago.[14]

Before his death, American diplomatic icon, George F. Kennan, the man who originally helped to create NATO and America's containment policies of the Soviet Union during the Cold War, warned American leaders about the threat NATO expansion posed to U.S. national security. Kennan said that "In trying to place NATO ahead of the EU as the focal point of European unity, and at the same time in looking to Germany to be, together with the U.S., the greatest military power on the European continent, the NATO leaders are, as I see it, making a mistake of historical dimensions. They are trying to revive all the disturbing ghosts of the modern European past."[15]

Look at the hellish fighting occurring in Ukraine today between the NATO-backed forces loyal to Kiev and the Russian forces: so-called "strategic bombing" of civilian infrastructure; a conflict in which the frontlines are often static and honeycombed with muddy trenches chock full of cold, scared, and uncomfortable soldiers who are just waiting to die. The American push to expand NATO into all aspects of Europe has indeed revived the disturbing ghosts of the modern European past: a European past that countless Americans spent the twentieth century helping Europe to move away from.

The Minsk II Agreement was not a panacea. It was a start, though. If the United States and its NATO partners were not so evangelistic about NATO expansion, they might have gotten the Russians to play more fairly with them, as Putin wanted to end the conflict in 2014. The Minsk Agreement ultimately should have led to real peace in Ukraine. Sadly, it merely led to a seven-year armistice during which both sides ramped up for a greater conflict. And a greater conflict is precisely what the world has gotten. It won't end well for any of us at this rate.

By January 2024, even the stubborn Ukrainian President Volodymyr Zelensky, who for two years had refused to negotiate with the Russians for a peace deal, extended an olive branch to Vladimir Putin via the Swiss.[16] The only problem, as future will demonstrate in another chapter, is that the Ukrainians are negotiating from a place of strategic weakness in 2024. What's more, there is little incentive for Putin to negotiate with Zelensky. Even if Putin did agree to negotiations, given the power imbalances between Ukraine's depleted forces and Russia's galvanized military, the likelihood that any postwar settlement would be conducive to Ukraine's survival as an independent nation-state is small. The NATO alliance will have been defeated in its proxy war with Moscow for control of Ukraine's fate. Thus, the West will be less safe and the ceaseless quest for maximum security via NATO expansion will prove to have had the opposite effect.[17]

CHAPTER 11

HILLARY CLINTON, CONSPIRACY THEORIST EXTRAORDINAIRE

HILLARY RODHAM CLINTON looked haggard. The seven months since her shocking defeat at the hands of the improbable Republican Party 2016 presidential candidate, Donald J. Trump, had not been kind to her. Clinton's eyes drooped with extreme fatigue. The former secretary of state's face, now defined by canyon-like lines, told a story of sleepless nights running a presidential campaign and then, after having lost that campaign, a constant raging over the defeat.

Hillary Clinton appeared almost haunted; her pale appearance was matched by a voice that cracked with the disgruntlement of being a perennial "also ran" presidential candidate. Given her age, Clinton's last chance to become the first female president of the United States was over. This fact—that she'd never again be able to win the presidency, the office she'd coveted since she was an idealistic freshman at Wellesley College—must have rankled her endlessly in the months following her loss to Trump.

Forlorn and adrift in a sea of her own recriminations, Clinton concocted an intricate conspiracy theory to explain away her defeat to Donald Trump, a man she clearly viewed as uncouth and beneath her. She bitterly shared this theory with anyone who would listen to her complaints. It involved shady Trump campaign advisors clandestinely aligning with shadowy Russian intelligence operatives to "overthrow our democracy" in 2016.[1] You see, as Hillary Clinton screeched throughout 2017, the Trump Campaign had engaged in a "vast Russian conspiracy" to deny Clinton her rightful destiny.[2]

And since she was the belle of the Wall Street and academia; a woman who needed to be seen and heard by self-styled elites as much as she needed to vent out her frustrations to the world, Clinton had taken to the lecture circuit to lick her psychic wounds (and rake in the gobs of cash a sycophantic list of Wall Street donors and midwit, lefty academicians tossed her way) following her 2016 defeat.[3] The elite world listened to her whinging. Many of them believed her accusations because, they too, hated Trump.[4]

When a successful person like Hillary Clinton has been beaten as badly as she was in 2016, that person usually does one of two things: either she skulks away and hides from the public shame of her defeat or she shamelessly accuses the person who vanquished her of being a cheater. Hillary Clinton, a former first lady, United States senator, and secretary of state—a career politician *and* the wife of a career politician—chose to accuse Trump and the Republicans of having cheated. Clinton's claims of Trump's perfidy took on a life of their own, the more she proliferated them to the wider public. And, in classic Clinton fashion, the former secretary of state had no substantive evidence to back up her claims. Bizarrely, Clinton's lack of verifiable evidence for her wild claims only added to the mystique of those charges among those who wanted to believe her—namely the Western, globalist elites who had invested so heavily into her political future.

Of course, Hillary Clinton was no stranger to conspiracy theories.

A History of Insane Clinton Conspiracy Theories

CLINTON WAS one of the greatest disseminators of insane conspiracy theories in American politics. Before her Trump-Russia collusion delusion in 2017, Hillary Clinton made a name for herself sharing conspiracy theories about a "vast right-wing conspiracy" aimed at herself and her husband.[5] When Bill Clinton was serving as the forty-second president of the United States, he was accused of lying under oath about an affair with a White House intern, Monica Lewinsky.

Mrs. Clinton stridently defended her husband. She did this, in part, by claiming the Republicans were so vindictive against her husband that they were willing to spread lies of President Clinton's infidelity in order to destroy his presidency. For good measure, Hillary Clinton also coordinated a media hit team from the bowels of the White House that was designed to defame and denigrate any woman who came forward to accuse President Clinton of sexual indiscretions.[6] The longer the Lewinsky scandal played out, the more women came forward to accuse the forty-second president of infidelity.

As it would turn out, despite Hillary Clinton's conspiracy theories, Bill Clinton did, in fact, have an extramarital affair with the White House intern. The Republicans impeached President Clinton over his refusal to tell the truth about that matter while under oath.[7] But Hillary Clinton's claims of a "vast, right-wing conspiracy" took hold within certain quarters of the Democratic Party. They held onto the lie that the Clinton administration had been railroaded by deranged, hyper-partisan Republicans in Washington, D.C. This conspiracy theory fueled the Left for years after Bill Clinton left the White House with Hillary Clinton in tow.

Another doozie of a conspiracy theory Hillary Clinton and her loyalists had crafted concerned former President Barack Obama. The 2016 presidential election was not Hillary Clinton's first bid for the presidency. Indeed, eight years earlier, in 2008, she was the Democrat most experts believed would both handily win her party's presidential nomination and then trounce the Republican candidate.[8] Fate, as it were, had other plans. An upstart forty-something from Chicago, Illinois had his own designs on the office. More problematic for Clinton's 2008 campaign was that the upstart Democratic Party challenger was a highly educated African-American named Barack Hussein Obama.

Unable to beat Obama in a fair fight, and as the contentious 2008 Democratic Party primary wore on, Hillary Clinton grew ever more desperate to diminish Obama's standing before the Democratic Party's national convention. So, Clinton, along with her bagman, Sydney Blumenthal, began sharing a wild conspiracy-theory about Obama's supposed true origins.[9] According to the conspiracy theory—which was designed to appeal to working-class whites, most of whom then voted Democratic, and were skeptical of a black presidential candidate—Obama was not from Hawaii as he claimed. He was, in fact, born in Kenya—where his biological father originated—and his birth certificate was forged to make it appear as though he were born in America and, therefore, was eligible to run for president of the United States.

Almost 20 years after the Lewinsky scandal and Hillary's cogitations about a "vast, right-wing conspiracy" and eight years after Clinton tried to delegitimize Barack Obama's trouncing of her in the 2008 Democratic Party primary, Hillary Clinton again needed to excuse a defeat in 2016. It couldn't be that the American people just didn't like Hillary Clinton as a presidential candidate. It couldn't be that the American people just didn't like Hillary Clinton as a presidential candidate or that they did not like her, period.[10] Or, as former Obama White House political guru, David Axelrod, admitted following Clinton's 2016 defeat, "It takes an awful lot of work to lose to Donald Trump." Then again, Clinton was an awful candidate.[11]

No, according to Clinton and her supporters, there was yet another grand conspiracy arrayed against the Clintons. This time, the right-wing of America had betrayed our hallowed democracy and helped the Russians rig the election against Hillary Clinton. The reason? Vladimir Putin hated Hillary Clinton. Putin, you see, hated

Clinton for a variety of reasons, one of them being because she was a woman (and Putin was a chauvinist).[12] Another reason, according to Clinton's self-serving conspiracy theory, was that as Obama's first secretary of state, Hillary Clinton had proven herself to be a true threat to Putin's grand imperial plans. Had Clinton been allowed to ascend to the White House in 2016, free of alleged Russian meddling, then Vladimir Putin's days would have been numbered![13]

So, what better way for Putin to defend himself against the implacable Hillary Clinton than to remove the woman who quickly would have become one of the toughest Russophobes in the history of the Oval Office? And, of course, the Russians would align themselves with Trump. According to those who bought into Clinton's dark fantasy, Trump was a noted Russophile. In fact, he had deep ties with the Russian mob and even famously wanted to build a Trump Tower in Moscow! Therefore, in their minds, Trump had to have been compromised by Putin's intelligence services.

The conspiracy theory got nastier, too—and it was all put to paper by a former British spy named Christopher Steele. Steele was able to place his salacious dossier, supposedly proving that Donald Trump had been compromised by Russian intelligence, into the waiting hands of the FBI and the Clinton Campaign, which was desperate to find dirt on Trump to use against him in the 2016 campaign. Trump's enemies within the Republican Party, such as Senator John McCain, whose heroic service during the Vietnam War Trump had defamed during that year's primary, also helped to spread the great lie.[14]

According to the debunked Steele Dossier, while visiting Moscow to judge the Miss Universe pageant in 2013, Trump had paid two Russian prostitutes to micturate upon the bed in his hotel room— the same hotel room that then-President Barack Obama and his wife, Michelle, had stayed in just a few months prior to Trump's visit. It was an act of revenge, or so Steele claimed in his now infamous memo. After all, Trump's Moscow trip was shortly after President Obama had humiliated him in front of major American elites at the

White House Correspondents' Dinner in Washington, D.C. During that event, Obama ripped Trump for spreading the birther conspiracy theory—the same conspiracy theory Hillary Clinton and Sydney Blumenthal had concocted in 2008 to harm Obama's chances in that year's Democratic primary. Supposedly smarting from being laughed at by some of America's most powerful people and verbally castigated by the president, Trump got revenge by paying prostitutes to pee on the Russian bed previously occupied by the Obamas.

The Steele Dossier asserts that Russian intelligence had the room where Trump was staying bugged and they recorded the event. Because of that recording, the theory goes, the Russian intelligence services have compromising material on Trump and they black-mailed him into serving Russian interests during the 2016 campaign. After years of investigation and millions of public dollars spent to prove this theory, there is still not a shred of verifiable evidence that this theory is anything other than the musings of demented, angry partisans. Yet, these unfounded accusations dogged Trump for most of his presidency.

As it turns out, a subsequent Department of Justice investigation into the whole Steele Dossier fiasco, led by federal investigator, John Durham, determined that the source of this claim was likely none other than Charles Dolan. If that name seems unfamiliar, that's okay. It turns out that Dolan is a major PR executive and longtime associate of both Bill and Hillary Clinton, with extensive ties to the media. Just as with Hillary Clinton's Obama birther conspiracy, in which a long-time aid, Sydney Blumenthal, was engaged to do her dirty work, so too did a longtime aid perform this service of spreading the misinformation about how Russian intelligence had compromising material on Trump. They did not. It was all a fabrication of Hillary Clinton's.[15]

Just as Hillary Clinton's denials of her husband's infidelity and insidious claims that Barack Obama was an illegal immigrant were proven false, so too were Hillary Clinton's accusations that Donald Trump was a Russian Manchurian Candidate. Sadly, in modern politics the severity is often more important than the accuracy of the accusation. Clinton understood this. She was going to make life Hell for Donald Trump, who was entering politics as a relative naïf. The Washington bureaucracy was already suspicious of him. Clinton's deranged conspiracy theories about Trump gave that dubious bureaucracy all the ammunition it needed to stymie Trump's radical (in their eyes) agenda for reforming the Washington bureaucracy (the "Deep State" in the Trumpist lexicon) and ending, what Trump believed, was the needlessly provocative expansion of NATO into Russia's backyard.

The "mainstream" media unquestioningly spread Clinton's grand conspiracy far-and-wide, as they too had been burned by Trump's victory in 2016.[16] The "vast Russian conspiracy" myth was just one more accusation to hurl at Trump on top of all the other claims, ranging from Trump being a fascist to a sexual predator. Yet, the lie Clinton spread to the world was highly damaging for the country—not least because of the negative impacts it had on the U.S.-Russian relationship. The accusations stemming from Clinton's conspiracy theory hemmed Trump in while president, as he could not be seen as making good on his desire to lower tensions with Russia, out of fear such actions would be used against him by those investigating him in Washington, D.C.[17]

Putin Rages Against Hillary

INTERESTINGLY, VLADIMIR PUTIN and Hillary Clinton disliked each other long before the 2016 presidential election. According to a former White House National Security Council staffer, Philip Gordon (who today serves as Vice-President Kamala Harris' national security adviser), Hillary Clinton was always "skeptical" about Obama's reset policy with Russia while she served as the secretary of state. In 2008, she mocked former George W. Bush's statement about having looked into Putin's eyes during their first meeting and "seeing his soul." Back in 2008, Clinton claimed that Putin "didn't have a soul" because he was a former KGB agent.[18] It was downhill from there. By the time Hillary Clinton became the secretary of state under Obama, Putin had switched with Dmitri Medvedev, making himself the prime minister and Medvedev the president.

According to reports, when they first met at one of Putin's dachas outside of Moscow in 2010, Putin wanted to extend an olive branch to Clinton. He knew that she was fond of animals—notably elephants. So, Putin arranged for her to come down to the basement of his dacha and view the massive collection of animal heads he had taken as trophies from his various hunting trips. It was a bizarre gesture. While there, Hillary Clinton convinced Putin to support tougher sanctions against the Islamic Republic of Iran. Yet, after the successful agreement, Putin immediately took to the cameras and railed against American trade policy and NATO expansion.[19] Still, the Clinton-Putin relationship was better during Obama's first two years than it was by the time Clinton ran for president in 2016.

By 2011, however, as the Obama reset was ending in the predictable disaster that was its destiny, the relationship between Clinton and Putin was also at its lowest point. In the first chapter of this work, a brief history of the geopolitical situation with Russia and the United States following the Cold War showed how the Putinist regime viewed not only NATO expansion but American actions in the Greater Middle East as being part of a grand strategy of containment for the weakened, smaller post-Soviet Russian state.[20] Hillary Clinton was a loud-and-proud advocate for the Obama administration's war against Libyan dictator Muammar Gaddafi. In fact, Hillary Clinton was a leading figure in the Obama administration and she arranged to dissuade Putin's regime from disrupting the American and NATO push for more forceful measures against Gaddafi's regime at the United Nations.[21]

The caveat for Putin's non-interference in the UN vote to impose harsh sanctions on Libya and even a No-Fly Zone was that the

Obama administration would not allow for Gaddafi's regime to be overthrown.[22] We all know how that ended. Once the international community aligned with the West on punishing Gaddafi, it was seen as a blank check for the United States to assist in Gaddafi's ouster. Putin had egg on his face because he not only inadvertently helped President Obama remove Gaddafi, but he got little in return for his assistance. Remember, Vladimir Putin has been described as having become "obsessed" with Gaddafi's gruesome demise in 2011. Reports indicate that Putin essentially watched those events on a loop—and he often angrily referenced Gaddafi's overthrow and execution as an example of what the West ultimately intended to do to him. Putin was both humiliated by Clinton and, he believed, manipulated by her.

There is a famous interview with then-Secretary of State Hillary Clinton in which she is gloating about Gaddafi's gruesome demise. In that interview she gushes, "We came, we saw, he died," followed by Clinton's signature cackle.[23] To the hyper-paranoid Putin, Clinton might as well have been speaking about him rather than the North African dictator. Even more than Obama, whom Putin dismissed as the equivalent of an airhead, Clinton was the aging face of a Western elite that was deeply committed to the destruction not only of his regime, but to the dissolution of the Russian state.

With the collapse of the Obama era reset, it became increasingly obvious that Putin was no longer going to play the shadow president of Russia. He again was plotting a return to the presidency from his place as Russia's prime minister. Ultimately, Putin would switch places with Dmitri Medvedev. He'd again become president and Medvedev would return to the prime minister's office. Russia was set to have its parliamentary elections. That year's parliamentarian elections were rife with accusations of corruption and malign actions by the Putinist regime.

To be clear: Russia is an authoritarian state. In 2011, it was becoming increasingly authoritarian beyond what it had already been when Putin first came to power. But Russia has been authoritarian for much of its history. It shouldn't have shocked anyone who was paying attention that, of course, Putin would rig the election to enhance his own standing in Moscow and the standing of his political allies—all as he prepared to return to Russia's presidency. First, Putin needed to retain majorities in the Russian Duma to change Russian constitutional law so that he could, in fact, run for a third presidential term in 2012. It's not surprising at all that Putin and his cronies would manipulate the important Duma elections in 2011.

Yet, Secretary of State Clinton felt the need to meddle by commenting on the skewered results in 2011.

She made a show of publicly castigating Putin for his lack of democratic scruples. After the election results came in, Putin and his United Russia Party won majorities—surprise! Like they had always done since Putin and his *siloviki* came to power, Putin and his ruling cadre ensured they'd remained in power. But Hillary called them out for it. And she didn't just complain about the rigged election, shortly after her comments castigating Russia's 2011 election results, a crowd of 30,000 angry demonstrators gathered in Moscow and 79 other cities in what became the largest protests since the end of the Cold War.[24] Vladimir Putin, looking out his window from the Kremlin, undoubtedly began thinking he was in the same spot that Gaddafi had been in months before. He might even have heard the maniacal cackling of Hillary Clinton in his paranoid state.

Most experts agree, though, that Clinton's comments completely killed her working relationship with Putin as he had come to believe that she was engaged in a covert regime change operation directed against him. The pattern of a color revolution seemed to be on display in the chaotic days following the corrupt 2011 parliamentary elections in Russia. In response, Putin ordered a vicious crackdown in Russia on all political dissidents. He then initiated a wide-ranging plan removing countless numbers of Western non-governmental organizations, which he and his regime identified as being part of a covert Western plot to destabilize Russia from within. Putin wanted to avoid an even bigger problem with the upcoming presidential elections a year later.

During the protests against Putin, he lambasted Hillary Clinton for her remarks siding with the protesters. According to Putin, "[Opposition leaders] heard the signal and with the support of the U.S. State Department began active work." The Russian strongman continued his tirade against Clinton saying: "We are all grownups here. We all understand the organizers are acting according to a well-known scenario and in their own mercenary political interests."²⁵ Clinton escalated her war of words with Putin when she then reiterated America's commitment to human rights. She defended her public statements calling out Putin's rigged election and siding with the protesters opposed to Putin's continued reign.

Putin Has Déjà vu

BUT THE PROTESTS looked uncannily similar to the other "color revolutions" that swept across Europe and the Middle East over the years. Indeed, they looked very much like the Euromaidan revolution that would erupt in 2014 in Kiev, replacing the pro-Russian Ukrainian President Viktor Yanukovych with a pro-NATO government. Many people today, indeed those who were involved in government during the time that these events occurred, publicly deny Putin's claims. They say that he is merely trying to deflect from the fact that the Russian people did not want him to return to the presidency and that they voted accordingly. That might be a factor in why Putin manipulated the vote, although it is hard to distinguish the streets of Moscow in 2011 (and, again, in 2012) from what happened in Georgia's "Rose" color revolution, Ukraine's "Orange" color revolution in 2004, inevitably, Ukraine in 2014—to say nothing of the pro-democracy revolutions that ripped through the Middle East in 2011.

Regardless of what Western leaders think or say about Putin's fears, the fact remains that Putin and his *siloviki* believe there is a concerted conspiracy afoot to overthrow their regime in Moscow. They further believed that Hillary Clinton was the villain behind the protest movement in 2011. This is not merely a cynical talking point made by an embattled Russian dictator trying to deflect from his various failures. This is a decades-old belief that has been internalized by the top Russian political, military, and intelligence leadership.

In 2017, for example, the U.S. Army translated a paper written by two senior Russian generals, A.S. Brychkov and G.A. Nikonorov, that had been published by *Russia's Journal of the Academy of Military Science*. According to Brychkov and Nikonorov, "the United States and Western governmental and non-governmental organizations and programs create an appearance of grand-scale social transformations that were allegedly in consort with the hopes of the peoples."[26] Brychkov and Nikonorov then outline the way the pattern of color revolutions dogging Russia's periphery in the post-Cold War era resembles what they perceive to be a new form of warfare. By employing "controlled chaos" within a target country's polity, these Russian generals think that Western forces will ultimately be able to "reduce and degrade the Russian population and place their national resources under control of transnational corporations."[27]

In their paper, Brychkov and Nikonorov assert that the U.S. and their Western partners are engaged in a massive conspiracy designed to depopulate Russia and make its remaining population weak and pliable. In their seminal paper, the two Russian generals refer to the human rights agenda of the United States and Western-backed NGOs operating within Russia—which almost always includes support for what many cultures believe to be radical sexual mores—as part of that strategy of "controlled chaos." Specifically, the Russian generals believe that the promotion of "sexual freedoms, free love, and homosexuality" all add to the Western goal of weakening Russia's population and reducing it in overall size.

Brychkov and Nikonorov assert that, "A special office was formed within the US Department of State in charge of staging and managing 'democratic revolutions' in any country chosen by the US government [...] Chiefs of missions at US consulates and embassies in sovereign countries are tasked with executing these directives of the State Department." What's more, the two Russian generals warn their Russian audience to "expect increased activity from NGOs and non-commercial enterprises to apply pressure on public opinion and authorities" as the country entered another presidential and duma election cycle.[28]

The paper goes on to detail the various ways a color revolution is being plotted by the West within Russia. However accurate or inaccurate are the worries of Russia's elite about the prospects of a Western-backed coup in Russia, the fact is that they believe it. They say these things not just in public, but also when speaking to each other in private. Thus, Vladimir Putin truly believes the West is coming for him and his country—and he will do whatever it takes to rebuff the West. And Hillary Clinton, as Putin saw it, became the face of that movement to destabilize and degrade Russia as a sovereign nation.

No Russia Collusion

THIS HISTORY between Putin and Hillary Clinton led many to claim that the real reason for the Russian-sponsored hack on the Democratic National Committee's (DNC) computer servers was to prevent Clinton from winning the 2016 election in favor of Russia's preferred candidate, Donald J. Trump.[29] That is what those closest to Clinton would have everyone believe. Of course, the truth is more complicated than the partisan hacks on cable news let on.

In fact, many experts remain skeptical that the Russian attack on the DNC servers was intended to choose Trump over Hillary in 2016.[30] More likely was that the Russians were probing both the Democrats and the Republicans, looking for dirt to use on both parties. They ended up gaining access to the DNC servers and not the GOP servers. Because of this, Russian sources leaked the only incriminating and embarrassing evidence they had and not much was said about the fact that the GOP protected their servers far better than the Democrats had.[31]

This last point is key to understanding the origins of the Russia collusion allegations that dogged Trump during his first two years in office. Clinton's former 2016 presidential campaign manager, Robby Mook, wholeheartedly endorsed the theory that Putin targeted the Democrats and Clinton specifically because she was such a hawk on Russia. Other Democratic Party notables embraced this convenient theory explaining away Clinton's defeat in 2016. Clinton's own animus toward both Putin and Trump, as well as the very real bad history between Clinton and Putin, was the real source of this conspiracy theory.[32] Few of those perpetuating the Russian stolen election myth really believed in it.

Further, neither Putin nor anyone in his inner circle believed anyone other than Clinton would win the White House in 2016. All this shows is that Putin wanted to create a little chaos in our elections and sully Clinton's otherwise easy ascent to the Oval Office. Putin anticipated a Clinton presidency, though. In fact, he may ultimately have welcomed it since he'd have been able to predict what she would do.

As a former top Sovietologist from the Defense Intelligence Agency (DIA) remarked to me once about Trump and Russia, the Russians feared Trump because he was viewed as mercurial and unpredictable. They understood that flattery was the surest way to keep him happy. But that would only go so far. Other top presidential candidates in the United States, such Jeb Bush or Hillary Clinton, were well-known to the Russians. What's more, the people who those more conventional candidates would hire as their foreign policy advisers were known by Russian intelligence and their decisions about Russia could be better anticipated.

This was not the case with Donald Trump. But it didn't matter. The lie about Trump and Russia took hold in the press and among Trump's various political enemies in Washington, D.C., and it was off to the races with investigating him and undermining his presidency. After two years of doggedly pursuing Trump while he was in office, former FBI Director Robert Mueller, III, had to admit—through gritted teeth, I am sure—that there was no evidence of Russia collusion with the Trump Campaign in 2016. But Clinton had her revenge.[33] The Russia collusion delusion weakened Trump's presidency almost from the start. The Russians, too, got to have a good laugh at America's expense. For all the talk about the Trump-Putin bromance, the fact of the matter was that Trump was tougher on Russia than his predecessors had ever been but that was never once acknowledged by his opposition.

Left unsaid was the fact that it was not only Russia that was meddling in America's election in 2016. It was also Ukraine. And they were decidedly in favor of a Clinton presidency. As the next chapter will show, the 2016 presidential election in the United States became yet another front in the ongoing NATO-Russia conflict over Ukraine's fate. It wasn't only Russia interfering with our domestic politics. The Ukrainians were doing it, too. In fact, because of their decades-long lobbying efforts, notably of the Democratic Party, their role in influencing our 2016 presidential election may have been even more pernicious than the Russians' meddling.

[**A DISASTER OF OUR OWN MAKING**

CHAPTER 12

AMERICA BECOMES A BATTLEFIED IN THE RUSSIA-UKRAINE WAR

G O BACK TO 1994, when President Bill Clinton negotiated the removal of Ukraine's massive nuclear weapons arsenal, left there by the Red Army at the end of the Cold War. Implied within the Budapest Memorandum, at least as the Ukrainians interpreted it, were security guarantees by the Americans. To ensure that the United States remained committed to Ukrainian independence, with their nuclear deterrent removed, Kiev worked to ensnare America's political elites with intensive, lucrative lobbying techniques.

Taras Kuzio, a Ukraine specialist who teaches at the University of Alberta, described the relationship between Ukraine and Democratic Party donors (as well with Republicans) as being "America's real life House of Cards." According to Kuzio, both political parties were subjected to an unusually high amount of influence buying from Ukrainian oligarchs.[1] And beyond flagrant lobbying, many politicos in the 1990s went to work in former Soviet states, like Ukraine. They made deep connections with the political class of Ukraine, helping them in their campaigns. These political consultants then returned to the United States and continued working in American politics, while maintaining their ties to Ukraine.

Of course, that doesn't necessarily mean that these individuals were then determined to somehow compromise U.S. national interests in service to Kiev. But it should raise some eyebrows. At least it should raise the same kind of suspicions that the Trump campaign raised when they hired a handful of political advisers who had previously worked in the former Soviet states as political consultants. Yet, it did not evoke the level of scrutiny and, frankly, paranoia in the media and among the U.S. security services that Trump's hires did.

Everyone has heard of Paul Manafort. An otherwise shifty old school political operative with a taste for the finer things of life, Manafort had been a GOP operative for decades. He was a critical player for President Gerald R. Ford's reelection campaign in 1976. Back then, Ford was deeply unpopular among the GOP base. He was viewed as being too moderate and weak for the base's liking. The Republican rank-and-file liked a California governor and former Hollywood celebrity, Ronald Reagan. In 1976, the fiery conservative California governor was planning to challenge Ford's nomination on the floor of the Republican National Convention. Manafort was the man Ford hired to stop the floor challenge.[2] After that, Manafort went to work in the former Soviet Union, where the rules for political consultants were far murkier than in the United States and the opportunities for large payouts were greater.

Manafort went to work for the pro-Russia Party of Regions in Ukraine.[3] He met some truly unsavory characters there and had no compunction about working alongside them for the right price. This was not a guy you'd want over on a Sunday afternoon. Trump in 2016 needed skilled campaign staff and, because of the controversy his campaign engendered among the GOP elite, Trump was having difficulty finding capable people to staff his campaign. Trump found Manafort and hired him. Specifically, Trump needed Manafort to help him stave off a floor challenge at the Republican Convention. Manafort's unique experience from 1976 made him attractive as an employee for that specific job. It was claimed by the Democrats, though, that Manafort was the crucial element linking the Trump campaign to Russia's intelligence.

Manafort was convicted in a federal court for tax evasion.[4] But he was hounded by the Mueller probe with allegations that the Trump campaign colluded with Russian intelligence. It was finally determined that Manafort likely handed off some publicly available polls to a Russian oligarch closely aligned with Vladimir Putin.[5] Of course, sharing campaign data is not illegal. Nevertheless, Manafort would pay for daring to help Donald Trump in 2016. They couldn't get him on what they wanted to get him on: being a Russian spy. But they got him on tax evasion. And because they got a conviction, Trump and his movement were further sullied despite the provably false allegations that Trump colluded with Russia to steal the 2016 election.

For everyone who knows Paul Manafort's name, few know who Alexandra Chalupa is. While she has never been charged with wrongdoing—and she categorically denies all claims that are about to be made in this book—she was a consultant for the Democratic Party in 2016 with deep foreign ties. The only differences between her and Paul Manafort, at least on paper, were that Chalupa had deep ties to Ukraine's pro-Western political elite and she was working for the Clinton 2016 campaign whereas Manafort was known to commiserate with the pro-Russia, Yanukovych wing of Ukraine's political elite.

According to Kenneth P. Vogel and David Stern of *Politico*, Chalupa was "consulting for the Democratic National Committee [when she] met with top officials in the Ukrainian embassy in Washington in an effort to expose ties between Trump, top campaign aide Paul Manafort and Russia."[6] In fact, Chalupa's efforts against her foil, Manafort, were rewarded when Manafort was punished for his ties to pro-Russia elements in Ukraine. After all, Chalupa was an evangelical in her crusade to get key Trump campaign aides convicted for the crime of helping Donald Trump defeat Hillary Clinton in 2016. Yet, Chalupa's ties to and sympathies with Ukraine remained oddly obscured from the public by the same media that was hounding

Manafort for his foreign connections. Chalupa's role in taking down Paul Manafort and wounding the Trump campaign with accusations of colluding with Russian intelligence to defeat Hillary Clinton were venerated on the Left. When Republicans on the Hill eventually wanted to depose her, she was "on a mission to testify."[7]

And, as the Kenneth Vogel and David Stern 2017 exposé in *Politico* goes on to detail, it was Ukrainian government officials who provided her with intelligence about Manafort's dark activities as a political consultant in Ukraine, when President Viktor Yanukovych and his Party of Regions ran Kiev.[8] The Petro Poroshenko regime, which ran Ukraine at the time of the 2016 U.S. presidential election, insists that they remained neutral throughout the contentious presidential race.[9] The *Politico* investigation "found evidence of Ukrainian government involvement in the race." Per the *Politico* document, Chalupa sought out the influence of a foreign government—Ukraine's—to help their preferred candidate, Hillary Clinton, defeat Donald Trump.[10]

In the words of David A. Merkel, a former George W. Bush administration official and someone who served as an election observer throughout the 1990s in Ukraine, "It seems that the U.S. election may have been seen as a surrogate battle by those in Kiev and Moscow."[11] Chalupa was a key figure in fanning the flames of paranoid resentment among leaders in Ukraine. A Clinton supporter, researcher for the DNC in 2016, and attorney of Ukrainian descent, Chalupa allowed herself to be interviewed by the writers of the *Politico* piece. She talked about how, early in the 2016 campaign, she "felt there was a Russia connection" with the Trump campaign.

Chalupa then reached out to her high-level contacts in the Ukrainian government, such as Valeriy Chary, who was serving as Ukraine's ambassador to the United States as well as one of Chary's top aides, Oksana Shulyar. In fact, Chalupa had high-level meetings with Ukrainian government officials at the Ukraine embassy in Washington, D.C. At those meetings, she shared her thoughts about

Manafort's allegiances and the overall tilt of the Trump campaign and the Ukrainians likely reciprocated.[12]

Four days after that meeting between Chalupa and the Ukrainian ambassador, the Trump campaign officially announced Manafort's hiring. Overnight, then, Chalupa was a "high-demand" expert for the DNC. The Clinton campaign was seeking dirt on Trump, and they turned to Chalupa to provide it based on her deep ties with the Ukrainian government. Interestingly, four years later, President Trump's political enemies would attempt to impeach him on grounds that he had asked for dirt on his political opponent (Joe Biden) from the Ukrainian government. Clinton, of course, got a pass and the Democrats were able to project their own legally dubious behavior onto their great rival, Trump, just a few years later.[13]

As one unnamed senior DNC staffer admitted to the *Politico* writers in 2017, "with the DNC's encouragement, Chalupa asked embassy staff to arrange an interview in which [Ukrainian President] Poroshenko might discuss Manafort's ties to Yanukovych." The embassy apparently drew the line, at least officially, with that request. Yet, Chalupa herself acknowledged that she and the Ukrainian embassy devised what amounts to an underhanded way of trading sensitive information. "If I asked a question, [the Ukrainian embassy] would provide guidance, or if there was someone I needed to follow up with." Chalupa insists that she never shared documents with or received them from the Ukrainian embassy.[14]

But that doesn't really matter, especially if the same standards that were applied to the Trump campaign advisers in 2016 are applied to the Clinton campaign advisers. And whether one is trading documents or simply sharing specific information from foreign governments tailored toward damaging a domestic political rival that that foreign regime finds problematic, the fact remains that one is being used as a conduit for foreign disinformation.

The meetings with Chalupa and verbal exchanges of damaging information about senior Trump campaign officials occurred at a time when the Ukrainian embassy in Washington had no qualms about hosting events in which they made clear their support for Clinton's presidential campaign. For example, the Ukrainian embassy asked longtime Hillary Clinton confidantes, like Melanne Verveer, to give speeches alongside Ukrainian politicians discussing ways Ukraine could "fight Russia's aggression in the Donbas." Verveer was not only a longtime Clinton confidante, she was also a former close adviser to Hillary Clinton when Clinton had served as Obama's secretary of state. At the time she had given the speech at the Ukrainian embassy alongside major Ukrainian political figures, Verveer was serving as a Clinton Campaign operative.[15]

Again, even as the Ukrainian embassy was denying its role in disseminating disinformation to Democratic Party operatives during the 2016 election, a Ukrainian embassy official admitted to *Politico* that the embassy was helping "Chalupa research connections between Trump, Manafort, and Russia." The former Ukrainian embassy official, Andrii Telizhenko, claimed that, "They were coordinating an investigation with the Hillary team on Paul Manafort with Alexandra Chalupa." The embassy leadership, according to Telizhenko, "were keeping [the investigation] quiet [while they] worked closely with Chalupa."[16]

From there, Chalupa took the information on Manafort from the Ukrainians and contacted Michael Isikoff, a Washington-based investigative journalist, and even "connected [Isikoff] with Ukrainian officials" so that both she and Isikoff could begin weaponizing the information they received in the American press. All this was done to elevate Hillary Clinton's chances of becoming president. Everything that they accused the Trump campaign of doing (that was provably false), it turns out, they were doing to Donald Trump with the help of Ukraine.[17]

The tale continues on like this for the duration of the 2016 campaign.

Chalupa was certainly not the only example of the cross-pollination of Ukrainian interest with Democratic Party political objectives. The Ukrainian president at the time, Poroshenko, is believed to have coordinated the release of damaging information that his investigators discovered about Manafort's political consulting business in Ukraine to Western media outlets. Interestingly, the evidence of $12.5 million in payments from the Yanukovych government to Manafort for political consulting fees came from the same Ukrainian anti-corruption unit that then-Vice President Joe Biden had strongarmed into not fully investigating the alleged misdeeds of Biden's son, Hunter, in Ukraine (more on that later). According to one senior Poroshenko adviser, the findings of the anti-corruption investigation into the Yanukovych-Manafort relationship could not have gone forward—let alone have been released to Western media sources—without Poroshenko's tacit approval.

For the record, the accusations against Manafort in the Ukrainian anti-corruption probe have never been verified. Manafort denies the charges against him. More importantly, some Ukrainian officials have come to the conclusion that, "[the anti-corruption bureau] is backing away from investigating [Manafort] because the ledgers might have been doctored" to implicate Paul Manafort as part of a larger scheme to undermine Trump's candidacy in 2016. A candidacy that Ukraine's pro-NATO regime undoubtedly would have considered a threat.

The 2016 U.S. presidential election was little more than a proxy war between Russia and Ukraine. Everyone has heard about Russia's hacking of the DNC and how Putin supposedly had a "bromance" with Donald Trump. Yet, the real election interference did not come from whatever conspiracy theories people like Hillary Clinton created in their rageful delusions about Trump and Russia. The actual election meddling was from Ukraine, in support of Clinton's shambolic candidacy, and against the campaign of the Republican Party's candidate, who the Ukrainians viewed as a direct threat to their interests.[18]

[**A DISASTER OF OUR OWN MAKING**

CHAPTER 13

THIS WAR WOULDN'T HAVE HAPPENED UNDER TRUMP

THIS LINE BEARS repeating as one might recite Yoga chant or as a monk would repeat a prayer: NATO is the most important defensive alliance in history. Embrace this as an article of faith. Let it become a new law of thermodynamics. Now understand that this is the degree to which the Washington establishment has internalized the concept of NATO as the most important defensive military alliance in history, and with it one is now able to see the great vision.[1]

What is that vision?

An endlessly expanding NATO bureaucracy to encompass Europe, of course!

But what is NATO's purpose other than to continuously expand into former Soviet states?

Let's look at this another way, too. If NATO's mission is one from God, as the proponents of the alliance seem to believe, then why have most of the NATO member states spent decades underfunding the alliance? Of course, no one in the neoconservative-neoliberal cabal dares to ask these questions. Partly this is because they are simply incapable of conceiving these queries on their own. Another reason they dare not ask these questions about NATO is because their commitment to NATO is quasi-religious. No true believer questions the existence of God, after all.[2]

Since the end of the Cold War, only one American politician has dared to countenance these existential questions about NATO. That person was Donald J. Trump.[3] An outsider to the political class that purports to rule the West, Trump was instantly reviled. He was uncouth. Trump did not look, act, or speak like the elites who run things today. Because he held unorthodox views on things like NATO and Russia, Trump found himself in the crosshairs of several bad actors, and from both major political parties, for daring to raise these points in his 2016 presidential campaign.[4]

Trump was never anti-NATO as his critics said. Like most ordinary Americans, he was ambivalent about the alliance. Trump just wanted NATO's members to stop, as he saw it, bilking the already cash-strapped United States to cover for the fact that most members weren't paying their share of NATO burdens.[5] In Trump's estimation, if the Russians were as serious a threat as the European leadership often claimed, then European NATO members should *at least* have been paying two percent of their national GDPs toward their defense. After all, Russia was right next door to Europe. These countries shared a massive land border with Russia, whereas the United States was an ocean and a continent away.

That two percent figure was agreed upon by the NATO members' heads of state in 2006.[6] But most members of NATO were not meeting that standard more than a decade later, despite Europe having a combined GDP just shy of $15 trillion.[7] Many European NATO members were chronically underpaying and having other countries, namely the United States, make up the difference.[8] Trump understood that it was neither fair nor appropriate to expect the U.S. taxpayer to fund NATO as lavishly as it did to combat a Russia that was nowhere near the threat to the United States it supposedly was to Europe—not when there were so many other problems that required America's attention both at home and in other parts of the world.

During the 2016 campaign, Trump said that he believed the United States coming to the defense of a NATO member that was attacked would depend on whether that country "paid [its] bills." Trump wasn't done, though. "They have an obligation to make payments. Many NATO nations are not making payments, are not making what they're supposed to make. That's a big thing. You can't say forget that."[9]

Just look at the numbers. Until the Russian invasion of Ukraine in 2022, the Germans had so chronically underfunded their military that the German Army's tank force was comprised mostly of dilapidated units.[10] Yes, Germany has the magnificent *Leopard* II-class Main Battle Tanks (MBT). But those units did not represent the bulk of Germany's force. Most of Germany's tanks were poorly maintained when Trump was running for office, there were far too few reliable tanks in Germany, and many of those units were old. Ditto on Germany's navy. Back in 2017, Germany's entire submarine fleet was out of commission.[11] That same year the German Defense Ministry reported that, "less than a third of Germany's military assets were operational."[12] I chose 2017 in this case because that was the situation Trump was inheriting when he assumed office. Back then, the German financial commitment to NATO (in GDP terms) was 1.98 percent.[13] That was a painfully small sum of money for a country that, back then, was the fourth-largest economy in GDP terms.[14]

After Russia's illegal invasion of Ukraine in 2022, Germany made a big show of announcing that—*finally*—they would begin paying a minimum of two percent GDP on their national defense, as per the requirements agreed upon by NATO's leaders in 2006.[15] In August of 2023, however, Germany had to walk back that commitment.[16] Although Germany's economy has been put through the ringer, between COVID-19 and the economic impact of the Ukraine War, the fact remains that Germany currently has a GDP of around $4 trillion and is ranked as the fourth richest economy in the world. Germany could easily fund its defense (and, therefore, its NATO commitments) to the tune of a measly two percent of its GDP. It's simply choosing not to do so. If our betters in Washington had been minding the U.S. taxpayer as much as they were obsessed with containing post-Soviet Russia, they might have asked themselves why a prosperous and advanced nation such as Germany hasn't taken the opportunity to stand up for itself ... that is, if the Russians truly are the great bogeyman of Europe that many assume them to be.

Much like questioning a religious fanatic's core beliefs, it is likely that those who unflinchingly support NATO expansion would not like truthful answers to such incisive questions. As George Smiley said in the 2011 film adaptation of John Le Carré's novel, *Tinker, Tailor, Soldier Spy*, "the fanatic is always harboring a secret doubt [about their own beliefs]." It may be that Germany secretly disagrees Washington's judgment that NATO expansion is as inexorable as the laws of gravity and cannot be denied or slowed. Perhaps Berlin does not have the heart or patience to have such a conversation with its allies in Washington (and it's likely those allies in Washington would be incapable of hearing such skepticism from Berlin's leaders, in any event).

And Germany is not alone in underfunding its NATO commitments.

On July 7, 2023, NATO shared data detailing how much each of its 31 members were paying for the alliance. Of the 31 members, according to NATO, only 10 of the 31 members are meeting the 2006 era goal of two percent of their GDP spent on defense.[17] In 2023, Poland was the largest spender as a percentage of its GDP on defense. At 3.8 percent, Poland's commitment to NATO is clear (and understandable, given its bad history with Russia). The United States came in second with 3.49 percent, followed by Greece (at 3.01 percent), Estonia (2.73 percent), and Lithuania at 2.54 percent. The five smallest spenders were Luxembourg, Spain, Belgium, Turkey, and Slovenia. But it was in Eastern Europe where defense spending was explosive.[18] This, of course, makes sense because Eastern European nations are the ones with the worst shared history with Russia and are understandably threatened by Russia's aggressive turn against Ukraine.

Trump's commentary on NATO's delinquent payments was just one of several statements from the 2016 campaign that set the elite's collective hair on fire. In the words of Zack Beauchamp, "I have no idea how to convey the enormity of Trump's NATO comments. They literally make World War III more likely."[19] Setting aside the incorrect usage of the word "literally" to make an overwrought political point, Beauchamp's line of commentary was common among journalists or pundits in the mainstream media when it came to Trump's foreign policy, especially regarding NATO. One could have had quite a good time playing a drinking game in which the participants drank a shot each time Trump was supposedly—*literally*—going to start World War III with one of his tweets or off-the-cuff statements.[20]

Yet, the country was never at risk of entering a third world war when Trump was president, not least because of his skepticism about NATO and his desire to reach a peaceful settlement with the Russian Federation. The first sacred cow he slaughtered, NATO expansion, made him a madman about to start a world war in the eyes of the mainstream media. The second, the suggestion that we should give up refusing to engage with Putin, made him a Russian spy—*literally!* Indeed, Hillary Clinton, one of the chief architects of the Russia collusion conspiracy theory, said of Trump's remarks about NATO in 2016, "It is fair to assume that Russian President Vladimir Putin is rooting for the Republican candidate." She would later claim that "there's no doubt [in her] mind that [Putin] wanted me to lose and wanted Trump to win."[21]

In both cases, the supposed mainstream opinion was dead wrong. Trump kept us out of major wars when he was president.[22] In fact, Trump got many of the NATO members who were delinquent on their payments to NATO to increase their funding for the alliance.[23] And while the outcome of Trump's outreach policy toward Russia garnered mixed results, the fact of the matter is that he had far better relations with Putin than does Trump's successor, Joe Biden. Ukraine never had to face a Russian invasion as it did under Obama and again during the Biden administration while Trump was president.

Senior Trump adviser, Stephen K. Bannon, likely echoing Trump's feelings, derisively referred to NATO as a "protectorate" of the United States in 2024.[24] A protectorate does not have to pay its fair share of anything ... because it is not an equal with the larger country (in this case, the United States). It merely exists as cannon fodder. A protectorate has no agency of its own. It is, in fact, part of the larger state or empire. This is not what NATO was founded to be—and it certainly is not what most Americans want. Remember, after World War II, the United States had a chance to create an empire. The U.S. purposely refused to do that.

For all the talk about Article V of the NATO charter which calls for all members to go to war on behalf of a NATO member that is attacked, little is said about Article III of the NATO charter:

In order more effectively to achieve [NATO objectives], separately and jointly, by means of continuous and effective self-help and mutual aid, will maintain and develop their individual and collective capacity to resist attack.[25]

In other words, all NATO members must pay their fair share to support the alliance *and be able to withstand an attack* for at least some period before the Americans intervene. Yet, until very recently countries like Germany did not pay their fair share, to say nothing of the smaller European states. Americans are expected to hold Article V as the eleventh commandment, "Thou Shalt Send Our Sons to Fight Russia," while ignoring Article III.

Aren't all the articles of NATO's charter equally important?

Come to think of it, maybe Bannon was wrong when he described Europe as an "American protectorate." Perhaps the truth is far darker (for the American people, at least). Increasingly, it seems that, far from being an imperialistic power ruling over a subservient Europe, the United States is a hostage to the peculiarities and geopolitical whims of this hodgepodge of tiny, European states, with deep (and understandable) historical resentments toward neighboring Russia. And now, with Ukraine, a non-NATO member, apparently the United States is also a hostage to the irresponsible behaviors of the most corrupt nation in Europe regarding its terrible relationship with Russia. As we've seen in the Ukraine War, after all, America is allowing itself to be drawn deeper into a conflict that most Americans do not seek with Russia.

Trump Courts Putin (By Killing Hundreds of Russian Mercenaries in Syria)

BACK IN 2009, when President Barack Obama enacted his failed reset policy with Russia, the forty-fourth president was hailed by the elites as being a peacemaking wiseman. When Donald Trump merely said that he thought he could get along better with Vladimir Putin than Hillary Clinton could, he was accused of being Russian agent provocateur. The key difference between the Obama era reset and Trump's attempt at restarting healthy relations is that Vladimir Putin truly disliked Obama and the Obama advisers. For the American side, the key difference was that Obama was part of the elite—a man who, the allegedly conservative columnist, David Brooks, claimed sent a tingle his leg whenever he saw Obama speak. Trump, on the other hand, was viewed as a garish byproduct of America's low-rent middle and working classes.

Yet Trump *was* viewed differently in Moscow than his post-Cold War presidential predecessors had been. This is *not* because he was a Russian agent. It was because Trump spoke the language of brute force, while at the same time not having any real ideological commitment to Europe. Trump was widely seen in Moscow as a transactional player.[26] Trump wasn't what Gary Dorrien described as a crusading "democratic-globalist."[27] Trump's lack of elite pedigree, the precise thing that alienated him from Washington's elite circles, endeared him not only to ordinary Americans but also to Russia's leadership. Trump had heterodox views on foreign policy and was, as his first *New York Times* bestselling book alluded to, a dealmaker. Russia believed they could work with Trump, not because he was one of their spies, but because he wasn't a quasi-religious zealot about NATO expansion into Ukraine.

Neoconservative and neoliberal ideologues would be kept far removed from any Trump administration. Or so, that was what most had assumed. The reality of former President Trump's governance was far different from what was promised—or even what Trump may have envisioned while campaigning for the office in 2016. Nevertheless, Trump sought to have healthier relations with Russia. And he seemed sincere. Further, his constant criticism of NATO on the campaign trail was geopolitical music to Putin's ears. Of course, Trump never truly seemed committed to disbanding NATO, as his detractors in Washington argued. He was merely ambivalent about continuing the primacy it had been given by so many previous presidents. So, just as so many others in the West had done, Putin was likely pouring his best hopes and wishes into what, ideologically, he thought to be an empty vessel.

When Trump told audiences repeatedly that he could—and wanted to—get along with Putin, he was excoriated by the recalcitrant elites in Washington, D.C. Yet, back in 2009, when Obama had chided Putin for "having one foot in the old ways of doing things and one foot in the new," many of the same people upset with Trump for his supposed love for Putin were also complaining that Obama had been too "clumsy" and forceful with Putin; Obama's hectoring remarks meant that his relationship with Putin was "dead on arrival" in 2009, in the words of Peter Rutland, a Russia expert at Wesleyan University.[28] Plus, the same people who said Obama in 2009 had been too tough on Putin and that Trump had been far too kind to Putin in 2016, were the same people who harangued George W.

Bush—the most hated Republican president before Donald Trump came along—for his "cowboy" diplomacy.

Whatever problems the elites in D.C. had with Trump's diplomatic enchantment strategy *vis-à-vis* Putin, Trump's gambit did bear some fruits. And because Trump was a practitioner of what Nixon would have referred to as the "madman theory," Putin and the Russians were kept off-balance.[29] This was especially true at the start of the Trump administration.

It's also true that Putin was able to discover Trump's kryptonite: his ego. Like so many others who have had to deal with Trump, inevitably, Putin recognized that by stroking Trump's ego, he could keep himself ingratiated with Trump.[30] At the same time, however, this bought the United States the maneuvering room it needed to cool tensions down on the international stage and focus on more pressing concerns (such as destroying the Islamic State of Iraq and Syria, which Trump did within his first two years in office). Even while Putin was blowing smoke up Trump's derrière, the wannabe tsar was still keeping his sword sheathed because he knew that upsetting Trump could seriously destabilize Russia's near abroad.

Consider this: in 2017, after Trump's daughter, Ivanka, played on his heartstrings about the Syrian children who were suffering after a chemical weapons attack was conducted on their village by the Russian-backed Syrian government, Trump decided to bomb the airfields where the Syrian warplanes had deployed from.[31] There were Russian troops at those airfields, too. Russian-built S-300 and the even more advanced S-400 air defense systems ringed Syria. These Russian-built air defenses could "easily blow out" the American Tomahawk cruise missiles that were fired at the Syrian airbase in retaliation for the alleged chemical weapons attack.[32]

Officially, Russian-trained Syrian troops manned the defense batteries but it is likely that Russia's military had a higher degree of operational control than what official Russian sources would have us believe. Moreover, we know that by 2019, Russia and Syria officially linked their air defenses to stunt the threat of U.S. airpower over the skies of Syria.[33] Despite having been given advanced warning, the air defense batteries stood down as American cruise missiles entered Syrian airspace and landed on their Syrian military targets.

Several months after this incident, the Russians were feeling their oats and decided to have their "private" military contracting force, the Wagner Group, launch a widescale assault on the entrenched American positions at the oil fields of Deir ez-Zour. An intense, four-hour battle ensued for control over the oil fields in Syria in which President Trump ordered the destruction of the Russian attacking force.[34] After four hours of intense fighting, Trump, the man who Hillary Clinton had convinced her cronies in the "mainstream" media was a Russian asset, ordered the deaths of 400 Russian mercenaries in a series of airstrikes, heavy artillery strikes, and direct engagement between U.S. Special Forces operators and the Russian forces.[35] The attack was gruesome. The Russian forces were far more aggressive and effective than what American planners had anticipated.[36] At the end of the day, though, the Russians were clearly defeated by the American forces.

U.S. intelligence was able to decrypt the Wagner Group's transmissions back to their base that day and recorded them for posterity. The Russians could not believe the ferocity with which the Americans fought. "To make it short," began the exasperated Wagner Group Russian commando over his radio, "we've had our asses f-cking kicked." The Russian mercenary then detailed the damage that had been inflicted upon his men. "So one squadron f-cking lost 200 people ... right away, another one lost 10 people ... and I don't know about the third squadron, but it got torn up pretty badly, too..." The Wagner commander then explained how the Americans deployed artillery and how Russian air cover was nonexistent, meaning his men got slaughtered even more than they might have done with that air cover.[37]

According to one report, the reason Russian air cover was not available was due to diplomatic efforts by Washington to pressure Moscow not to escalate the situation. The Russians complied with the Trump administration's request and immediately began deescalating. In the meantime, however, the Americans killed hundreds of Russian mercenaries defending the oil refinery.

Trump, the purported Russian spy in the White House, aggravated his intelligence chiefs by then publicly bragging about how he orchestrated the annihilation of a massive Russian force in Syria. Trump allegedly even rubbed Putin's nose in the news. This is not the work of a man who was a pushover for Putin. What these moves did was display to Putin that Trump was a serious player. Unlike Obama, who was constantly handwringing and second-guessing, Trump could modulate his hopes for a better relationship with Putin by applying decisive, though proportional force when Russia threatened perceived U.S. interests. Essentially, Trump was establishing meaningful boundaries in his relationship with Putin.

As a result of Trump's dual-track approach with Moscow, he managed to keep the supply lines into Afghanistan open, supporting our war effort there. Further, Trump was able to better coordinate the war on ISIS, as Russia had a role in that fight. Meanwhile, as previously noted, Trump provided far more lethal aid to Ukraine than did Obama—all while maintaining a peace with Russia that was otherwise unknown during the Obama or now, the Biden years.

"We've Got a Lot of Killers. What, You Think Our Country Is So Innocent?"

TRUMP AVOIDED the caterwauling over Russia's various human rights abuses. What good would that do? Russia is a nuclear-armed power and an alien culture with different values than our own. Why spend precious diplomatic capital on antagonizing Russia when we could be working together on important issues?

One of the first men to have made America his home, the Puritan leader, John Winthrop, proclaimed that America would be a "shining city on a hill." In other words, the United States would be a free land and the freedom we established would *inspire* others around the world. George Washington, the greatest American who ever lived, urged his people to avoid entangling alliances in Europe (here's looking at you, NATO). John Quincy Adams would later admonish Americans not to, "go abroad in search of monsters to destroy."

Far from representing some radical departure from traditional American foreign policy, Trump was merely following in their footsteps. Why create tensions over matters that amount to irreconcilable differences? Let's instead have an effect on matters where we have shared objectives, and over time, perhaps enough trust would be built to peacefully engage on matters, such as human rights. But that time was not going to be during the Trump administration—not after the total breakdown in U.S.-Russia relations over which Obama had presided.

Trump further bewildered audiences, both in America and Russia, with his infamous interview with former *Fox News* host, Bill O'Reilly. The combustible newsman demanded to know why Trump wanted to get along with Putin when Vladimir Putin was "a killer." To which, Trump nonchalantly replied, "We've got a lot of killers. A lot of killers. What, you think our country is so innocent?" The media, of course, misinterpreted the entire interview. The context was O'Reilly wanting to know why Trump desired to have a good relationship with Putin. Before Trump's infamous response, he explained that, while he hoped to have a healthy working relationship with Putin, there was no guarantee that he would get along with the man. As with everything that Trump did, it was conditional; transactional.[38]

Trump was communicating with Putin in that interview. He was signaling that he was open to a restart of relations with Russia. But he also wanted to be clear that he would not be a pushover and he would not beg for a deal, as did Obama. Contrary to what so many elites thought at the time, Trump was in the driver's seat in the relationship. This was why Ukraine was never invaded when Trump was in office.

Putin is on the record as having complained about the "men in gray suits" (the permanent bureaucracy) being the ones who were really in control of the United States government.[39] After decades of dealing with a host of U.S. presidents who were beholden to that group, since the days of Bill Clinton, Trump was an anomaly to Putin. Trump wasn't welcomed in the elite circles other U.S. presidents were. Plus, Trump had little real interest in politics until shortly before running for office. Meanwhile, his skepticism about NATO expansion bought him a degree of goodwill with Moscow, allowing the United States to finally push forward with Russia on the things that most mattered to both countries.

The neoconservative-neoliberal elite, however, could not countenance this. They were wedded to NATO expansion as an article of faith. The inexorability of Ukraine's admission into both NATO and the EU, Moscow's concerns be damned, was fundamental. Anyone who dared to question it, such as the uncouth Trump and his boorish followers, were to be considered heretics and treated accordingly by the Washington foreign policy elite and NATO zealots.

Helsinki Blues

THE APOTHEOSIS of Trump's outreach to Russia was to come in Helsinki in July of 2018. It was here that the forty-fifth president had hoped to create a new *modus vivendi* with the Russian Federation: a restart in relations and a restoration of the kind of partnership the U.S. initially enjoyed with Russia immediately after the Cold War. Thus, the pressure on Trump's outreach to Russia was most intense from his domestic political opponents. Within the intelligence community and within the elite political circles that run Washington, D.C., the pushback against Trump's Russia agenda was unlike anything he had yet experienced. The resistance from certain free-rider nations in Europe, which for so long had enjoyed NATO protection on the dime of U.S. taxpayers, was great as they feared the kind of reckoning Trump had in store for them.

Before heading into the conference at Helsinki, Trump tweeted a scathing condemnation of what he described as, "U.S. foolishness," for being responsible for the awful state of U.S.-Russian relations.[40] As you've seen, Trump was merely pointing out true history. An obsessive commitment to NATO expansion, an obsequious faith in the sclerotic European Union, and an almost paranoid view that Russia was going to come for everyone to the west of Belarus, compelled a succession of America's leaders to avoid acting pragmatically in their post-Cold War dealings with Moscow. And their extremism begat Russia's extremism.

The Robert Mueller investigation into allegations that the 2016 Trump Campaign colluded with Russia to rig that year's election in Trump's favor was in full swing, too, meaning that President Trump was further hemmed in. Anything the president said or did that appeared respectful toward Russia was immediately perceived through the lens of the Mueller investigation and the unfounded allegations—the Clinton conspiracy theory—that was designed to stymie Trump's ability to conduct meaningful diplomacy with the world's largest nuclear weapons power. This was a fact Trump himself acknowledged in a series of tweets leading into his meeting in Helsinki with Putin.[41] Of course, Trump's acknowledgement of how damaging the baseless Mueller probe was for U.S.-Russia relations only added to the pressure Trump was receiving from his domestic political opponents during the Helsinki conference.

The most complicating factor in Trump's attempts to normalize relations with Russia at Helsinki was the way the media kept linking his trip with the Mueller probe. This sidetracked Trump and made him paranoid. At the end of the summit with Putin, when the two leaders were to make their cursory statement summarizing the meeting, Trump ripped into a reporter who asked him about whether he brought up Russia's alleged election interference in 2016. With his typical bombast, the forty-fifth president insisted that Russia had not interfered in the 2016 election. When pressed by reporters as to how he knew this, Trump said because Putin "strongly" denied the accusations. Everything Trump said and did after that point made him politically dead in the eyes of the neoconservative-neoliberal elite.[42] Trump, ever the competitor and wanting to make sure no one could besmirch or take away his historic win in 2016, began reciting the number of electoral votes he received over Hillary and castigating the media as spreading a scurrilous lie meant to diminish him in the eyes of the American people.

American intelligence and media sources were angry over these claims because they thought Trump was siding with Putin over his own intelligence professionals. In a way, he was. While it was an inappropriate remark to make in front of the Russian leader, the fact of the matter was that there was no collusion in 2016. Mueller's investigation was a waste of time and resources. Trump was defending himself from vicious, partisan attacks—domestic political assaults that were now railroading his attempts to stabilize the U.S.-Russia relationship and were being conducted by rogue elements of his own intelligence community. Trump then raged against the FBI's apparent inability to get its hands on the server that the DNC claimed had been hacked by Russian intelligence during the 2016 campaign.[43] That was the server that caused so much consternation during the campaign and was the source of the embarrassing WikiLeaks reports on the Democrats in 2016.

This is a strange, key point in the saga of the DNC hacks from 2016. You see, the Democrats refused to turn over their compromised servers to the FBI team investigating the breach. Instead, the Democratic Party handed the server over to a company called CrowdStrike.[44] A firm with a stellar record in the cybersecurity industry, one that had multiple contracts with the United States Department of Defense, CrowdStrike was a private actor and was not accountable to the FBI.

It worked for the DNC. The FBI relied on the conclusions of the CrowdStrike investigators rather than demanding that they be given direct access to the server. It was CrowdStrike that concluded the Russians had hacked the DNC server. The intelligence community, like they did with the former MI6 spy, Christopher Steele, simply took CrowdStrike at its word.

Despite the unsubstantiated conclusion of CrowdStrike, the determination that Russia hacked the DNC servers was taken as an undeniable fact. Yet, while testifying before the House Intelligence Committee on the matter, CrowdStrike President Shawn Henry was forced to admit that, "We did not have concrete evidence that the data was exfiltrated [moved electronically] from the DNC, but we have indicators that it was exfiltrated."[45] So, when pressed, the group charged with proving the claim that Russia hacked the 2016 election to favor Trump had no verifiable evidence proving their claim. Further, the Democratic Party refused to let the federal government investigate their server directly, making many observers ponder if there was some cover-up occurring.

Trump was wrong to have thrown the U.S. intelligence services under the proverbial bus in front of Putin, irrespective of what he believed about the reliability of their conclusions about Russian interference in the 2016 election. He took their claims as a personal affront; that they were somehow arguing his win in 2016 over Clinton was illegitimate. As a politician who won the most important office in the world against all odds, Trump wanted to dispel these perceptions that he was somehow an illegitimate president. His method for defending himself was wrong. But as a matter of fact, Trump was right.

Inevitably, Mueller would have to abandon his investigation, and Trump would walk away as the victor. But much damage—not least to the U.S.-Russia relationship—was done. That damage would prove irreparable, especially considering that Trump did not win the 2020 election.

The Results of the Helsinki Conference: Not Great, Not Terrible

AS FOR THE SUBSTANCE of the talks, it was a variegated matter. Though it was certainly not the failure Trump's critics claimed, neither was it a smashing success. In typical Trump fashion, the big takeaway was that the United States and Russia would work, however slowly, to restore their economic relationship. Putin envisaged using intermediaries in industry to be the vanguard in restoring economic ties between the West and Russia.

Regarding Crimea, according to Putin himself, he and Trump had such a contentious exchange over the status of the Black Sea peninsula that the two men "agreed to differ." Contrary to what the media was saying, Trump did *not* sell out Ukraine. To indicate where Putin's mind was, the Russian leader urged Trump to use his leverage over Ukraine to compel them to fully implement the Minsk accords. Putin then demanded that NATO never allow Ukraine to join its ranks. But pleading with the U.S. leader to get its Ukrainian ally to follow a treaty and insisting on respect for longstanding Russian fears of Ukraine's admittance to NATO should be distinguished from threats of hostility if those conditions were not met. These pleas, contrary to the narrative that they showed Trump's willingness to cave, in fact demonstrate how strong Trump's diplomatic hand was at Helsinki. It is too bad the media did not take a moment to consider that perspective rather than allowing partisan biases to dictate reporting.

In addition to these matters, the two world leaders spoke about the Syrian Civil War and their countries' interest in that conflict. Specifically, Putin needed to crush the Islamist rebels in southwest Syria, while keeping Syrian forces from clashing with Israeli forces along Syria and Israel's shared border. Because of the expanding presence of Iranian forces helping the Russians defend Bashar al-Assad's embattled Syrian regime in his war against Islamist groups, Israel was striking at Iranian targets in Syria. Eventually, Syria's military was going to respond to the Israeli incursions into their territory. Putin said that this was required under international law, as defined by the 1974 treaty that ended the Yom Kippur War between Israel and Syria (as well as other Arab nations). Trump, a hawk on Iran and one of America's most pro-Israel presidents, refused to acquiesce to Putin's demands. Trump explained himself to Putin by saying that, "the United States will not allow Iran to benefit from our campaign against ISIS."

Then came the matter of nuclear arms talks. The nuclear issue has defined U.S.-Russian relations since the earliest days of the Cold War. Putin was concerned that the U.S. was going to allow the START Treaty to expire in 2021. He asked Trump to be willing to renegotiate the START Treaty rather than to abrogate it. Again, the old Russian bugaboo about U.S. missile defense systems was raised. Putin wanted to keep the Americans in the Intermediate Nuclear Forces (INF) Treaty that was originally signed between Moscow and Washington in 1987. And, rather than insist that the U.S. and Russia remain fixed in the INF Treaty as it was originally written, Putin agreed that it should be updated. (Most U.S. hawks wanted to simply tear the agreement apart, which is what ultimately happened).

Putin and Trump both adopted a conciliatory tone regarding energy. Specifically, on the matter of the Nord Stream II (NS2) pipeline Russia was building to link Russian natural gas with Germany through the Baltic Sea, Trump showed a willingness to negotiate. For years, Trump had opposed the pipeline, fearing it would make Europe—specifically Germany—far too dependent on Russia.[46] Trump changed his tone on the NS2 pipeline, however, once it became clear that there was a way to permit it and to help the Ukrainians and their flagging economy at the same time.

Ukraine was a key destination, as well as a hub, for Russian natural gas flowing into Europe. It was feared, however, that once NS2 was built, the gas flowing from Russia through Ukrainian pipelines would be reduced. This would have hit Ukraine's economy hard because it partly relied upon transit fees from Russia. In order to ensure Ukraine did not lose those transit fees, Trump horse-traded with Putin: In exchange for Trump removing pressure from the Germans regarding NS2, Putin would not harm Ukraine's economy by slowing the flow of natural gas to pipelines cutting through Ukraine.

Putin said he would fulfill Trump's request so long as a dispute between the Russian gas company, Gazprom, and the Ukrainian firm, Naftogaz, was settled in Russia's favor. At that time, Naftogaz had won an arbitration case against Gazprom because the Russian firm cut the flow of gas into Ukraine, thereby breaking Gazprom's contract with Naftogaz. The Russians were ordered by a court in Stockholm, Sweden, to pay Ukraine $2.5 billion for losses. Gazprom was appealing the decision and even blocked an attempt to seize its assets in Europe.[47]

These sorts of conversations, though, were normal for diplomatic talks. They were not indicative of Trump being some kind of Manchurian candidate or Russian prop. In fact, at several key points, Trump held his ground against Putin on issues that Putin believed were essential for Russia. The elites who run Washington and the Western world expected the American president to go in and essentially lecture Vladimir Putin, as Obama and other post-Cold War presidents loved to do. Where did this hectoring and faux moralism get those post-Cold War U.S. leaders with Russia? It got us closer to conflict and an insuperable rupture in key diplomatic relations. Instead, Trump talked with the man. He and Putin moved the diplomatic needle forward—without the American side giving up the proverbial store to Russia (and without Russia feeling encircled by the West).

Of course, that was not the public takeaway because Western media had so thoroughly clouded the Helsinki talks with their Trump Derangement Syndrome. After leaving Helsinki, Trump faced a hell storm unlike any other when he returned to Washington as the narrative of supposed disaster at the summit merged with the on-going, salacious claims of the Mueller investigation. Trump would not attempt another major summit with the world's largest nuclear weapons state for the rest of his presidency. This sad commentary is owing entirely to Hillary Clinton's paranoid conspiracy theories, the media's outrageous Trump Derangement Syndrome, and the deep state's religious commitment to NATO expansion-at-all-costs.

What Could Have Been

SINCE THE COLD WAR, Russian and American leaders have danced to a complex tune of brinkmanship and détente. American presidents have had to navigate this complex relationship. At times, they've done it seamlessly. At other points, they've failed miserably. Some presidents, like Reagan, who ultimately got the best of the Soviets by defeating them bloodlessly and ending the Cold War, had a mix of failed and, ultimately, successful meetings. These summits were key for U.S. and Russian leaders coming to an understanding of one another. They allowed the forging of ties in relative peace so that when the risk of war arose, the parties would be more inclined toward de-escalation rather than escalation.

Recall Winston Churchill's line about Russia being a "riddle wrapped in mystery inside an enigma." American and Russian leaders are inherently different. Our two countries are not naturally aligned. Because of their size and nuclear weapons arsenals, though, the two nations must have healthy, working relationships. Trump was attempting to build on the example set by the likes of other U.S. presidents who had maintained successful relations with Moscow, such as Richard Nixon and Ronald Reagan. Without their tireless efforts at diplomacy, the world might have been engulfed in a nuclear hellfire decades ago.

Today, too many think of diplomacy—especially when it comes to Russia—as a four-lettered word. The so-called elite who rule

Washington believe there are no downsides to NATO expansion and they cannot believe that anyone who dares to question that assumption, such as Donald Trump, is acting in good faith. Instead, he must be a Russian stooge whose agenda (and presidency) needed to be destroyed using all available means. If Trump had been allowed to build upon his somewhat successful meeting with Putin with more summits, it is possible Russia might become a partner in peace rather than a geopolitical impediment to U.S. interests. At the very least, Trump might have gotten Putin to stop poking the Americans in the eye at every turn. And Ukraine—the most corrupt nation in Europe, a nation on behalf of whose interests Americans are apparently expected to court a nuclear world war—actually would have been better defended if Trump been able to fully restart relations with Russia. Even if this had meant tabling NATO expansion and maybe even minimizing NATO altogether, the result would have been better for all of us.

To repeat a famous Trump tweet, "SAD!"

CHAPTER 14
THE PHONE CALL FROM HELL

DONALD J. TRUMP'S worries didn't end with the failed Mueller probe or the collapsed Helsinki Summit with Russia. In 2019, a whole new (albeit familiar) debacle unfolded surrounding his relations with Ukraine. Trump was heading into a presidential reelection year and convinced he would face Joe Biden as the Democratic Party's 2020 nominee. Former New York City Mayor Rudy Giuliani had become a key adviser for Trump's 2020 reelection effort. In that role, Giuliani had been calling for deeper investigations into years' old claims that Joe Biden's family, through his son, Hunter Biden, had benefited from illicit dealings in many countries—notably Ukraine—while Joe Biden served as vice president during the Obama administration.

Remember that early in the Obama presidency, the forty-fourth president had handed the bulk of responsibility for Ukraine over to then-Vice-President Joe Biden. From that moment on, Joe Biden ran everything related to Ukraine. Hillary Clinton, Obama's first secretary of state, and John Kerry, Obama's secretary of state during his second term, had to coordinate all Ukraine policy with Joe Biden's office. During the effort to remove Viktor Yanukovych from power, for example, senior State Department officials had to run everything through Biden's national security team. Recall, if you will, the infamous call between Victoria Nuland and the Obama administration's ambassador to Ukraine during the 2014 Euromaidan protests. In the transcripts of that recorded phone call, Nuland and the ambassador discussed how they were seeking approval from top Biden advisers, such as Jake Sullivan. (Sullivan would later become a key member of Hillary Clinton's 2016 presidential election and then became Joe Biden's national security adviser when he was elected in 2020).

Key members of then-Vice President Biden's entourage were involved in some of the darkest geopolitical movements in Ukraine. They would continue being involved in such dealings when Biden returned to the White House in 2020. More specifically, though, Trump was concerned about how Joe Biden used his power and influence over the post-Yanukovych Ukrainian government to engorge himself (and his family) with foreign aid money flowing into Ukraine from the West (foreign aid money that he was managing as the senior Obama administration official for Ukraine policy).

President Donald Trump wanted more information on what Hunter Biden was up to during his business exploits in the wilds of Ukraine. Giuliani discovered evidence that Joe Biden had used his power over Ukraine to get the Ukrainian President Petro Poroshenko to fire a Ukrainian prosecutor general, Viktor Shokin. Indeed, Joe Biden admitted to this—bragged is actually a better word—at a public event he was participating in for the Council on Foreign Relations in 2018. At that event, Biden recounted how he waded into Shokin's corruption investigation of the Ukrainian natural gas firm, Burisma, by financially squeezing then-Ukrainian President Petro Poroshenko to fire Shokin.

"I looked [at Petro Poroshenko] and I said: 'I'm leaving in six hours. If [Shokin] is not fired, you're not getting [the aid money].' Well, son of a bitch, he got fired. And they put in place someone who was solid."[1] Biden said proudly to an audience of rapt CFR members, grinning from ear-to-ear as he recounted the sordid tale.

Left unsaid at the time, of course, was that Biden's son, Hunter, had been made a member of the board of Burisma Holdings, earning an astonishing $50,000 a month in 2014. While Shokin's investigation, officially, was about claims of corrupt dealings by Burisma two years before Hunter Biden joined the board, the fact of the matter is that the Ukrainian oligarch, Mykola Zlochevsky, did not want *any* investigation into his firm. Having the son of the U.S. vice president—the man charged with running America's Ukraine portfolio—on the board of his firm was a wonderful way to shield Burisma from the kind of anti-corruption probe that Shokin was conducting. It should be noted, however, that Shokin later claimed in an interview with *Fox News'* Brian Kilmeade that he was looking for evidence that Burisma had illegally produced and sold natural gas during Hunter Biden's time on the board. According to Shokin, had he been allowed to continue his investigation, he'd have not only discovered damning evidence of Zlochevsky's nefarious deeds, but also uncovered evidence of Hunter Biden's participation in the corruption. And, if that is true, Shokin undoubtedly would have found financial linkages between Hunter Biden and his father, Joe.[2]

Zlochevsky is on the record as having bragged about bringing Hunter Biden onto the board of his energy firm, Burisma. The Ukrainian oligarch's testimony answered some important questions, such as why any natural gas firm would hire Hunter Biden and pay him a sum total of $11 million for his time. Hunter Biden is not an expert on natural gas. He is, however, an expert on influence-peddling. At least, that's what many researchers, notably Peter Schweitzer, determined in the course of his deep investigation into the Biden family's foreign dealings. As if to demonstrate how obvious it is that Hunter's appointment to Burisma's board was as an act of influence-peddling, Zlochevsky stated that, "Hunter Biden was stupid [and Zlochevsky's] dog was smarter!"[3]

If Hunter Biden was so dumb then why have him on the board of your massive energy firm that was under serious investigation from authorities in your own government?

Zlochevsky further testified that, as vice president, Joe Biden participated in business transactions along with Burisma and Hunter Biden. What's more, Zlochevsky's testimony corroborates the testimony of Devon Archer, a longtime business associate of the Biden family.[4] In 2023, Archer was sentenced to a year-and-a-day of prison for having fraudulently sold $60 million of tribal bonds. After his indictment Archer testified that, as Hunter Biden's longtime business partner, the two men would often leverage their ties with Hunter's father, Joe Biden, to finalize tough deals. In the case of the Shokin investigation, both Archer and Zlochevsky claimed that they got Joe Biden to put the kibosh on Shokin's unwanted investigation into Burisma Holdings by having the then-vice president threaten the delivery of Ukraine's much-needed foreign assistance money until Kiev fired Shokin.

It worked like a charm.

Biden threatened Poroshenko with cutting him off from U.S. foreign aid unless Poroshenko fired Shokin. And, poof, Shokin was gone—and so was an investigation that could have proven Hunter Biden's corruption. Interestingly, a few years before Devon Archer's explosive testimony detailing how Joe Biden was an essential part of his son's global schemes, another of Hunter Biden's business associates, Tony Bobulinski, sat down with then-*Fox News* host, Tucker Carlson. Like Archer years later, Bobulinksi spoke in vivid detail about how Hunter's entire business model relied on trading access to his vice-presidential father in exchange for gobs of money from foreign actors.[5] Ukraine was one of Hunter Biden's biggest clients. Part of the business arrangement, according to Bobulinski, entailed "ten percent for the Big Guy," in Hunter's formulation. The Big Guy, in this case, was none other than Joe Biden.[6]

Hunter Biden once lamented in a text message exchange with his oldest daughter about how his father made him conduct these international transactions, peddling access to Biden's office in exchange for money, and then took upwards of half of the money Hunter had earned. Hunter was telling his soon-to-be adult daughter that, like him, she'd have to earn her keep as a Biden family member. "Don't worry," Hunter wrote, "Unlike Pop, I won't make you give me half your salary."[7]

Interestingly, a few years after Hunter Biden joined the Burisma board, another individual deeply linked to the U.S. intelligence community also joined: J. Cofer Black, the legendary former Counterterrorism Center director at the CIA.[8] Along with Black and Hunter was the former Polish president, Aleksandr Kwaśniewski, who enjoyed longstanding ties with NATO.[9] For his part, Kwaśniewski, while denying any corruption, admitted that Hunter Biden was only brought onto the Burisma board because of his connection to the U.S. vice president at the time.

So, let's see, the vice president's son, the retired head of CIA's Counterterrorism Center, and a former president of a major NATO member were all on the same board of directors for a Ukrainian state-owned natural gas firm that was legendary for its high degree of international corruption. There were numerous testimonies of former Hunter Biden business associates amid other shocking forms of evidence casting doubt on Hunter Biden's claims that he was doing legitimate business in Ukraine. Certainly, if Joe Biden had been a Republican, rather than a Democrat, and had Hunter behaved similarly under those circumstances, the Washington establishment would have destroyed the entire Biden family. But they were Democrats-in-good-standing. So, they get a pass in the eyes of the law and media.

Donald Trump, however, did not swim in the same circles as Hunter and Joe Biden. He wanted answers, not only for his own political gain, but for the good of the country (he had consistently vowed to "drain the swamp"). Thus we were told that President Donald Trump was the bad guy for asking questions about it in 2019 during a phone call with Volodymyr Zelensky, who at that time was the newly elected president of Ukraine. Asking any hard-hitting questions of or about the Biden family was forbidden, even back then.

Something certainly smells rotten in Kiev.

Meanwhile, the proof of Hunter Biden's alleged illegal behavior has come from Hunter Biden himself. In April 2019, Hunter Biden dropped off his laptop at a computer repair shop in Delaware. Assuming it was just another job, the technician began his work of clearing the hard drive and tweaking the operating system when he came across a seemingly endless array of inappropriate photos stored on the laptop. The photos were not just your run-of-the-mill pornographic content. What was there, according to the technician, was a plethora of legally damning photos showing Hunter Biden engaged in illicit activities, using copious amounts of drugs, while engaged in varying states of coitus with prostitutes—some of whom, according to the technician, appeared to be underage. When Hunter Biden did not retrieve the laptop after many months, the computer technician contacted the authorities, who did nothing. Ultimately, he handed the computer over to the Trump Campaign.[10]

During the 2020 presidential campaign, Miranda Devine of the *New York Post* broke most of the stories related to what she ruefully dubbed the "Laptop from Hell." Hunter Biden as the son of the Democratic Party's presidential nominee should have attracted far more attention than he ultimately did. The Right covered it throughout the campaign, but the left-leaning mainstream media ignored it. Hunter's defenders insisted that the information contained in the laptop was both obtained and shared with the public illegally. Others claimed that it merely showed a man who was battling addiction and other demons. But all of that is beside the point. It wasn't just crazy details about Hunter Biden's drug-induced sex romps that earned this discovery the appellation "Laptop from Hell." Embedded within that data were tranches of documents related to Hunter Biden's ongoing international business dealings. These dealings can be described—and have been described by critics of the Biden administration—as nothing more than a blatant influence peddling operation.[11]

Of course, the Trump Campaign desperately wanted to deploy

this information as a sort of "October Surprise" against their rivals in the Democratic Party. They weren't interested in humiliating Hunter Biden. They were rightly trying to expose the Biden family as having illicitly benefited from Joe Biden trading access to his various elected offices in exchange for lots of money. The Biden Campaign downplayed the significance of things like the "Laptop from Hell." At the time, 51 former high-ranking U.S. intelligence officials signed a letter denouncing the "Laptop from Hell" scandal as little more than overwrought Russian propaganda.[12]

Because of that denunciation by 51 senior intelligence officials, the mainstream media—which was champing at the bit, along with their compatriots in Big Tech, to censor the story—was able to claim that the story was disinformation. In the post-Russiagate hoax and post-Trump 2016 victory era, the media was not going to give any credence to controversies and news stories that might empower Trump's reelection campaign. Years after the Hunter Biden stories were censored by the media, it was discovered that the letter castigating the Hunter Biden laptop story was a manufactured document crafted by none other than senior Biden Campaign staffers, such as Antony Blinken and Jake Sullivan. The text was written by them and then the letter was circulated to fellow "Never Trump" types in the intel community.[13] Many of those who signed that letter were also instrumental in pushing the "Trump-Russia collusion" myth that had weakened the Trump administration.[14]

For the record, the House Republicans would conduct a comprehensive investigation into the Biden family's finances as part of their inquiry into Hunter Biden's allegedly illicit international activities. They determined that Hunter Biden was taking the money he earned from his various international business transactions and redistributing it into his family's coffers. According to House Oversight Committee Chairman, Representative James Comer (R-KY), "at least two Biden family members were paid $1.3 million from an associate [of Hunter Biden's] who had links to a Chinese energy company."

In fact, Comer's long-running inquiry into Hunter Biden's purport-edly illicit dealings overseas uncovered direct (albeit small) payments from accounts associated with Hunter Biden's business to that of Joe Biden, beginning in 2018. Meanwhile, Hunter Biden's firm paid Joe Biden's brother, James, $40,000 after it completed a questionable transaction with Chinese state-owned firms. According to investigators, that $40,000 wound up in Joe Biden's account, too, after his brother transferred it over to him.

Much of this information came out only two years after Joe Biden became president and after the Democrats had lost the congressional midterm election in 2022 to the Republicans. Once in the majority, the House GOP were eager to dig up dirt on Biden. The GOP wanted to exonerate Donald Trump, too, by proving his rationale for want-ing information from the Ukrainian government regarding alleged Biden misdeeds going into the 2020 election. So, the elite helped Biden cover up evidence allegedly showing his family's wrongdoing in order to ensure Biden could win the contentious 2020 election. Understanding the pattern of the Biden family's corruption helps one to see how deeply enmeshed with corruption the Bidens must have been in Ukraine. That they were often seen as being aligned with CIA assets only helped to shield Biden more from the Right's criticisms. After all, Ukraine is more than just a place where U.S. tax dollars go to get laundered to special interests in Washington, D.C. It is at the epicenter of a major geopolitical fight between the West and Russia.

It all goes back to Ukraine, though. Ukraine is the key. And the information that has come out since the Republicans reclaimed the House of Representatives in 2022 was all, for the most part, com-mon knowledge among the elite well before House GOP initiated their investigation into the Biden family. Rumors abounded about the Biden family's escapades overseas, in places like Ukraine, for many years before they were finally brought to the public's attention. But it's not just the Bidens. The activities of the Biden family have

become standard operating procedure for the members of both political parties in the swamp.

Which gets us back to Rudy Giuliani and President Trump's phone
call from Hell with Ukraine's President Zelensky.

Because Trump's phone call with Zelensky in 2019 inquired about
alleged Biden misdeeds in Ukraine from his time as vice president—
specifically related to the gutting of Viktor Shokin's prosecution of
Burisma's corruption—it became the trigger for a second wave of
attacks launched against Trump's presidency. The first wave came
in the form of Hillary Clinton's "vast Russian conspiracy" that was
utterly disproven. But the problem for the deep state remained:
Donald Trump was still in office. And given that the Russia investigation concluded in Trump's favor, as the country was more prosperous (and secure) than it had been in decades under Trump, it seemed
likely that he would skate to reelection in 2020.[15]

The Phone Call

PRESIDENT VOLODYMYR ZELENSKYY was a unique figure in
Ukraine's politics. Like Donald Trump, he was a celebrity and came
from outside politics. Ukrainian voters were tired of the constant
corruption of both the pro-Western and the pro-Russian sides of
their political elite. They wanted change. They wanted someone who
was untainted by the corruption. Ukrainian voters desired for their
leader to "drain the swamp" in Kiev just as Americans had wanted
President Trump to "drain the swamp" in Washington, D.C. Part of
the reason Trump chose to call the recently elected Zelenskyy was
because Zelenskyy's political party, Servant of the People, had just
swept the parliamentary elections in Ukraine. Trump wanted to
congratulate his Ukrainian counterpart.

Of course, there was more to the call.

Ukraine receives massive amounts of U.S. tax dollars in the form
of foreign aid. With the changes in leadership in Kiev, the phone call

was meant to cement the ties between Ukraine and the United States by having the leaders of the two respective countries meet to discuss the geopolitical situation. This was the moment, though, that Trump wanted to press the need for Ukraine to share any insight or evidence about Hunter Biden's purportedly illegal activities while in Ukraine. Trump's critics would later insist that this was a self-serving conversation. Of course, in part, it was. But there was a legitimate need to rein in the U.S. role in furthering whatever corrupt activities occurred in Ukraine's politics by demanding a more thorough accounting of where the money we were giving Kiev was really going.

Interestingly, several years after Trump's phone call from Hell, it would be revealed that the bulk of the foreign aid money sent to Ukraine was spent in the United States. According to an official at the Ukrainian embassy in Washington, D.C., a "significant portion [of U.S. aid money to Ukraine] is utilized in the United States for construction of new weapons or to replenish those dispatched to Kyiv from U.S. reserves." The Ukrainian embassy official concluded that, "an analysis found that nearly 90 percent of aid granted by Congress is benefiting American interests."[16] Well, it's certainly benefiting special interests in Washington, D.C. and Wall Street. Whether it's benefiting ordinary Americans is another matter entirely.

Recall there was a report after Donald Trump unexpectedly won the White House in 2016 that detailed how the then-Ukrainian President Petro Poroshenko spent $600,000 buying the services of former Republican Mississippi Governor Haley Barbour's lobbying firm, BGR Group (previously Barbour, Griffith & Rogers LLC), so that Ukraine's leadership could gain access to the Trump Administration.[17] Where do you think those funds came from?

On its own, Ukraine's economy cannot produce the wealth required for its government to be blowing it on massive weapons and influence operations in America. Poroshenko likely took a chunk of some of the aid money and repurposed it to buy access to Trump's court when he was elected. That is just a microcosm of what Ukraine has been doing with U.S. aid money. The money that the United States continues to shovel into Ukraine's coffers; the funds that the Ukrainian embassy openly admits are spent back in the United States on things like weapons for their war against Russia, are going to feed Washington's war machine (which, incidentally, took a huge blow when the Biden administration so horribly fumbled the U.S. withdrawal from Afghanistan in August 2021). What Washington has established for itself in Ukraine, irrespective of the morality of the cause, is the equivalent of a self-licking ice cream cone. Considering how much President Biden loves ice cream, this seems fitting.[18]

Five years after that fateful phone call, we now know that Ukraine is playing fast-and-loose with American aid dollars. Further, we now know that the Biden family, through Hunter, was benefiting financially from an allegedly illicit influence peddling scheme in Ukraine. Beyond that, we have Ukrainian embassy officials freely admitting that they are washing U.S. aid dollars and reinvesting it in the United States—while key American elites and firms in Washington, D.C. take a cut of the action. (It's no accident that seven of the wealthiest counties in the United States ring Washington, D.C.)

Therefore, as president, Trump was well within his rights to inquire with his foreign counterpart about alleged corruption perpetrated there by American officials and the family members of prominent Americans. Whatever benefit this information may have been to Trump politically was far outweighed by the fact that the president has a responsibility to oversee where large sums of U.S. tax dollars are spent. It is far more likely that he was impeached for interrupting the corrupt cycle between Kiev and Washington than for doing anything outside the bounds of his office. Trump complicated the financial windfall of the elites who were benefiting from the dark business in Ukraine. These elites became concerned about Trump's inquiries into their behavior. They became convinced that Trump was becoming like a pitbull with the bit between his teeth, refusing to let go, and making a bloody mess everywhere. That the alleged misdeeds of

America's elite in Ukraine might come out as a result of Trump's inquiries during an election cycle only made the elite more committed to ousting Trump from office at all costs.

The phone call itself was innocuous. It did not last very long, and the Hunter Biden issue was not even brought up until the end as a sort of afterthought. One almost gets the sense that Trump was bringing it up to appease the excitable Rudy Giuliani, who had zeroed in on the story of Hunter Biden's exploits in Ukraine like a heat-seeking missile. But it is interesting that the moment that Hunter Biden was brought up—on a recorded line, on which dozens of federal national al security staffers were listening—somehow the entire conversation was leaked to partisans in Congress who were desperately looking to drag Trump through the political mud after the abject failure of the Mueller probe. At that point, it became a national political scandal and the basis of Trump's first impeachment.

Trump was convinced that "Ukraine had tried to take me down!" during the 2016 election. And, as has been demonstrated, there is ample evidence to suggest that there was a negative influence operation afoot—in conjunction with the DNC and Hillary Clinton campaign—to do just that. Giuliani was convinced, too. That's why Trump brought up both the Hunter Biden corruption concerns as well as claims that the private cybersecurity firm, CrowdStrike, had sent the supposedly Russian-hacked DNC server from 2016 to offices in Ukraine (rather than handing it over to the FBI). Of course, both CrowdStrike and multiple defense experts have denied these allegations. Instead, they chock up the crisis over CrowdStrike to Russian disinformation. Regardless of whether this is disinformation, Trump believed that the Ukrainians had organized a campaign against his election effort.

But the deep state wanted its pound of flesh from Trump for daring to question their carefully laid plans against the Russians in Ukraine; their religious commitment to expanding NATO into Ukraine at all costs. Because Trump had used the colloquialism, "Do me a favor?"

in his conversation with Zelenskyy, and the fact that he brought up Hunter Biden's alleged corruption and the unproven claims that CrowdStrike was working with Ukraine's government to protect the Democratic Party from Trump and the Republicans, the bureaucrats who were listening into Trump's conversation became convinced, or *said* they were convinced, Trump was seeking an illegal *quid pro quo* from Ukraine. Lethal aid that Congress had allocated for Ukraine was held up for 55 days by the Trump administration. The members of the permanent security state who were aware of what was said on the Trump-Zelenskyy call insisted that the aid was withheld because Trump was trying to squeeze Zelenskyy into doing Trump's bidding. According to these bureaucrats, Trump was undermining the will of Congress, which had already allocated the funds to provide Ukraine with lethal aid—meaning that the chief executive, Trump, did not have the right to slow-walk the delivery of that aid.

In typical fashion, the elites in D.C. were accusing Trump of having done *exactly* what Joe Biden actually did while he was in office: use American aid to Ukraine to pressure Ukraine's leadership into *kowtowing* to U.S. domestic politics. After all, it was Biden who giddily recounted to an audience at the Council on Foreign Relations about his showdown with former Ukrainian President Poroshenko and how he threatened to deny Ukraine much-needed U.S. aid unless Ukraine's chief prosecutor investigating Burisma was fired. The Democrats are masters of projection. Trump never did what they said he did. It was the Democrats—and specifically Joe Biden—who did these things.

Beyond that example, no one bothered to find out that, despite Congress having authorized the sale of lethal aid to Ukraine during the Obama administration, the forty-fourth president did not deliver that aid as legislated by Congress. No one back then complained. In fact, Obama was hailed as a wiseman for refusing to hand over the lethal aid. As Obama's CIA Director, John Brennan, argued in 2019, "arming Ukraine would hand [sensitive U.S. military technology] to Russia."[19] Obama never faced calls for impeachment for having violated the Constitution's separation of powers. This standard of impeachment for slowly fulfilling Congress's wish to supply lethal aid to Ukraine was only applied to Trump. Ultimately, Trump delivered more lethal aid to Ukraine than did his predecessor, despite the Obama White House having been more explicitly pro-Ukraine than Trump ever was.

The "Never Trump" Crusade of Ukraine's "Amen!" Corner in the U.S. Government

THERE WERE SEVERAL VILLAINS in the sinister tale that was the first Trump impeachment. Many of them were affiliated with the same forces that had tried to kneecap Trump's presidency with the fake Russia collusion investigation—like the now-retired U.S. Army Lieutenant Colonel Alexander Vindman and the mid-level CIA staffer, Eric Ciaramella. Both of these characters have been shown to have had an outsized role in furthering the whistleblower complaint against Trump for his allegedly improper phone call with Zelenskyy that became the basis of the impeachment trial against Trump.

Eric Ciaramella was a CIA analyst who had been detailed over to the White House National Security Council when the Trump-Zelenskyy call occurred in 2019. Ciaramella was a 33-year-old registered Democrat at the time of the call. He had previously served in the Obama White House and, in fact, had been held over in his White House role when Trump assumed office in January 2017. According to my colleague at *Real Clear Investigations*, Paul Sperry, Ciaramella had worked directly for Joe Biden when he was vice president and with former CIA Director John Brennan (Brennan, of course, was a key figure in pushing the Trump-Russia narrative in the first half of the Trump term in office). Ciaramella had maintained very close contacts with Biden's team long after he had moved on professionally from working with Biden.

What's more, Ciaramella worked directly under Susan Rice when she had served as President Obama's national security adviser during his second term in office. Biden, Susan Rice, John Brennan, and many others were not only central figures in undermining Trump on the Russia collusion lie, they were the architects of the shadow campaign against Trump in Ukraine.

Sperry reported that Ciaramella had previously been removed from the Trump NSC in 2017. The analyst was suspected of having leaked the contents of sensitive calls between Trump and other world leaders. The point of these leaks, of course, was to undermine Trump's foreign policy at the start of his presidency.[20]

In Washington, however, one's career is never truly killed off after having been accused of undermining a GOP presidential administration. That's just part of doing business. So, two years after being removed from his normal position on the NSC, Ciaramella again found himself liaising with the very same White House that he had worked to weaken. Of course, he was up to his old tricks: leaking the contents of presidential phone calls with foreign leaders to impugn the forty-fifth president. This time, he leaked Trump's call as a supposedly confidential whistleblower.

Yes, while pretending to be a concerned steward of the national interest, Ciaramella went to the anti-Trump bureaucracy to disclose the contents of a classified phone call between two world leaders. Once Ciaramella brought forward his whistleblower complaint alleging illegal *quid quo pro* between Trump and Zelenskyy, Representative Adam Schiff (D-CA) got wind of it. Schiff was one of Trump's most virulent opponents in the Democratic Party. Schiff was given an early briefing about Ciaramella's supposedly secret whistleblower account by one of Ciaramella's former CIA colleagues and one of his best friends, Sean Misko. Both Ciaramella and Misko had served on the Obama NSC together in 2015. Misko would go on to join Representative Schiff's staff in August 2019.[21] Just a few months later, Ciaramella's complaint became public knowledge, thanks to Misko's unhinged boss, Representative Schiff.

Once he got a hold of Ciaramella's whistleblower complaint, Schiff convinced then-Speaker of the House Nancy Pelosi to turn the whistleblower complaint into the basis of the Trump impeachment. To be clear, the impeachment was based on exaggerations and outright lies. It was more than a political witch hunt. Trump's first impeachment over his Ukraine call was a grotesque abuse of power by permanent bureaucrats who were more loyal to the Democratic Party (and Ukraine) than they were to their oaths as officers of the U.S. Constitution. They wanted Trump out. Sure, they didn't like him generally. But that weird zeal for NATO expansion and brinkmanship against post-Soviet Russia was the real driving force. And they'd risk tearing the country apart, lying to protect Joe Biden's chances of winning in 2020, and Lord knows what else to ensure that Trump didn't get a second term that might complicate their carefully laid plans for a wider war with Russia.[22]

When one does even a cursory examination of the facts surrounding the impeachment, one cannot help but to conclude that this historic event was merely the continuation of the long-running Ukrainian plot to oust Donald Trump way back in 2016. Indeed, our old friend, Alexandra Chalupa, had met with Eric Ciaramella when he served on the Obama NSC staff. Chalupa discussed her efforts to get Ukraine to assist her in stopping Trump from winning the 2016 election.[23]

There were several other notables who had met with Ciaramella during the early days of the 2016 presidential campaign while he served on Obama's NSC. These included the lead anti-corruption prosecutor in Ukraine, a senior aide from then-UN Ambassador Samantha Powers' office (her fingerprints were all over the Russia collusion lie), and the ever-present Victoria Nuland. Indeed, Nuland was reportedly a key member in both the Hillary Clinton-funded Christopher Steele dossier that led to the Robert Mueller investigation as well as the attempt to smear Trump with members of Congress just hours before he was sworn in as president in January 2017.[24]

Eric Ciaramella, though, is not the only senior NSC staffer who had a hand in this nefarious ordeal. It gets weirder. The lead Ukraine expert for the Trump White House NSC was a U.S. Army Lieutenant Colonel Alexander Vindman. A Ukrainian by birth, his family emigrated to the United States after his mother passed away when he was a small child. Vindman's father moved him and his twin brother, Yevgeny from Ukraine to Brighton Beach, New York, when the Vindman twins were three. Growing up in a middle-class American family, Vindman excelled in academics and was patriotic enough to join the U.S. Army. Vindman served in Iraq at the height of the bloody insurgency and was wounded while in combat. He received a Purple Heart as a result of his combat wounds. Upon his return to the United States, Vindman attended Harvard University where he earned a master's degree. Inevitably, Vindman found himself billeted over to the National Security Council under Trump where he employed his Ukrainian background and expertise in Russian as the lead Ukraine expert for Trump's NSC.[25]

During Trump's impeachment, both he and his twin brother (who served as a national security lawyer on the NSC) were let go by Trump because of their suspected role in getting Trump impeached. There's much more to Alexander Vindman than meets the eye, though. The *Washington Examiner*'s Byron York did a deep dive on Alexander Vindman and his true role in the Trump impeachment for his 2020 book, *Obsession: Inside the Washington Establishment's Never-Ending War on Trump*. What York determined with his intensive research is that Eric Ciaramella "was a diversion" to keep people distracted from the much bigger fox guarding the Trump NSC henhouse: Alexander Vindman. According to York, Ciaramella was basically a cut-out used by Vindman to get the classified contents of Trump's call with Zelenskyy into the hands of rapacious Democrats on the Hill looking for dirt on Trump.

Ciaramella would have been a subordinate to Vindman on the NSC. And since the two men shared an affinity for Vindman's country of birth, Ukraine, it stands to reason that Ciaramella would have been willing to take the hit to his career in order to become the face of the whistleblower complaint. Vindman, with his years of experience and his high rank in the system, likely was far too useful to sacrifice in the first round of the impeachment fight against Trump. Using Ciaramella as a cut-out for Vindman was an attempt to keep Vindman in place as a senior leader overseeing Ukraine policy on the NSC.

Ultimately, Vindman was fired by Trump.

Of course, the damage had been done. It's important to explore Vindman beyond what his official CV says. On paper, Vindman appears to be an upstanding member of the military and a patriot. Officially, Vindman defended his actions in helping to spur the impeachment investigation into Trump because, in his words, he didn't "think it was proper to demand that a foreign government investigate an American citizen."[26]

Too bad for Vindman this was a specious argument. Even if he meant it, the fact of the matter is that the U.S. government routinely asks foreign governments to spy on U.S. citizens. In fact, this was the basis of multiple National Security Agency (NSA) counterterrorism programs. Because there were constitutional limitations imposed upon U.S. government agencies spying on U.S. citizens, the government figured out workarounds. One was to contract electronic surveillance of U.S. citizens to allied foreign governments. The goal was to remove Trump because, as the Ukrainian-born Vindman saw it, the forty-fifth president was a direct threat to Ukraine and a "useful idiot" for Russia's Vladimir Putin.[27]

The impeachment failed. Vindman was fired. But not before much damage was done to the country's political institutions going into the 2020 election. It would set the stage for the divisiveness that defined the country during what was then the as-yet-to-occur COVID-19 pandemic. Everything centered around Ukraine, Russia, and NATO expansion. The fact that the forty-fifth president wanted to distance the United States from Ukraine, rekindle relations with

Russia, and slow NATO expansion made him a threat to the elite in Washington, D.C., whose ideological pretensions aligned perfectly with their financial interests in using Ukraine as a money-laundering machine. Trump threatened that entire gravy train. Thus, he had to be removed. Ultimately, Trump was removed from power and replaced with the very same man who had overseen so much of Obama's (failed) foreign policy toward Ukraine, Joe Biden.

While the discussion of the Clinton conspiracy theories about Trump in 2016, the ongoing Hunter Biden scandal, and the alleged Ukrainian attempt to oust Trump from the presidency may be controversial, they are essential components of the disaster that is of our own making in Ukraine. The instability and chaos on the home front since the 2016 election has been the direct result of foreign actors waging a proxy war within our political system. The Democrats and Ukrainians have been entwined since 1994, when President Clinton negotiated the removal of Ukraine's nuclear weapons arsenal. Given that Ukraine's existence remains on the line today, and Donald Trump is again running for office, the same forces that corrupted our domestic politics are at it again—this time, with all their ire fixated exclusively on Trump.

[**A DISASTER OF OUR OWN MAKING**

CHAPTER 15
BIDEN BLUNDERS INTO WORLD WAR III

E VERYTHING CAME TOGETHER for the Ukraine lobby in America
when Joe Biden became the forty-sixth president of the United
States. Joe Biden was the man who ran the Obama administration
Ukraine portfolio. He brought many of the same foreign policy advisers who were key players in the Clinton and, later, Obama administration's foreign policy toward Ukraine and the former Soviet
Union. Thus, the assumption that NATO would ultimately expand
into Ukraine and other places near Russia's borders was ingrained
in the very policy preferences of the Biden administration. Further,
the belief that former President Donald J. Trump was an enemy
agent serving the interests of the Russian government and that the
Republican Party had somehow been similarly compromised per-
vaded the minds of virtually every member of the Biden team.

Joe Biden had campaigned in 2020 as the man who would hold
Vladimir Putin accountable. According to Ron Nichols of *Axios*,
throughout the 2020 campaign, Joe Biden "sounded like Ronald
Reagan" who was "setting up a potential Day 1 confrontation with
Russian President Vladimir Putin." Biden himself was emphat-
ic about his hostile position on Russia throughout the 2020 campaign. At one point, Biden attempted to highlight the differences between himself and then-President Trump on Russia. In Biden's view,

"Russia is an opponent [whereas] China was merely a competitor, a serious competitor."[1]

While serving as Obama's vice-president, though, Biden believed in Obama's reset policy that dominated his first term in office. What could have possibly changed in the intervening years? Well, for starters, Hunter Biden was paid gobs of money by both the Ukrainian and the Chinese governments.[2]

It remains a matter of dispute that Hunter Biden's business ever accepted funds from the Russians.[3] The House GOP investigation into Hunter Biden, however, indicates that the First Son did, in fact, "receive millions" from Russian oligarchs (along with millions from Kazakhstan and Ukraine).[4] Perhaps Ukraine and Russia, on top of using America's presidential elections as a proxy war, got themselves into a nasty bidding war for the Biden family's loyalty—assuming that Joe Biden would be president and hoping that they'd curry his favor. Alas, it looks like the Ukrainians won that fight with Russia!

A cynical person might immediately conclude that the Biden family would craft policies that favored countries and firms that had paid them over the years. Well, Ukraine certainly wanted America's support to oust the Russians from their territories in the east and from Crimea. What's more, the Chinese benefited mightily by having the United States (and NATO) initiate a serious conflict with Russia over Ukraine, as it would distract Putin's Russia from focusing their geopolitical attention on their Chinese neighbors and allow for China to possibly embrace the Russian Federation as an ally.[5]

Thanks to the Ukraine War, this is precisely what has occurred. China and Russia are closer today than they have been since the early days of the Cold War, when there was much fear and consternation over the Sino-Soviet alliance (which broke down in the 1960s).[6] Western support for Ukraine, which proved so damaging to Russia since the outbreak of the war in 2022, has forced Moscow to seek allies outside of the Western world. Hence, Putin and China's Xi Jinping have become, in Xi Jinping's words, "best friends."[7] Despite

the resistance to Russia's actions against Ukraine, in the face of onerous Western economic sanctions, Beijing has made clear their intention to stand beside Russia at all costs.[8] And this new axis of resistance to Western power and the U.S.-led world order is being joined
by a who's-who of America's geopolitical foes (including Iran, North
Korea, Venezuela, Syria, Cuba, and even NATO member Turkey, to
name just a handful of states).[9]

Hardly any of this would have been possible, though, had not the
Ukraine War so totally divided the West from Russia. Which, again,
should demonstrate just how effective those millions of dollars shov-
eled into the Biden family's coffers were, both for negatively influencing U.S. policy and for empowering America's enemies. After all,
Russia and China are not natural allies (which is why their original
alliance during the Cold War fell apart, despite both of them being
communist countries at the time).[10]

During the Trump administration, in fact, there were several in-
stances of tension between the two powers. At one point, China
moved nuclear missiles near the northern border with Russia.[11]
Actually, the only silver lining to have come out of Obama's generous New START Treaty with Russia in 2011 was that, as soon as the
ink dried on the document, Putin refocused his attention away from
Europe and turned it toward Asia. Shortly after the signing of the
New START Treaty, Russia launched the largest military exercises in their Far East (which borders northern China) since the Cold
War had ended.[12] According to Roger McDermott of the Jamestown
Foundation, one of the main opponents in that Russian military
exercise was not the United States. Instead, the threat Russia was
training against was China.

All that went away, though, once Biden was elected. He entered
office seeking a harder line against Russia. That was precisely what
he got. The problem was that Joe Biden is preternaturally incapable
of being the kind of hawkish president that he wanted to be. His age
and liberal ideology prevent him from being an effective hawk, in

any case. And whereas Ronald Reagan could afford to be hawkish with the Soviets when he first took power, the state of the world in the wake of the COVID-19 pandemic from Wuhan, China, was such that Biden had to deal with multiple, pressing conflicts at once. Each time the Biden administration fumbled on the world stage, therefore, Moscow took notice—and ratcheted up the pressure. They knew Biden and his team of neocons and neoliberals were wanting to do the same to Russia.

One display of Biden's incompetent hawkishness was the sudden and poorly planned evacuation of U.S. forces from Afghanistan in August 2021. Whatever one's opinion on the war in Afghanistan, it was incumbent upon any U.S. leader pulling out from that war to do it in such a way that America did not look like a declining power. Russia watched with glee as the Americans cut-and-ran from Afghanistan, returning the Taliban to power, and leaving behind billions of dollars in U.S. military equipment for them. This ensured that the U.S. would lose whatever geopolitical leverage it once had in Russia's backyard the moment the last U.S. military plane exited Afghanistan's airspace. As I wrote at the time, Russia, along with China, were watching the American withdrawal and taking notes. Their lesson was that Biden was incompetent and weak, that they could take what they wanted, and no one would stop them.[13]

It should come as no surprise, therefore, that less than a year after the botched Afghanistan withdrawal, Russia invaded Ukraine. Mind you, the Russians had spent the previous seven years dancing around the issue, partly out of the fear of U.S. military reprisals—particularly while President Trump was in office. But with Biden, it was an entirely different affair. Moscow understood that Biden was a weak president leading a divided nation that was also war weary, after 20 years of ceaseless, inconclusive conflict in the Middle East. Putin further understood that Biden was surrounded by people who wanted to risk war with Russia over Ukraine's acceptance into both NATO and the EU. And with a completely mixed message coming from the Biden White House, Putin assumed that his time to strike was in 2022.

The Wannabe Tsar and the Part-Time President

THE UNITED STATES and Russia had been eyeing each other since Biden and his neoconservative-neoliberal team wrenched power from the hands of Donald Trump. Tensions between the two sides had reached new highs surrounding the issue of Ukraine since Biden became the forty-sixth president of the United States. A meetup for the summer in 2021 between the two leaders was established. "[Biden is not] seeking a reset of [the U.S.-Russian] relationship, at least not in the way that term—fairly or unfairly—has come to be defined in the U.S.-Russian lexicon since the Barack Obama administration used it," thundered a *Politico* assessment written in the run-up to the summer 2021 meeting between Biden and Putin in Geneva. Biden was not interested in forgiving or forgetting the past. Instead, he was going to seek a "stable and predictable" relationship with the Russian strongman.[14]

The Geneva Conference was scheduled for the week of June 16, 2021, a pleasant time of the year for a peace conference in the bucolic setting of cool Switzerland. Initially, it seemed there was cause for hope at the conclusion of the conference that U.S.-Russian relations would avoid escalation. They would not warm but would remain chilled (harkening back to the "Cold Peace" that Boris Yeltsin warned President Clinton about in 1994). Putin's only real concern was Crimea and ensuring that the world accepted the Russian annexation as a fact. Eastern Ukraine was a sideshow for him. It was all about geopolitics. Russia needed Sevastopol for access to the Black Sea.[15] Since the conference ended without Putin and Biden vowing to wage war upon one another, there seemed to be a real chance that, over time, the U.S.-Russia relationship could heal.

In fact, right before the Geneva Conference was scheduled to commence, Russia had scheduled what many in the West had described as a provocative, large military exercise on its territory and inside of Crimea. A pressure campaign was mounted by the West for Putin to abandon these exercises as they would likely scuttle whatever chance of forward momentum existed from the Biden-Putin summit. Putin acquiesced to the demands, sensing a diplomatic opportunity to build up goodwill with the new American administration.[16]

It is likely that this move by Putin not only saved the conference but gave the appearance of *some* positive developments, despite the overall frosty tone of the meeting. Putin had made clear his desire to resolve the problem with the West over Ukraine via the flawed Minsk II protocols. Before and during the Geneva conference, there were no new Russian provocations to warrant any escalation from the West over Ukraine.

The Black Sea Incident

OF COURSE, Biden had surrounded himself with Russia hawks who would rather have entered a shooting war with Russia over Ukrainian admission into NATO than to simply have stabilized the relationship between two of the world's largest nuclear weapons states. The Russia hawks who surrounded Biden immediately went to work destabilizing the tenuous U.S.-Russia relationship following the conference. In a strange twist, a PowerPoint planning presentation, labeled "Most Secret," was discovered left unattended in a "soggy heap" at a bus stop in Kent, England, by a "random member of the public." That file detailed a series of provocations that NATO was ready to take immediately after the Geneva conference.[17]

Like clockwork, the world was subjected to a geopolitical crisis off the coast of the Black Sea. As per the uncovered classified documents, the British and American militaries supposedly had discussed in detail three possible responses to a proposed "Freedom of Navigation Operation" (FONOP) to be conducted by the British warship, the

HMS *Defender*, near the Crimean coastline in the Black Sea. A U.S. Navy *Arleigh Burke*-class destroyer and a Dutch destroyer would operate alongside the HMS *Defender*. The three possible responses from Russia ranged from "professional" to "aggressive." Given how close the HMS *Defender* would come to the Russian naval base at Sevastopol and how sensitive Moscow was to their tenuous hold on Crimea (from an international legal standpoint), the Russians were not going to take the provocation from NATO with serene contemplation.

Shortly before the NATO mission took place a U.S. Navy P-8 spy plane took off from Crete to provide air support for the NATO flotilla as it was transiting through the Black Sea. The moment the plane took off, though, the Russians determined that NATO was readying for a provocative move against their holdings in Crimea. Things went downhill from there. Having been alerted that NATO forces were on the way, the Russian forces were waiting for whatever was coming.

A diplomatic fiasco ensued.

The HMS *Defender* breached what the Russian military considered to be their national territory. Specifically, the *Defender* sailed within twelve nautical miles of Crimea. This prompted twenty Russian military aircraft and two Russian coast guard ships to shadow the British warship. When *Defender* got too close to Crimea for the Russians' comfort, a Russian patrol ship fired multiple warning shots in the direction of the British warship. What's more, Russian warplanes buzzed the destroyer and dropped two bombs in the path of the *Defender*. For their part, the British government disputes the claim that the Russians ever fired on the HMS *Defender*. But, of course, they would because the goal was not to start a conflict with Russia over Crimea but to "show solidarity" with Ukraine.

What fools would think that an already tense Moscow would not view the provocative action in the Black Sea as anything other than an attempt to trigger a war? In fact, it was the response that NATO was hoping for. The goal of the NATO mission was to place Russia on its backfoot; to make it look like Russia was the provocateur. It did not work. What it did was make Putin think greater provocations were coming.[18] Whether NATO actually yearned for conflict over Ukraine or if they truly were virtue-signaling their support for Ukraine, the result was that Russia did not believe the Biden administration—or their NATO allies—were acting in good faith ... or that Biden was even in control of his own government. Putin likely was haunted once again by his delusions of the faceless "men in grey suits" coming for him and his Mother Russia the way they did for Qaddafi and Saddam.

What's more, for Putin, as always, Crimea was his red line.

Meanwhile, President Biden himself was completely oblivious. At the Geneva conference, he likely reminded Putin of the old Soviet Premier, Konstantin Chernenko, who was a sclerotic and absent-minded old man, merely a placeholder for the Soviet *apparatchiks* who governed the Soviet Union. In other words, Biden was both weak and incompetent. And whatever he had told Putin was meaningless because the cabal running his administration was decidedly anti-Russian for an assortment of reasons (most of which were listed earlier in this book).

More bizarre provocations by NATO were to come that would only force Russia into a corner when it came to Ukraine. Of course, the Western establishment would have the world believe that it was the nasty Russians who acted as crazed villains. If only that were the case. Instead, NATO yet again pushed Russia into a defensive position that prompted its leaders to take on the geopolitical equivalent of a fight-or-flight response over Ukraine. And for the Kremlin, which had overseen the destruction of the vast Soviet empire 30 years earlier, there was nowhere left for them to flee.

Countdown to World War III?

LATER THAT SUMMER, the United States and Ukraine militaries would lead a NATO military exercise in the Black Sea codenamed "Sea Breeze." The exercise would consist of 5,000 troops, 32 warships, 40 aircraft, and 18 special operations and dive teams. The militaries of 30 different nations would participate in this massive—and provocative—exercise near Russian-held territory.[19]

Between the NATO flotilla and the subsequent Sea Breeze exercises in the Black Sea, it is likely the Putin regime no longer believed the Americans and NATO were interested in maintaining the status quo. The fact that Ukraine *co-hosted* the NATO exercises with the United States effectively meant that Ukraine was a member of NATO in all but name.[20]

Indeed, NATO could never have accepted Ukraine's membership in the organization outright because NATO guidelines explicitly state that potential members cannot have ongoing territorial disputes within their borders. The presence of Russian forces in Eastern Ukraine and Crimea clearly meant that Ukrainian accession into NATO was a non-starter.[21] Nevertheless, there Ukraine was, co-hosting massive military exercises in the Black Sea, dangerously close to Russian forces in Crimea. Russia believed the West was going to launch some military campaign to reclaim Crimea—and for Putin, that was an unacceptable outcome.

In September 2021, the Biden administration would host their counterparts from Ukraine. At that White House summit, the two sides agreed on the need for "reinvigorating" the Strategic Partnership Commission (SPC). The SPC solidified the special commitments that the United States had made to Ukraine at the end of the Cold War (after Clinton got Ukraine to give up its massive nuclear weapons arsenal). It was effectively a backdoor for Ukraine to receive NATO support without having to go through the troubling NATO accession process—which other NATO members, notably Germany and France, would scuttle. The move helped Ukraine avoid the messy NATO regulations that specifically denied entry of states into NATO with preexisting territorial disputes. Instead, the Americans (and British) got Ukraine a *de facto* membership.[22]

Throughout the rest of 2021, Russia's leadership begain to try to get the Americans to back away from supporting the obviously provocative move of incorporating Ukraine into the NATO military sphere. On December 7 of that year—Pearl Harbor Day, ironically—Putin and Biden held a two-hour video chat in which the American president threatened Russia with increased sanctions in response to a massive Russian military buildup across the border from Ukraine. This was the last shot at a diplomatic settlement, as both sides had backed themselves—and each other—into a corner. Putin's stance was consistent with his previous stances on Ukraine: in exchange for Russia ending its provocative military buildup, the United States and its NATO partners needed to first guarantee that Ukraine would never formally enter NATO. All Biden had to do was simply say that he was open to reaffirming that which his predecessors had agreed to do at the end of the Cold War: keep Ukraine as a neutral buffer between Russia and NATO. Had Biden done that, at the very least, a devastating war could have been delayed.

Neither Biden nor the other NATO leaders would even consider Russia's request. It makes one wonder if the provocative actions taken by NATO in 2021 were just examples of naïve virtue-signaling, or if there was something more intentional about them—possibly even something more than the dementia-addled president could fathom? Was Washington's permanent bureaucracy, committed as it had been to endless NATO expansion, taking advantage of the fact that Joe Biden was an empty vessel ripe for their manipulations? Earlier in this book, you read about Robert H. Wade's article in the London School of Economics online blog from May 2022 asserting that NATO had effectively tricked Russia into invading Ukraine. Is the above proof that Wade was correct in his assertions?

Everything after that exchange between Putin and Biden in 2021 was mere posturing and preparing the Ukrainian battlefield for the war—a war as unnecessary as it was insane—to come. The Russians are not heroes. But they had made their position clear and indicated a willingness to avert greater calamity if NATO would simply honor the pledges it had made to Russia at the end of the Cold War (even though most Russians never seriously expected NATO would hold to them).

The real question on the minds of many experts was just what, precisely, prompted Russia to pull the trigger on the gun they had been holding to the heads of Ukraine and NATO for years? NATO had wanted to expand into Ukraine for decades. Why was the winter of 2021-22 such a game-changer?

Again, this gets us back to the man in charge of the White House. Joe Biden is an octogenarian who has serious difficulty speaking in public. He looks weathered and is always worn. Rumors abound about his cognitive decline. The Russians know all this. Add to that the fact that Biden has filled his administration with Russia hawks who are deeply committed to NATO expansion at all costs, and Putin likely felt he could not chalk up the various aggressive displays by NATO forces throughout 2021 to mere posturing. Russia has its own problems, both economically and demographically. For the Russians to have had a chance at a successful war, they needed to move fast. Biden's (and NATO's) botched withdrawal from Afghanistan only further solidified the notion that Putin could beat NATO in Ukraine.

To show you how uneven the Biden administration's Russia policy has been, on the eve of the Russian invasion of Ukraine, after Biden had refused to countenance abandoning Ukraine as a possible NATO member, the forty-sixth president made one last plea against a Russian attack. Inexplicably, Biden conceded that the United States would not stop the Russian invasion before it began.[23] He then added the bizarre kicker that Washington could accept a "minor incursion" by Russian forces into Ukraine. For Moscow, this was the greenlight for an invasion.[24] Even when trying to be hawks on Russia, the Biden administration was haphazard and shambolic.

The real concern for most people, though, is how does the Ukraine War end?

Throughout the conflict and at various intervals, Russian forces have threatened nuclear reprisals. The one red line, as always for

Russia, is control over Crimea. And control over Crimea is the one consistent objective for NATO-backed Ukraine. Would NATO simply fire a Parthian shot at the Russians for having obviously beaten them in Ukraine?

Before you roll your eyes at that question recall everything that happened in 2021. As aggressive and prolific the Russians are at violating human rights, the fact remains it was NATO, not Russia, that precipitated the Ukraine situation. What could have been the start of a new relationship between Biden and Putin at Geneva in June 2021 rapidly devolved into a shooting war shortly thereafter. Some of it was Russia's fault. But the provocative actions of the NATO side were responsible for much of it. And NATO has already proven desperate to maintain its ongoing war against Russia, so much so that, as you'll see in the next chapter of this book, the U.S. might have covertly attacked Germany to keep them onboard with the destructive Ukraine War.

CHAPTER 16

WORLD WAR III OR A PHONY WAR?

THE ENTIRETY of the Ukraine War has been shrouded, as most wars are, in a series of lies. The only problem facing the West is that those lies have so distorted truth that the lies are preventing decision makers in Western nations from making accurate assessments. Is Ukraine winning or losing? Western leaders say one thing and then another depending on the time of the day. Is Vladimir Putin dying of cancer?[1] Will Putin be overthrown tomorrow? Again, the answers vary one day to the next. These aren't just the questions on the minds of those in the public. There seems to be real disagreement from those in power, too.

Meanwhile, the facts on the ground are this: since 2020, Ukraine's population has declined from around 42 million people to about 28 million.[2] Most of that depopulation occurred because of the Russian invasion, which was likely prompted by NATO's provocations in 2021 and the Biden administration's muddled approach to Russia. No significant amount of territory has been gained by Ukraine or lost by Russia. In fact, Russia has hardened its hold on Crimea and does not appear to be at risk of losing Eastern Ukraine. And, in mid-February 2024, Russian forces were in the process of capturing the strategically important city of Avdiivka.[3] Whereas the Western propagandists' rumor mill is in overdrive about Russia's inevitable collapse or Putin's ultimate demise, little is being said about the horrible condition of Ukraine.

When the invasion began in February 2022, the NATO-trained Ukrainian forces were able to exploit Russian weakness and successfully defend Kiev. That moment was the time for the Zelenskyy government in Kiev to sue for peace. Instead, that was the moment Kiev's truculent NATO backers demanded Ukraine go on the offensive against the Russians.[4] Ukraine—entirely dependent on NATO, specifically, the United States—did as it was told. The result has been that the Ukrainian military is broken in the field.[5] On the flipside, the Russians today are more empowered. There is enough food within Russia to allow this fight to go on indefinitely, despite Western sanctions.[6] Gone are the days when the West could hold Moscow hostage with the threat of sanctions on their vital natural gas exports to Europe.[7] Because Russia is a commodities superpower, and because it has ravenous neighbors, such as India and China, Russia has avoided most of the bite from the Western sanctions.[8] What's more, while the Russian military was forced to adapt to very difficult conditions in Ukraine, by early 2024 it appears to be doing far better than its adversary.

Ukraine's economy has been devastated. It continues to spiral the longer the war drags out. Meanwhile, Russia's economy has been reinvigorated.[9] Sure, it's not as potent as the American economy (or even China's or India's), but Putin doesn't need it to be. He just needs to ensure that his economy is moving along well enough to avoid political backlash at home. And while pressure on his regime has increased as many people are understandably upset that Russia is fighting a war, the political opposition to Putin in Moscow has not been strong enough to overthrow him. Further, there is no guarantee that any possible replacement for Putin would be any better for Western interests than he has been.

In January 2024, the Biden administration's Undersecretary of State Victoria Nuland was again skulking about the frigid streets of

Kiev in the dead of night. Like she did in 2014, Nuland gave an impromptu press conference to Ukrainian news services in which she reasserted America's solidarity with Ukraine and insisted that everything was going well for the struggling nation. She added that new weapons systems—more powerful than those given to Kiev in the past—were coming in 2024. She insisted that Ukraine was about to use these new weapons in a devastating way to beat back the Russians. Whatever the truth of the matter was, most military experts today believe Ukraine will be unable to dislodge the Russians from their entrenched positions in Crimea and Eastern Ukraine. The Ukrainians are a spent force and the arsenals in the West have been dangerously depleted by the high tempo of the Ukraine War.

At the time, I went on the air to describe how Nuland's presence might have been much more than a show of solidarity with the embattled Ukrainians. For months before her visit, Zelenskyy had been cracking down on his own people.[10] Specifically, Zelenskyy was purging his government of anyone who dissented from his war plans. During that time, Valerii Zaluzhnyi, the supreme commander of Ukraine's forces since the start of the war, had been falling out of favor with Zelenskyy. This was because Zaluzhnyi had resisted Zelenskyy's extreme orders and had dared to express skepticism about the efficacy of Zelenskyy's (really, NATO's) strategy of constant offensives against the entrenched Russian lines of Eastern Ukraine that were only draining Ukraine's already limited manpower and resources—all while Russia retained its combat effectiveness.

Rumors abounded that the Ukrainian president and his popular, top general had suffered a falling out. It was an insuperable divide, according to people in the know. Reports circulated in early 2024 that Zelenskyy wanted to remove his top general. Out of Russia, came claims that Zaluzhnyi was fomenting a coup against the U.S.-backed Zelenskyy. Whatever was really happening, things were not going well in Kiev.[11] For all the talk about whether Vladimir Putin's days as the wannabe tsar of Russia were numbered, few in Western media circles truly wanted to have the discussion about whether Zelenskyy's days as leader of Ukraine were coming to an end. It is likely that the reason behind Nuland's visit at the start of 2024 was to handle the very serious leadership crisis that was tearing apart Ukraine's government—a crisis that the Western media dutifully ignored.

The only reason there was dissent in Kiev among the top players is because the war, contrary to what the West has been told, is not going well for Ukraine. It is unlikely to end in a Ukrainian victory. The Russians know this. Many in the West are waking up to this fact, despite the best efforts of the Western press to obfuscate. And if the Western elite are lying about what's really occurring within the U.S.-funded, NATO-backed government in Kiev, there is no reason to assume this is their only lie.

Manipulations Galore

INFORMATION WARFARE, from both the Western and Russian sides, has defined this war. But once one understands the objectives of the two sides, it suddenly becomes clear what is really going on. For example, the West has been desperate to prove to the world that Ukraine is the aggrieved party and that NATO is merely helping a wounded, smaller country evade the predation of a larger neighbor. And while Putin certainly initiated the invasion of Ukraine, and his troops have committed many human rights violations, the fact remains that the war is over one thing: keeping NATO away from Ukraine. Russia does not want Ukraine to be used as a base from which NATO can directly threaten the Russian western borders or deprive Russia of its access to the Black Sea.[12]

If Ukraine had been able to join NATO as they had wanted to do, Russia would have had to accept that strategic reality. But why would anyone imagine Moscow would have allowed for this reality to occur? It is particularly unimaginable given that Putin was viewing the chaos within the United States following the COVID-19 pandemic and the raucous presidential election year. After a very weak Joe Biden was elevated to the White House, Putin knew that he had to act fast. The military moves by NATO in 2021 reinforced the belief in the minds of Russia's leaders that NATO was planning to integrate Ukraine into the alliance.

In response to the Russian invasion, Western leaders enhanced the sanctions that had already been placed on Russia following that country's illegal annexation of Crimea in 2014. But by then we already should have seen how the Russians were able to maneuver around those sanctions and continue to be an effective threat, despite the economic hardships imposed by the West. Nevertheless the West—notably those in former Soviet states as well as Britain, Canada, and the United States—were determined to further disentangle the economies of Europe from Russia. The Americans needed to break Europe of its addiction to cheap, readily available, nearby Russian natural gas.

Going back to the Trump administration, the forty-fifth president had warned his German counterparts about becoming overly reliant on Russian natural gas. After all, the Germans and the rest of Europe were known to be active proponents of the position that Russia was dangerous to the world. Trump could not fathom how, if the Europeans believed this, they could allow their economies to become so totally dependent on Russia for their basic energy requirements.[13] Indeed, Trump had made U.S. energy independence a key tenet of his administration. Because of that, American production of oil and natural gas were at all-time highs. Not only was fossil fuel far cheaper in those days than it is now, but there was such an excess capacity that America could sell its fossil fuels to Europe to offset some of their dependence on Russia.

An Energy Bridge to Nowhere

BUT THE GERMANS PERSISTED in their reliance on Russia for energy. There were a variety of reasons for this. One of them goes back decades: Berlin's leaders, like those in Paris, have long fretted about being too reliant on the United States, a country for which they harbor deep suspicions. Another reason, as Thane Gustafson writes about in his book, *The Bridge: Natural Gas in a Redivided Europe*, the Europeans had envisioned using natural gas as a bridge to move away from the supposedly "dirty" fossil fuels, like coal and oil, and toward a "clean" energy future. It was critical to their Green Energy transition policies. But many countries, like Germany, became stuck on Russian natural gas.[14] This was especially so after Germany mothballed all its nuclear reactors following the Fukushima nuclear reactor meltdown in Japan (France, meanwhile has dozens of nuclear reactors powering that nation).

The German government had been steadfastly committed to enhancing its reliance—and therefore, Europe's overall reliance—on Russian natural gas through their support for the Nord Stream 2 pipeline project. Germany's insistence on keeping the pipeline open, even as the war raged, was a sore spot among Germany's NATO allies. It was an entirely understandable move by Germany, though. Germany is an economic dynamo. As noted earlier in this work, it is the fourth largest economy in the world (in GDP terms). Before the Ukraine War began, Germany was one of the most prosperous and diverse economies in the world and the economic beating heart of the European Union. Germany's economic miracle was, in no small part, the result of its easy, consistent access to cheap Russian natural gas.[15] Remove that from the equation and you diminish Germany's economic potency.

Wasted Tanks, Wasted Time

THROUGHOUT THE OPENING YEAR of the Ukraine War, the United States hectored Germany (and other recalcitrant NATO allies) for not doing enough to support Ukraine. It should be noted, however, that Germany was the third largest supplier of weapons to Ukraine (next to the United States and Britain).[16] Still, Germany had an arsenal of sophisticated tanks—known as *Leopard* 2-class Main Battle Tanks—that NATO wanted Germany to give to Ukraine.[17] Further, Berlin was blocking many other countries that were in possession of the *Leopard-2s* from handing them over to Ukraine. Ultimately, Germany would allow Poland to hand their *Leopards* over to Ukraine, but only after much caterwauling.

One reason behind the German reluctance to be more helpful to Ukraine was their concerns that providing such weapons to the embattled nation would prompt an aggressive action by Russia directed against Germany. Berlin was more than happy to be seen as going along with their partners in NATO, but they did not want to take the lead by providing such sophisticated systems to Ukraine. They knew such weapons would likely be used to kill and maim many Russian soldiers. Escalation, at all times, has been a concern of German policymakers (if only U.S. policymakers were as concerned about this prospect).

After much hemming-and-hawing, though, the Germans acquiesced. A sum total of eighteen measly *Leopards* were handed over to Ukraine from Germany.[18] And, wouldn't you know it, a handful of tanks—no matter how sophisticated they may have been—could not turn the tide of battle in Ukraine's favor. Particularly not when Ukraine is faced against the bulk of the Russian Army.

The British sent an additional fourteen *Challenger-2* MBTs and the Americans promised countless numbers of M1 Abrams tanks.[19] The French plied Ukraine with a handful of old, lightly armored tanks the Ukrainians complained were little more than death traps and "impractical" for launching the kinds of offensives against the hardened Russian positions on the frontline that Ukrainian leaders envisioned.[20] Similarly, the Abrams tanks sent by the United States were of an older variant and were in disrepair. So, on top of everything else, NATO was pumping much of its junk into Ukraine.

Germany's tanks were the only MBTs of any value. But they were in too short supply to be made useful at the tactical level. Throughout the entire period Germany deployed tanks to Ukraine, German leaders engaged in what they referred to as, "Scholzing" which is a play on the name of Germany's Chancellor Olaf Scholz. It means to, "communicate good intentions, only to use/find/invent any reason imaginable to delay [the delivery of weapons to Ukraine] and/or prevent them from happening."[21]

Pipeline Politics Goes Bust

LEFT UNSAID was the real reason for Germany's reluctance to supply weapons systems that might fundamentally alter the battle against Russia: their dependence on Russian natural gas. Specifically, the Nord Stream 1 and 2 pipeline networks that ran from Russia through the Baltic states and into Germany (where it was then pushed out to other points in Europe). The pipeline project itself had been negotiated between the German government and Russia's major state-owned energy firm, Gazprom. The person in Germany who had acted as intermediary for the negotiations of the Nord Stream 2 pipeline deal was none other than Gerhard Schröder, the former president of Germany who shared a close relationship with Vladimir Putin. Thus, most of Germany's political elite supported the pipeline.[22]

Speaking in the tense run-up to the Russian invasion of Ukraine, Victoria Nuland ominously warned that, "If Russia invades—that means tanks or troops crossing the border of Ukraine—there will be no longer a Nord Stream 2." Shortly thereafter, President Joe Biden bleated to a room full of reporters, with Olaf Scholz standing beside him looking shocked that, "We will bring an end [to the Nord Stream 2 Pipeline] ... I promise you, we'll be able to do it."[23]

Shockingly, on September 26, 2022, the world awoke to news that the Nord Stream 2 Pipeline had been irreparably damaged in an odd explosion that occurred in the dead-of-night. Understand that the loss of the Nord Stream 2 did immense harm to the German economy.

The expert class in the West immediately took to the airwaves to manage the perceptions of their confused and frightened people.

On the one hand, it was asserted that the pipeline was destroyed due to catastrophic mechanical failure. On the other hand, many in the West asserted that those pesky Russians blew up their own pipeline.[24] In both scenarios, the West was exonerated from any suspicion. But the neoconservative-neoliberal cabal running the Western alliance simply could not help themselves. They gloated. They wanted the world to see their ugliness on display. Rather than continuing to downplay any potential role of NATO forces in the destruction of the pipeline, or maintaining plausible deniability, they gave up the game.

U.S. Secretary of State Antony Blinken gushed that the totally random destruction of the Nord Stream 2 pipeline presented the West with a "tremendous [strategic] opportunity."[25] Yet again, Victoria Nuland pronounced in her congressional testimony on the event that, "I am, and I think the [Biden] administration is, very gratified to know that Nord Stream 2 is now … a hunk of metal at the bottom of the sea."[26] Beyond U.S. officials, though, European leaders, like the former Polish prime minister and chair of the European Parliament's Delegation for Relations with the United States, Radek Sikorski, tweeted an image of the pipeline smoldering with the caption, "THANK YOU, USA!" Sikorski later deleted that tweet and insisted he was being facetious.[27]

But investigative journalist, Seymour Hersh, once the doyen of the old Left and now a darling of the New Right, wrote an eye-opening exposé showing that the Nord Stream 2 pipeline was, in fact, destroyed by NATO forces. According to Hersh's exclusive reportage, an elite team of U.S. Navy divers secreted themselves to the base of the part of the pipeline that cut across the Baltic Sea during the BALTOPS-22 NATO military exercises in the Baltic Sea. At a depth of 260 feet, the Navy divers proceeded to plant C4 explosives along the pipeline's base underwater. The explosives were set on a 48-hour countdown. By the time it went off, all NATO personnel would have been long gone from area, further clouding any certain attribution to the Americans. According to Hersh, though, Biden got cold feet and, at the last minute (and much to the annoyance of the Navy divers who had been meticulously training to plant timed explosives), ordered that remote detonated C4 explosives be used.

The covert Navy mission was designed to give President Biden maximum maneuvering room when addressing the Ukraine War. The U.S. Navy divers were used rather than U.S. Special Forces operators because the Navy divers are not required to share their covert actions with the "Gang of Eight" in the Senate. Thus, Biden was given plausible deniability—a key feature of any covert operation.

Although there is some degree of comfort in the realization that our military and intelligence services are still able to conduct truly daring covert operations of the kind that we once read about from the Cold War, it is important to remember that the target was a pipeline that was a critical component of Germany's economy. And Germany, supposedly, is a close U.S. ally in Europe. The Biden administration was effectively attacking a NATO ally. This, of course, raises the question of the degree to which the collective security agreement—Article V that binds NATO together—is actually sacrosanct. If the United States did, in fact, conduct the attack against fellow NATO member, Germany, then shouldn't Berlin invoke Article V and take NATO to war with the Americans?

The whole thing, of course, is absurd. It highlights the bastardization of itself that NATO has become. And it should reinforce the idea that NATO is a construct long past its prime in dire need of being put out of its misery before it creates even more misery for the West than it is already creating.

The goal, obviously, was to deprive Russia of a key leverage point over Europe's most economically important state, Germany, while forcing a reluctant Germany to pivot away from Russia and embrace the United States more fully. The strategic logic (if you can call any of this logical) went something like this: If the Germans could be cut off from Russian natural gas, they'd be forced to rely more heavily on American sources of energy. In becoming more reliant on the U.S. to meet their energy needs, Germany would become a more willing participant in the Ukraine War as they would no longer fear escalation might threaten their access to energy.

The actions of the Americans against German interests lend credence to Steve Bannon's controversial claim that NATO is more of a protectorate of the United States and less of an alliance of equals. True allies don't attack each other or target each other's critical infrastructure in a cockamamie plot to ensure maximum adherence to the preferred agenda of one partner—even as that agenda is inimical to the other partner's interests. But imperial powers hellbent on imposing their will on everyone and everything around them most assuredly do act like that. A punishing blow of the kind that NATO imposed on Germany by attacking that pipeline was designed to subordinate Germany to the United States.

It worked—to a point. After all, you've already read how Germany reneged on its promise to adequately fund their contributions to the NATO alliance. That decision has not been reversed in the aftermath of the Nord Stream sabotage.

Norway proved to be a vital player in the American scheme, too. The Norwegians helped the Americans identify the best place to target where the two sets of pipelines got closest to each other in the Baltic Sea. Hersh (accurately) speculates that Norway was more than happy to help the Americans blow up the Russo-German pipeline as that would have forced Germany to purchase more natural gas from nearby Norway.

As for the rest of NATO, they were kept in the dark.

Sweden and Denmark were given a last-minute cursory overview by the Norwegian and American intelligence services in order to prevent their navies from accidentally interfering with what would be unusual maritime activity at night. Ultimately, though, the circle was kept tight. In fact, the Swedes abruptly shut down their investigation into the event. Their conclusion was: "We have a picture of what happened, and what the picture consists of we cannot get into more detail, but it leads to the conclusion that we do not have jurisdiction."[28]

That's some crackerjack investigative work there.

In the first eleven months of 2022, U.S. energy sales to Europe exploded by about 137 percent.[29] That number only increased after the Nord Stream explosion. Because U.S. natural gas sources are more expensive to ship across the ocean from America than the pipelined Russian natural gas, Europe is also paying a premium price to U.S. domestic energy producers. So, Germany's economic miracle was murdered, not by the Russian bogeyman, but by Germany's purported American ally. For the low cost of attacking an ally, eviscerating their economy, and risking greater escalation with Russia over Ukraine, the Americans were able to position Germany into a subservient position, possibly forever.

Not to worry, though, Europe—notably Germany—insists that the destruction of the Nord Stream pipelines will only expedite their much-ballyhooed transition to completely "sustainable" sources of energy. Alas, a reliance on alternative energy such as solar power, for example, will only ensure that Europe becomes ever more dependent on China. Thus, America is again pushing another group of countries out of its orbit into the waiting arms of its only real geopolitical foe in the world today, China. Again, no one does strategy in Washington, D.C. anymore. Even when they try, as the neoconservative-neoliberal cabal does, their strategies are less like real plans and more like playing the game of Risk while drunk—with similarly disastrous results.

In the meantime, anyone who dares to question the official narrative about the Nord Stream 2 explosion is immediately denounced and declared to be a Russian stooge by the Western elite.

The Ukraine War is a Giant Lie Factory

THE CONFLICT has been one giant lie factory. Each lie is more extreme, and absurd, than the last. We in the West are made to consume the lies so much that we are beginning to choke on them. Despite what we have been told, Ukraine is losing the war. This is why the very popular Ukrainian General Valery Zaluzhny, who wanted his government to sue for peace, was released from his job by President Zelenskyy. But the Ukrainian government is not so much of a government as it is part of a larger Western machine that is two-parts money-laundering and one-part power politics. The Ukrainians cannot end the war because Zelenskyy is not fully in charge. The Ukrainian president is beholden to his masters in Washington—and the extremists in his own ranks, who will likely murder him, if he actually tries to sue for peace with Russia. None of these forces want the war to end. Therefore, it will continue.

We know this is true. Vladimir Putin's forces were unexpectedly repulsed from their brutal attack on Kiev by the Ukrainian defenders. Russia had a plan to take Kiev quickly, arrest the Ukrainian leaders there, and either ship Zelenskyy off to Siberia or, more likely, to murder him, thereby ending the war. Ukraine's forces stopped that from happening. But Ukraine's forces were limited in what they could do. Ukraine is much smaller than Russia. It has significant limits in what it can achieve against a hulking adversary like Russia. Yet the Russians attacked Ukraine with far fewer troops than they would have needed to conquer a territory as large as Ukraine. Putin's decisions at the start of the war have remained a matter of debate among observers in the West. Was it actually a mistake? Or was Putin attempting to achieve something else altogether?

Sensing an opportunity for peace, Zelenskyy reached out to Putin through intermediaries, seeking a ceasefire. Putin, for his part, was interested in this as he did not want the war, which was not going the way he had planned, to drag on.

Peace Denied

THE FORMER Israeli prime minister, Naftali Bennett, revealed how he was attempting to broker a ceasefire between Russia and Ukraine. Bennett claims that both Zelenskyy and Putin were ready to meet in Turkey and finalize a much-needed end to the war. Unfortunately for everyone, certain powerful members of NATO were simply too committed to the Ukraine War to have it end so soon.[30]

To stop the unwanted peace deal from happening, Britain's leader, Prime Minister Boris Johnson, boarded a plane and, in his signature scruffy style, appeared in Kiev. Ostensibly, he was there to show support for the Ukrainian cause; to rally the troops, as it were. Unofficially, however, Johnson was there to remind Zelenskyy that he was merely a passive observer in this war. Sure, it was Zelenskyy's people who were being slaughtered *en masse* and his country that was being ripped apart by the war. But there were larger concerns for Britain and its primary ally, the United States.

A pressure campaign conducted by the British and American governments ensured that the Ukrainians would not negotiate from their position of relative strength. The war would grind on. All that leverage Zelenskyy had acquired by presiding over the successful defense of Kiev was gone. Two years after the start of the war, it is now the Russians who are in positions of strength and the Ukrainians who are at their breaking point.

Here's the kicker to the whole story: the Russians claim the only reason they pulled their army back from Kiev in April 2022 was because Moscow was given certain guarantees by the West that negotiations for a peaceful settlement to the conflict would take place.[31] Once the Russians pulled their forces back from Kiev, however, the West reneged on their promises, and the war continued on. This claim was made by Vladimir Putin in his interview with independent American journalist, Tucker Carlson, in early February of

2024. Many in the West challenge Putin's assertion. It should be noted, however, that my colleague, Lee Slusher, a former U.S. intelligence analyst with experience in Russia, believes that this is true. The Russians, according to Slusher, did pull back as part of a larger movement toward peace that the NATO side ultimately broke (and likely never had any intention of respecting).

The insistence of the Americans and the British that the war drag on is based a dangerous assumption about their interests. In 2023, I was speaking in an off-the-record conversation with several uniformed leaders at the Department of Defense. At one point in the conversation, one of the generals in attendance became incensed at the direction it was taking. "Don't you see, Mr. Weichert, what's happening out there?" He demanded. "We're breaking the Russian Army in the field—for cheap!" He huffed. Similar sentiments have been expressed in public by former U.S. Army generals who have experience serving in Europe.

It's all wrong. And the lies that we are being forced to choke down by our own leaders about this war are obscuring the fact that every assumption of theirs about this war is incorrect. Is anyone all that surprised, though? The same group who led us into the failed Mideast wars of the last twenty years have been the same people banging the drum for this conflict with Russia.

A month after the end of the Siege of Kiev, I argued in a piece at *The Washington Times*, that Western leaders should be careful about demanding Ukraine go on the offensive against the Russians. Even if the Ukrainian Army could be successful in its fight to reclaim the lost lands of Eastern Ukraine and Crimea, the fact that American and Western arsenals are dangerously low—with little industrial capacity to quickly replenish—means that Western suppliers will be unable to meet the Ukrainians' demands. The longer this war drags on, the more true this is.[32]

The level of hate mail and angry tweets from the Military-Twitter crowd was astonishing (especially because I work as a

consultant with many of these organizations). But the Biden administration was committed to "breaking the Russian Army in the field."
Unbeknownst to these geniuses, however, we were merely breaking
ourselves in Ukraine.[33] Rather than admit they were wrong and had
miscalculated badly, the Western elite, in their hubris, continued
deepening NATO's involvement in the Ukraine War.

An air of make-believe permeated the minds of every Western
leader as it related to Ukraine. It's almost as though the Ukraine War
is a phony war. It's not like Iraq or Afghanistan in that there are no
U.S. servicemen and women dying in combat (although there are
some Americans who are fighting in Ukraine and have already died).
Drunk on the concept that they were Captain America to Putin's
Thanos, the NATO leadership kept speeding down the highway of
death, avoiding all off-ramps lest they be seen as weak. Putin, meanwhile, kept plugging along. Each time the delusions of the West were
shattered by reality, such as the claims that Putin was about to be
overthrown or that Russia's economy was set to collapse under the
weight of Western economic sanctions, NATO doubled-down on
failure—as so many elephantine bureaucracies desperately seeking
to justify their existence (and cost) do.

The Psychic Wounds of Vietnam Still Sting

PART OF THE PROBLEM is that the Western military establishment
views Ukraine merely as a proxy war. It's no different than, say, what
the Americans did in funding the Mujahideen anti-Soviet resistance
in Afghanistan during the 1980s. We all know what happened to
the Mujahideen after the Soviets left Afghanistan in defeat in 1989:
Many of them went on to become al Qaeda and the Taliban! We
funded and trained the terrorists who attacked us on 9/11. Besides,
Ukraine is not the equivalent of Afghanistan in the minds of most
Russian leaders. It's much more akin to Hungary in the 1950s. And
we know that the Soviet Union was willing to go to world war to

prevent Hungary from leaving the Soviet Union, as the coup against communist rule there almost did cause Hungary to do. Russia was at peace with a Ukraine that was independent yet neutral. After 30 years of NATO attempting to change that dynamic, the Russians punched back at the West.

What's more, the blasé attitude toward the Ukraine War on the part of American and Western leaders is perplexing. It traces back to their view of the conflict being just another proxy war. The Western elite seem to forget that the Vietnam War was just another proxy war against Moscow—specifically, the spread of communism. In fact, the attitude and nature of America's involvement in Ukraine is shockingly similar to the way in which America handled the Vietnam War.

People forget that the Vietnam War lasted far longer than what they were taught in school. American involvement in what was then known as Indochina began almost as soon as the Pacific Theater in World War II ended. Communist guerillas led by Ho Chi Minh took the northern portion of Vietnam and were agitating to invade the southern, U.S.-backed portion. From the 1950s until 1964, a covert war was fought between U.S.-led-and-trained South Vietnamese forces against the communist-backed North Vietnamese insurgents planted in South Vietnam. President John F. Kennedy, shortly before his death, recognized the folly of becoming embroiled in a proxy war with Russia over the fate of tiny Vietnam. Yet, his vice-president (and successor), Lyndon B. Johnson, believed that preventing Vietnam from falling into the Soviet Union's orbit was a critical strategic objective for the United States. As soon as JFK was killed, LBJ began escalating in Vietnam.

That war, too, was shrouded in absurd and unnecessary lies. The lack of honesty with the American people eventuated in some of the worst excesses in U.S. military history. It also destabilized the United States at home—much as the Ukraine War today is helping to do. Just as with the Vietnam War, the Ukraine War today can easily be resolved by diplomatic negotiations. Yet, the NATO side will not countenance it. All their stunning hubris, combined with denial about how badly things are going for Ukraine, has led to some fairly insane possibilities.

The South Vietnamese army was effective but could not defeat the North Vietnamese military without U.S. military aid and support. LBJ knew the American people would never allow for a direct war in Vietnam so he and his team manipulated events in Vietnam—specifically, off the coast of Vietnam—to ensure that an inciting incident could be used as a pretext for launching the war with direct U.S. military involvement. This became known as the Gulf of Tonkin incident. It was believed that North Vietnamese torpedo boats launched torpedoes at the U.S. Navy Destroyer, USS *Maddox*, on August 4, 1964. After allegedly evading the torpedoes, the crew of the *Maddox* sent their report to the Pentagon. The Defense Department then alerted LBJ, who went postal, and took the incident to Congress, demanding they give him the power to invade Vietnam.

The U.S. Congress, rather than officially declare war on Vietnam, handed their warmaking powers over to President Johnson, who then went about committing the U.S. military to a war that he and his team thought would be over rather quickly. At each stage of that war, though, the arrogant American politicians misinterpreted the intentions of the enemy. Further, those leaders, for political purposes—as well as to preserve their own pride—continued to expand the war rather than seek a negotiated settlement (which is ultimately how America's involvement in the Vietnam War ended in 1975). Hundreds of thousands of young Americans were committed to a bloody war that was being waged less for U.S. national interests and more to preserve LBJ's honor ... and the image of the United States as a dominant military power abroad.

But for almost twenty years before the first U.S. Marines landed in Vietnam, Washington had waged a shadow war against the communist North Vietnamese. That proxy war ended in failure. The failure should have been obvious because, the point of waging the covert campaign against North Vietnam was to ensure that a larger, more conventional war was unnecessary. Of course, the proxy war ended so badly for the United States, that the American political leadership believed they needed to fully commit to a major war in that country. After a decade of fruitless fighting, Vietnam ended as it was always going to end: with a U.S. withdrawal and North Vietnam poised to reclaim their land.

Today, I see many troubling comparisons between Ukraine and Vietnam. It, too, was a war of choice. As with Vietnam and the Gulf of Tonkin incident, the reason behind the Russian invasion was not as straightforward as the democratic-globalist elite who purport to rule over us would have you believe. Yes, Russia invaded Ukraine. But Moscow took the action it did, as has been demonstrated in this work, because of the constant poking done by the U.S.-led NATO alliance. Similarly, as there was in the proxy war in Vietnam, there are many members of the U.S. military serving as "advisers" on the ground in Ukraine. And, as with the U.S. military advisers to the South Vietnam Army, it is unlikely that these American advisers are simply staying out of the fight against Russian troops. So, while officially U.S. forces are not (yet) fighting in Ukraine against Russian troops, the probability that Americans are fighting in a covert capacity is real. We've already been advised of the names of many Americans who have died fighting in Ukraine.

More troubling than that is the political situation in the United States. The country is as divided as it was during the Vietnam War. It has a president in Joe Biden who is not in control of either his faculties or his own administration. He and his team also are convinced that he is the next FDR or LBJ, both of whom had sweeping Progressive domestic programs as well as major wars under their watch. Plus, Joe Biden is banking on it making him look good if he is considered a wartime president in the midst of the contentious 2024 election cycle. At least that's what his team thinks. It certainly worked for both FDR (who served an astonishing four terms as president) and for LBJ (who bested Republican senator of Arizona, Barry Goldwater, in the 1964 election).

All this lends itself to the fear that phony war in Ukraine between NATO and Russia is about to become a very real conflict, possibly a third world war. There's another part of this scary equation that could become more frightening. In his interview with Tucker Carlson, Vladimir Putin reiterated multiple times that he remains open to a negotiated settlement of the Ukraine War. Yet, the West continues blocking any such peace talks (because they are still deluded and arrogant enough to believe they have a chance at breaking the Russian Army in the field). Instead, the longer Ukraine is delayed from getting a peace deal with Russia, the more likely it is that Russia will simply bleed the Ukrainians dry and take whatever they want from them. Meanwhile, in Washington, rumors abound from those involved with managing this failed war that, at some point, a negotiated settlement will be needed to end the conflict.

If this work has done anything, I hope that it has been to highlight the hubris of Western leaders. These people have gotten everything wrong about this war, from the logistics to the strategy, to their assumptions about who will win and when the war will end. Why assume that they will get the peace correct (or that they even want peace)?

NATO wants war. They have spent the last several decades pressuring Russia with everything NATO has to put Russia in a permanently weakened state. The final domino to fall for NATO would have been the absorption of Ukraine into the alliance. The Russians have identified that the real reason for this NATO obsession with Ukraine is to deprive the Russians of access to the Black Sea. And any serious threat to Crimea, as Moscow has explicitly stated, will lead to a nuclear conflict. That is a red line Putin will never allow the West to cross. Yet, the West keeps escalating.

Desperation Fuels the War

BY THE SUMMER OF 2023, it was obvious that the war had reached a stalemate. If something was not done quickly to terminate the conflict, the war would shift decisively in Russia's favor through sheer attrition. Hubris was again defining the West's decisions. Rather than admit the war was over and without the ability to fundamentally alter the conditions on the ground, a strange event occurred. It looked as though the hopes of the desperate NATO alliance about overthrowing Vladimir Putin were about to become reality.

Inexplicably, Yevgeny Prigozhin, the infamous leader of the Russian mercenary force, known as the Wagner Group, took his forces that had been leading the Russian offensive in Ukraine on a merry race from the Ukrainian frontlines to Moscow itself.[34] Western news media sources breathlessly reported every movement Prigozhin's Wagner Group took on its hard-charging march toward the seat of Putin's government. But what triggered Prigozhin's sudden turn against Vladimir Putin? After all, Prigozhin rose to infamy by being a loyal sidekick to Putin. He was so loyal that Prigozhin had earned the nickname, "Putin's Chef" (no, it was not because of Prigozhin's mean *Borscht* recipe).

Officially, Prigozhin claimed he was leading a mutiny against his old mentor, Putin, because of the awful conditions on the frontline. To be fair, Putin's government had tasked the mercenary group with some of the nastiest assignments in the war. And the Wagner crew were more than able to get their hands bloodied and muddied—on a far greater scale than the ordinary Russian Army was able (or willing) to do.

In the closing weeks of June 2023, the Pentagon made a stunning announcement. According to the bean counters at the Department of Defense, they had overestimated the value of the weapons sent to Ukraine—by about $6.2 billion. This created a surplus "that will be used for future security packages," as the Associated Press reported at the time.[35] This occurred, however, a week before Prigozhin turned on Putin. I mention this because there exists a real possibility that Prigozhin, who was one of the world's greatest mercenaries, was paid off by U.S. intelligence services in yet another quixotic bid to overthrow Putin.

The Western press tells us that U.S. intelligence only learned of Prigozhin's plot a few weeks before he initiated it.[36] But this does not mean that the Western intelligence services could not have convinced themselves that they might get out of the massive hole into which they had dug NATO by handing over a massive amount of tax dollars to the mercenary leader, Prigozhin. I have long suspected that the West, at least in part, bankrolled Prigozhin's abortive coup attempt against Putin.

After the initial shock of Prigozhin's move wore off, the Russian government was able to get its bearings and repel the Russian mercenary—bloodlessly. It was the strangest non-coup coup in the history of warfare. Ultimately, Prigozhin negotiated with Putin's proxies, the Chechen leader, Ramzan Kadyrov, who promised Prigozhin that, "If you stay with us, I promise you that we will give you more, create better conditions, than you have today. We will try to make everything top notch for you." Following discussions with Putin ally, Kadyrov, the Russian defense minister, Sergei Shoigu, supposedly met with Prigozhin and the two men spoke for several hours. It all ended after Prigozhin determined that he could not rally the Russian military's leadership to his cause.[37] He stopped the coup, claiming that he did not want to shed "Russian blood" but, in fact, it's because he overestimated his pull relative to that of Putin's in the Russian system.[38]

Ultimately, Prigozhin went to Belarus and hid out for a while. It was rumored that he'd eventually go to Africa, where the Wagner Group had many missions.[39] The coup evaporated ... along with whatever money it seems likely to me Prigozhin was given by Western intelligence services. Just when all seemed to have been smoothed over between Putin and Prigozhin, on the two-month anniversary of the failed coup attempt, Prigozhin's private jet was shot down while flying over the skies of Moscow.[40]

And Prigozhin would not be the only Putin rival to be killed as part of the Russian strongman's victory tour. Consider Alexei Navalny, who had been Putin's most strident opponent and had been viewed by the Western elite as the best hope for replacing Putin. While in exile in Germany, Navalny elevated his standing in the Western press with his strident opposition to Vladimir Putin's reign. Despite being a Russian nationalist, like Putin, Navalny became a darling of the liberal establishment.[41] Many in the West believed that he would overthrow Putin's regime and replace it with a true democracy (whatever that means in the Russian context). In their desperation to overthrow Putin at all costs and to get out of the unwinnable Ukraine War without conceding defeat to Russia, Western intelligence services filled Navalny's head with bogus claims about how he'd be greeted as a liberator. Defying all logic and reason, Navalny returned to Russia, where he was promptly arrested and sent to a horrific penal colony north of the Arctic Circle.[42] While at that wretched prison, Navalny died under mysterious circumstances. Another of the Western intelligence community's shambolic, half-baked schemes had gone awry.

Meanwhile, it was Putin's hand that was strengthened.

CHAPTER 17

NATO'S PARTHIAN SHOT?

THE ART of the "Parthian shot" was developed by the ancient Parthians, although it was employed by many other ancient powers. The Parthian shot was often deployed as a feint whereby an enemy could be tricked into a false sense of security as galloping horsemen thought to be retreating would turn their arrows rearward and fire them at the enemy behind them—the enemy from whom they were purportedly fleeing. A Parthian shot, then is attacking one's enemy when they assume they've won and let their guard down. A Parthian shot is a parting salvo meant to bloody the nose of the rival; it's the ultimate "f-ck you."

I do not know what form a possible NATO Parthian shot would take. I do, however, understand that the hubris displayed by NATO in its dealings with post-Soviet Russia and its commitment to expanding the alliance at all costs, will make any kind of negotiated settlement very difficult. The Russians have made clear they will not give ground on any of the territories they have captured in Eastern Ukraine since 2014. More importantly (and this has been a key sticking point preventing any real negotiated settlement from taking shape in the past), the Russians will not negotiate on Crimea. It is theirs. They will not abandon it. The Ukrainians, acting on behalf of NATO, meanwhile, won't drop their obsession with taking back

Crimea. This is one reason behind Zelenskyy's removal of Zaluzhny. The Ukrainian general vociferously opposed Kiev's, frankly lunatic, plans for risking everything to recapture Crimea from Russia.[1]

Given the arrogance of Western leadership and the dire consequences if Ukraine, and therefore, NATO, lose the War in Ukraine, there is a high probability that NATO will do what LBJ did in Vietnam: create the preconditions necessary for U.S. troops to be deployed into Ukraine. Victoria Nuland herself intimated as much when she visited Kiev in early 2024 during the leadership crisis between Zelenskyy and Zaluzhny. Nuland said that, "Putin is going to get some nice surprises on the battlefield."[2] Little details were given by Nuland as to what systems she was referring. At the time of that statement, the U.S. Congress had stopped any new aid from reaching Ukraine because of a legislative battle occurring between the Democratic and Republican Parties over funding increased security measures at the U.S. southwestern border. Although reports circulated in February of 2024 that Congress was looking at separating Ukraine funding from the contentious U.S. border security fight Nuland's promises to Ukraine—and implicit threats to Russia—could materialize later this year.

Speaking of the legislative battle in 2024, the Democrats' Senate Majority Leader Chuck Schumer went on *MSNBC* to advocate for the passage of the Ukraine aid bill. He had a strange way of doing it, though. Rather than make the standard arguments that Ukraine should be free and that we shouldn't allow for larger countries, like Russia, to bully their smaller, democratic neighbors, Schumer came on the air breathlessly arguing that, unless the $113 billion aid package was sent immediately to Ukraine, then the war would expand beyond Ukraine. Russia would easily capture Ukraine. The pro-Western government in Kiev would be annihilated. Then, Ukraine would be used by Russia as a base from which the Russian military could attack Poland. Schumer then went beyond that paranoid fantasy. He argued that if the aid package didn't get to Ukraine and the country fell—or looked to be in danger of falling—then U.S. troops would be used to stop Putin from annexing Ukraine.[3]

It was a stop the presses moment that was conveniently glossed over by the Democratic Party controllers at *MSNBC*. There were no follow-up questions to this display from one of the most powerful men in the U.S. government; no attempt to get elaboration on his caustic statement. The absurd claim was taken at face-value because it fits the preferred narrative of the elites in Washington, D.C. that actually rules over us. Most Americans, however, were taken aback by the senator's exasperated prognostications about American troops being deployed to fight Russia.

Just as with Vietnam in 1964, most Americans would be unable to find Ukraine on a map. Moreover, if one had asked Americans in 1964 if they supported sending their kids over to fight in Vietnam, even against the Soviet-backed communists of North Vietnam, most would have said it wasn't worth the bones of a single G.I. Yet, the American political establishment wanted a war at all costs. They arranged to have it. And then they got burned because the war ended up going badly for the United States—to the point that it ended in a strategic defeat for America. We are still today licking the psychic wounds of that conflict. Now the democratic-globalist elite are gearing up to engage in an even nastier war in Ukraine.

Schumer is not the only powerful American leader to have insinuated that U.S. troops would soon be patrolling the streets of Kiev. In 2022, while visiting U.S. forces stationed in Poland, President Biden explicitly told the men and women in uniform that they'd be deployed into Western Ukraine "soon" and that some of them might be fighting Russian forces.[4] Almost as soon as Biden had stuttered out those words, his staff, as per usual, came in to do damage control. The president misspoke, we were assured. Of course, no U.S. forces would be deployed. Why would they be? Haven't you been listening to the Western press? The Ukrainians were running circles around the Russians! The war would be over in days. Crimea and Eastern

Ukraine would be returned to Kiev's control. The Russians would be kicked out, as they were in Afghanistan in 1980 by the local resistance. And then, just as with the end of the Soviet-Afghan War, Russia herself would implode, and Uncle Sam—with its multinational corporations—could move in and absorb the immense natural resources of Russia all while using Russia as a base to further contain China.

The dissolution of Russia is what it always seems to come back to with the lot running Washington. No matter how impractical, undesirable, or utterly delusional such a plan may be, they're wedded to it.[5]

Of course, the Ukrainians are not winning. If what Putin said about the willful Russian withdrawal from Kiev on the promise of a negotiated settlement with the West was true, then even the Miracle at Kiev was part of a NATO propaganda operation directed at their own people. Two years on, Russia is stronger than it was in 2022, more self-reliant, and enjoying dominance on the battlefield. The Ukrainians, meanwhile, are struggling and will likely lose soon.

As I noted in an apparently controversial column at the *Asia Times*, Russia does not need to negotiate. They can just wait out the Ukrainians, who are already crumbling before the sustained pressure Russia is exerting on Kiev's forces on the frontlines. With American aid slowed, critical gaps in Ukraine's ailing defenses will be revealed, leaving Moscow's forces with a key moment of opportunity.[6] That is, unless the Americans and the rest of NATO come rushing in to fight.[7]

Ultimately, at the end of April 2024, the House Republicans buckled under pressure and approved the funding bill for Ukraine. Despite his promises to the contrary, Speaker of the House Mike Johnson (R-LA) did not get funding for border security along the United States' border with Mexico in exchange for Ukraine funding. He apparently just gave in to the Democrats' demands.

Although, it should be noted, that there was one sacrificial lamb made to appease the angry political gods of Washington. Shortly before the funding bill passed, Victoria Nuland announced that she was retiring from the State Department. She would no longer haunt the policy discussions about Ukraine, Russia, and Eurasian affairs at Foggy Bottom as she had done for so long. Never forget, though, in Washington, one's career is never truly dead. Political resurrections occur frequently. That is especially true if one is an upstanding member of the ruling cabal, such as Nuland is. Expect to see her hitting the lecture circuit, appearing on *MSNBC* as a "national security expert," and either teaching at the elite college of her choice or serving as an expert for one of Washington's countless think tanks, where she will leverage her contacts in government in exchange for continuing to push the cabal's globalist agenda.

Ukraine Has Been Trying to Rope NATO in For Years

THERE IS ALSO something else to consider: Kiev has been desperate to make their little territorial spat with Russia a full-blown NATO war. One of the important NATO partners that has been supporting Ukraine in its fight against Russia has been neighboring Poland. Essential supply lines coming from America and the rest of the Europe run through Poland into Western Ukraine. Without Poland's assistance, the support of Ukraine would be impossible.[8] In fact, Poland has one of the largest contingents of soldiers fighting in Ukraine (sheep-dipped in Ukrainian uniforms, of course).[9] Yet, the government that ran Poland during the first two years of the Ukraine War was right-leaning and was careful not to allow itself to be pulled into direct confrontation with Russia.

On November 15, 2022, a little more than a month after the sabotage of the Nord Stream pipelines in the Baltic Sea, the Russians engaged in their usual terror campaign against the poor Ukrainian people. A missile fusillade rocketed from Russian positions toward Ukrainian cities in Western Ukraine. During that attack, it was claimed that the Polish village of Przewodów was attacked by a Russian missile.[10] An international scandal erupted as, unsurprisingly, the American and British governments were licking their lips at the prospect of getting Poland to invoke Article V that would have allowed for U.S. troops and other NATO forces to be deployed directly against Russian forces in Ukraine.

The Polish government at the time was skeptical, though. Even though the Ukrainians were insisting that the Russians had attacked Poland, Warsaw was unsure. Kiev mounted their own pressure campaign to get Poland to declare that the Russians had, in fact, attacked Poland with a missile, that it was a clear sign of escalation by Moscow, and that it was time for Poland to invoke Article V. At the time this was occurring, Western media outlets barely covered the story. They buried the story deep among other trending news topics. So people do not realize how close we came to World War III—how serious the Phony War could have become.

Ultimately, Warsaw determined that it was not a Russian missile attack at all. What had hit Przewodów was actually a Ukrainian missile. The Polish government conducted an investigation at the time. The president of Poland back then, Andrezj Duda, declared that "the missile was an S-300 rocket made in the Soviet Union, an old rocket, and there is no evidence it was launched by the Russian side." Duda concluded that it was, "highly probable [the S-300 was] fired by Ukrainian anti-aircraft defence [sic]" and "unfortunately fell on Polish territory." The NATO secretary general concurred with the Polish assessment.[11]

There was no sign that Russia was interested in escalation with NATO. It took the Poles a few days to confirm that the Russians were not behind the attack. Yet, that never stopped Zelenskyy from screaming that Russia attacked Poland. At no point after what should have been an embarrassing display by the Ukrainian leader did Zelenskyy or anyone in his government walk back the initial accusations against Russia. It is obvious that Kiev didn't care about the truth. They were desperate to get NATO directly involved because by that time, Ukraine was losing. Washington knew they were losing, and the more aggressive members of the alliance were desperate for the pretext to get direct American involvement.[12]

Ukraine couldn't help but to alienate Poland in 2023. According to sources in Poland, during the Fall of 2023, the Polish government had come to the conclusion that "a series of absolutely unacceptable statements and diplomatic gestures appeared on the Ukrainian side." Specifically, Polish farmers had become incensed by their government's largesse toward Ukrainian grain imports. While most Poles supported Ukraine's cause as a matter of necessity (they believed that Poland would be next on Putin's menu if they didn't stand with Ukraine), the war was hurting Polish farmers because Warsaw had been helping to prop up Ukraine's economy with generous trade deals. And, after a year of being disrespected by Kiev, Poland's right-wing government had had enough. So, in September of 2023, Warsaw discontinued transferring weapons to Ukraine.[13]

Warsaw's necessary move in protecting their national interests, even in the face of increased pressure from their NATO partners—notably those in the Biden administration—seems to have set faceless forces against that country. Conveniently, a month after their decision to cut off most lethal aid to Ukraine, the right-wing Polish government lost the Polish national elections and was replaced by a left-leaning government. Donald Tusk was sworn-in as prime minister after his pro-European Union coalition defeated the conservative, anti-EU government run by the Law and Justice Party.[14] Tusk was previously Poland's prime minister from 2007-14. Donald Tusk is also a devout globalist. After he lost his spot in Poland's government in 2014, like so many failed globalist politicians throughout Europe, he was given a sinecure in the European Union Parliament. Tusk ascended to the top spot in the EU.

Tusk belongs to the same loose democratic-globalist cabal that runs the West presently. The realignment of Poland with the rest of the globalist elite means that the next time there is a crisis between Poland and Russia, cooler heads are unlikely to prevail. Ten days after the pro-EU Tusk government was sworn in, Warsaw called in the Russian ambassador to Poland to issue an official warning to

Moscow, after a Russian missile briefly flew through Polish airspace on its way to targets in Ukraine.[15]

Upon his swearing in, the EU-loving Donald Tusk declared that "We will ... loudly and decisively demand the full mobilisation of the free world, the Western world, to help Ukraine in this war. There is no alternative."[16] Gone are the days of Poland and other rational governments looking for off-ramps to the end of the Ukraine War. Tusk has made clear his intention to escalate. And that means the Americans and the rest of NATO are readying to do something completely insane.

Team NATO is on its last legs. It has picked a fight with Russia over Ukraine and almost none of its grand plans for Ukraine have gone according to plan. In fact, many of them have completely backfired. So, the only thing the neoconservative-neoliberal cabal knows to do is to continuously escalate, assuring themselves that there would be no way that the Russians could match the escalations. Or that Russia would dare risk nuclear war.

When it looked as though the Republicans in Congress were going to put an end to the funding for Ukraine in early 2024, however, the Biden administration made a desperate pronouncement: that Russia was readying to deploy a new anti-satellite space weapon.[17] No further details were provided by the White House. Of course, Russia has possessed a coterie of devastating anti-satellite weapons (as I documented in my first book, *Winning Space: How America Remains a Superpower,* released in 2020). At the time, there was concern that the Russians were readying to deploy nuclear weapons in orbit.[18] For their part, Moscow vehemently denied the Biden White House's claims.[19] Whatever the extent of the purported threat, it was an obvious escalation from someone. Or, at the very least, a pretext for a possible escalation.

But, to what end? Was Russia sensing that NATO was preparing to conduct a Parthian shot of sorts against their forces in Ukraine and Russia was attempting to preempt that move? Was this a cynical ploy by the Biden administration to ensure that American funding continued flowing into Ukraine? Was it possible that, since the Russians had not yet deployed the weapons system in question, that they were merely trying to pressure NATO into coming to the negotiating table? Whatever the case may be, it is a highly dangerous moment in the annals of NATO-Russia relations.

Like so much in this war, though, Moscow has been very clear about what will prompt a nuclear escalation from Russia. And the Americans and their NATO allies keep ignoring Russia. At some point, the arrogant self-delusion will end. What's more, the democratic-globalists erroneously believe that they can manage Russia militarily in a fight. They do not understand that Russia is prepared for any contingency and they are more hardened against NATO attacks than the United States and Europe are for Russia's.

We already know that the democratic-globalists who purport to rule us have determined that Putin and his *siloviki* are planning to march on Poland, Estonia, and all the other former Soviet states in the Slavic world. These policymakers are desperate to prevent what they think is a far larger war from coming (here we go again with the dangerous echoes of the Bush Doctrine and the Iraq War of 2003). Just as they did with Saddam Hussein's alleged WMD arsenal, the neoconservative-neoliberal cabal thinks that by agitating for a conflict now with Russia over Ukraine they are somehow sapping the Russian military's capabilities *before* the Russians can move on Poland and the rest of Europe. What these democratic-globalists are doing in the name of preemption—inflating Russia's threat and fighting a war today on the notion that it'll somehow be cheaper than waging a war tomorrow—is a grotesque repeat of what they did in Iraq, only on a far grander, and more destructive scale.

Poland is the trigger point. And now the neoconservative-neoliberal cabal has fellow travelers in Warsaw. A Parthian shot might be next. Chuck Schumer's threat to his own people that their sons and daughters will soon be in a direct fight with Putin's troops in the muddy, blood-soaked killing fields of Ukraine might be more than just a scare tactic to pry more ill-gotten funds from America's coffers. Schumer might be telegraphing what is to come next for Americans.

In the coming days and months, as Ukraine's defeat becomes impossible to ignore, NATO might call for peace talks just as they did to save Kiev in April 2022. But, just as in 2022, the calls for peace from NATO might be a trap for a Russia. As Russia seeks to conduct peace talks, it is possible that a desperate and humiliated NATO goes too far and engages its Parthian shot in an effort to escalate the war. Sending U.S. troops into direct conflict with Russia under the false belief that the introduction of U.S. forces will end the Ukraine War in Kiev's favor immediately, is more likely to be a good way to discover that Russia won't surrender or renegotiate under those circumstances.

At that point, nuclear world war is just around the corner. All this was totally avoidable. But, contrary to what the Biden administration claimed when it assumed power in January 2021, there are no adults in the room. That's why every patriotic American should be worried about what comes next in Ukraine—and why NATO must be treated with far more skepticism from Americans than it has been.

Thucydides wrote that fear, interest, and ambition drove nations to wage war upon each other. Hubris, then, is the fuel for nations to wage war. NATO after the Cold War was adrift. At risk of being dissolved, the elite cadre ruling the West opted to hold the alliance together. But the loss of its Soviet enemy left a gaping hole in the heart of the Cold War era collective security pact. They replaced anti-Soviet communism with anti-Russian policies. The alliance stopped being a defensive collective security alliance of equals and became something very ugly. It devolved into that which it had defeated in the Cold War: an aggressive, ideologically-bound protectorate of a distant military power, the United States (just as the old Warsaw Pact was a protectorate of Soviet Russia during the Cold War).

Back in the heady days of the Cold War, NATO's equal members steeled themselves to the possibility that the ideologically expansionistic Communists might initiate a nuclear war at any moment. The alliance was prepared to defend Western Europe. At no point in the Cold War, however, was NATO interested in *starting* a nuclear war with the Soviet Union. They truly were the good guys in that fight. Interestingly, most modern Russians would likely agree with the statement that the Communists were the villains of the Cold War. Today, sadly, NATO is now the vehicle of instability in Europe. It has expanded five times in thirty-three years, even after it had assured post-Soviet Russian leaders that it would not do so.[20] The war in Ukraine is entirely the result of NATO expansion.

NATO's history will be one of tragedy. It began its existence as a heroic institution founded on the concept of defending the liberty of its members from vicious Communist ideologues to Europe's east. It did not seek to aggressively push itself or its ideas upon the Soviets to the East. NATO merely wanted to defend democratic and capitalistic Western Europe from the aggressive Soviet Union and the Warsaw Pact. When NATO collapses—and it likely will if the war expands into a direct conflict between NATO and Russian forces in Ukraine—historians will observe that heroic NATO survived long enough after the Cold War to see itself become the villain.

Let us hope and pray that an alternative route can be taken before the shooting begins. To achieve such a noble goal, however, requires an unconventional and even disruptive political leader in the United States. That person is Donald Trump, not Joe Biden. His policies, as outlined earlier in this work, protected NATO by forcing Europeans to prioritize the organization that they had spent decades underfunding all while deterring Putin from taking more aggressive action. Further, Trump's policies could again place the onus of European defense *on the Europeans*. In fact, if Trump is reelected, we may get lucky enough to either freeze the operations of NATO or disband the organization altogether in favor of a defensive alliance that doesn't engender the kind of war it was supposed to be preventing.[21]

Trump avoided conflict with Russia without acquiescing to

Moscow. Biden, on the other hand, has consistently invited conflict either through his weakness or his mindless commitment to the corrupt oligarchs in Ukraine. The 2024 presidential election in the United States is truly America's last, best hope to ensure it remains a great power in the next half of the twenty-first century—and to prevent a nuclear world war.

Even now that Biden is no longer running, his possible successor and current vice-president, Kamala Harris, will most definitely continue Biden's insanely aggressive policies in Ukraine if she is elected.

ACKNOWLEDGEMENTS

A Disaster of Our Own Making began as a scattering of ideas in print. While writing for the *Asia Times* contemporaneously with the Ukraine War, I began to see that the conflict was not what was being presented on our televisions. Having lived through the lies of the Iraq War (and having bought them at the time), I was immediately suspicious about what we were being told. It wasn't that Russia was the hero and Ukraine was the villain. Things rarely are that simple. Russia was wrong to have invaded, as I told my colleague Stephen K. Bannon on his hit podcast, *War Room*.

Russian forces, much like the Ukrainians, have committed egregious human rights violation. That is not the issue at hand, however. Instead the issues were understanding 1) how NATO involvement could assist Ukraine in preserving its sovereignty *without* risking wider war and 2) what was NATO's role in precipitating the conflict. From there, I attempted to understand—and explain—what we were actually seeing. For two years, the bulk of my articles at *Asia Times* centered on these issues.

At the end of 2022, I began to receive encouragement from an old friend, Tom Lipscomb. He had been sharing my articles questioning the official narrative about the Ukraine War and called me up one evening shortly after Christmas in 2022 to encourage me to write a book. I fiddled around with the concept for several months but finally tabled it because I didn't think there was anything I could do with it. Moreover, few reputable publishers wanted to talk to me because of the position the book was taking. Rejection followed rejection. For six months this dance continued. Finally, I set the project aside, not wanting to waste any more of my valuable time on something that wasn't going anywhere.

But then something happened in my analysis of the war that prompted me to pull the materials out in the Fall of 2023. Over that summer, there was a bizarre abortive coup attempt in Russia led by Vladimir Putin's former right-hand man, Yevgeny Prigozhin, the leader of the Wagner Group, Russia's largest mercenary force. I did not believe the official narrative that this was a spontaneous uprising against Putin. Instead, I believed that Prigozhin had fallen under the influence of Western intelligence services desperate to end this protracted war by getting rid of Putin. Needless to say, despite having heard these rumors from sources I trust with deep government experience, yet again no one was willing to say this in the media; no one was willing to speak the truth to the American people. So, I dusted off the incomplete manuscript, phoned up the folks at *Encounter* and asked if they wanted to do another project together.

They did. And I am grateful to Roger Kimball and his excellent team at *Encounter*. My previous book with Encounter, *Biohacked: China's Race to Control Life*, did exceedingly well for a book on such an esoteric topic. Their professionalism, patience, and persistence in getting a product out that represented their brand—and mine—is what made me want to go to them with this complex and controversial project in the first place.

I want to say here that this work is likely my most controversial. I resisted writing this for a long time. As you read in Curt Mills' brilliant foreword to this book, I was not initially in the restrainer camp. I thank everyone who encouraged me because doing this work could very well make me a pariah among my former colleagues in Washington, D.C., most of whom are committed neoconservatives and/or neoliberals. Regardless of the opposition from my former friends and colleague in Washington, D.C., I know that I have taken the correct position here.

I would like to thank the late, great Angelo Codevilla, who spent his final years with the folks over at the Claremont Institute. Angelo was more than just another academic. He was a former, high-ranking government official with decades of experience in U.S. intelligence policy. Codevilla wrote multiple bestselling books on the subject of national security that are still required reading for those of us who work in the national security space. I became personally acquainted with Codevilla in 2017. We had met at a Claremont Institute event in Washington, D.C. He approached me in his typical gregarious fashion and proceeded to tell me that he enjoyed my work (at that time I was working for *American Greatness* and *The American Spectator*). After that event, Codevilla and I remained pen pals writing emails intermittently and exchanging pleasantries.

Angelo died unexpectedly in 2020. But before he died, he had spent the previous several months giving me critiques and providing insight for my first book, *Winning Space: How American Remains a Superpower*. His hand can be felt throughout that work. Codevilla was a tough old bird. We didn't agree on everything. Who does? But we agreed on much. And as the terrible 2020s have progressed since his death, I find that, most often where we differed, he was right, and I was wrong.

F.H. Buckley is another man I must thank. A friend and colleague, Buckley is the reason I came to know the folks at *Encounter*. He is one of the best independent political thinkers and writers in America today. And he has been a steadfast supporter of my work. For that, I am eternally grateful.

Gordon and Lydia Chang are also two people who I would like to thank. After getting to know each other on the lecture circuit, we have maintained a wonderful friendship and an excellent working relationship. I appreciate them and their commitment to freedom.

Former Congressman Thaddeus McCotter (R-MI), who gave a highly enlightening talk about U.S. foreign policy toward Russia while we were on the lecture circuit together should get an honorable mention here. He's got a unique insight into the world and the many speaking engagements we have done together continue to enlighten and inform my work. His take on Russia is both original and unique and I incorporated some of his arguments in this this work.

I'd also like to tip my hat to Curt Mills of *The American Conservative* for being willing to write the foreword to this book. Curt is another rising star on the Right whose foreign policy insights are always worth noting. I know that I have followed his work for many years. I am honored that he took the time to write the foreword.

Relatedly, thank you to Reid Smith for facilitating some of the connections that were necessary for completing this project. His tireless commitment to the truth and his assistance at the end of this project were instrumental in helping me to finish this herculean task of taking on the conventional wisdom of our time on this issue. I hope to have many more interactions with him over the next several years.

My old editors at *American Greatness*, Ben Boychuk and Julie Ponzi, came through for me in a big way during this project. Because I signed the contract with Encounter Books to complete this project in an insanely short amount of time—with a newborn at home—I worried about the finished product here. I knew that all this work needed was a reliable editor who could talk sense into me when needed. I called Ben to vent a week before the manuscript was due and express my concerns about the need for an editor who understood me. Without missing a beat, Ben told me to call Julie and see if she'd be willing to take on this project. I did. She was willing. Encounter supported bringing her on. The rest is history. Julie edited my work at *AG* from 2016-2023. If there is any editor who understands my style and who knows how to tell me to drop something or to make a vital change, it's her. And the work is better for it. So, I thank Julie and Ben for coming through for me on this one.

There were many others who went into helping me with this book. I have been blessed to have a career in government as well as in consulting that has allowed for me to meet well-connected individuals in our intelligence apparatus. Specifically, there are people within the Defense Intelligence Agency (DIA), National Geospatial Intelligence Agency (NGA), National Ground Intelligence Center, the Defense Threat Reduction Agency (DTRA), and National Security Agency (NSA) who have proven to be essential in my work. All these people insist on remaining on background for fear of reprisals to their careers, reputation, and families. But they know who they are, and I am eternally grateful to them for their courage both in serving our country and helping to get the truth out.

My final shout out goes to Dr. Richard Farkas of DePaul University's political science department. Dr. Farkas was my professor for several components of Russian studies that I had taken as an undergraduate (one of those was a graduate level course I did as an undergrad during my senior year). A taciturn and rigorous educator, I learned more about Russia from a single quarter of being in his class than I ever did working in government. Although, he had an annoying tendency to call me, "Brian," (which I suspect he did to tweak me), his insight and knowledge of Russia made me a better expert on this most unique and confusing country that has simultaneously plagued and dazzled U.S. foreign policymakers for decades.

Lastly, given what is happening in our national politics—the censorship and the political witch hunts directed against people who lean to the Right—I have long believed that people like me will eventually be squelched by an increasingly authoritarian central government. At some point, I fear, my work will lead me to a very disturbing place both professionally and personally. I only hope that this book, like my other ones, will continue to provide insight and help others navigate this most dangerous and corrupt time in which we are living.

BIBLIOGRAPHY

"15 Years Ago, Russia Invaded Georgia Under the Pretext of Supporting Separatists." *The New Voice of Ukraine*. August 8, 2023. https://english.nv.ua/nation/15-years-ago-russia-invaded-georgia-under-the-pretext-of-supporting-separatists-50344641.html

(1985) The Battle at Kulikovo Field, Soviet Studies in History, 24:1-2, 11-44, DOI: 10.2753/RSH1061-198324010211

"A Fatal Friendship?" *Wall Street Journal*. December 17, 2010. https://www.wsj.com/articles/SB10001424052748704828104576021823816289798

Abelow, Benjamin. *How the West Brought War to Ukraine: Understanding How U.S. and NATO Policies Led to Crisis, War, and the Risk of Nuclear Catastrophe* (Great Barrington, MA: Siland Press, 2023)

Abely, Christina. *The Russia Sanctions: The Economic Response to Russia's Invasion of Ukraine* (London: Cambridge University Press, 2023)

Adams, Paul. "Classified Ministry of Defence Documents Found at Bus Stop." *BBC*. June 27, 2021. https://www.bbc.com/news/uk-57624942

Adelman, Ken. "Cakewalk in Iraq." *Washington Post*. February 12, 2002. https://www.washingtonpost.com/archive/opinions/2002/02/13/cakewalk-in-iraq/cf0930c-c6c4-4f2e-8268-7c93017f5e93/

Ahlander, Johan and Ringstrom, Anna. "Sweden Ends Nord Stream Sabotage Probe, Hands Evidence to Germany." *Reuters*. February 7, 2024. https://www.reuters.com/world/europe/sweden-ends-investigation-into-nord-stream-p pipeline-blasts-2024-02-07/#:~:text=The%20multi%2Dbillion%20dollar%20Nord,of%20methane%20into%20the%20air

Ainger, John. "NATO Members Ramp Up Defense Spending After Pressure from Trump." *Bloomberg.* March 16, 2021. https://www.bloomberg.com/news/articles/2021-03-16/nato-members-ramp-up-defense-spending-after-pressure-from-trump?embedded-checkout=true

Allison, George. "German Military Short on Tanks and Combat Aircraft for NATO Mission." *UK Defence Journal.* February 19, 2018. https://ukdefencejournal.org.uk/german-military-short-tanks-combat-aircraft-nato-mission/

Allison, George. "Less Than a Third of German Military Assets are Operational, Says Report." *UK Defence Journal.* June 21, 2018. https://ukdefencejournal.org.uk/less-third-german-military-assets-operational-says-report/

Al Maydeen English. "Polish EU Lawmaker Deletes 'Thank You, USA' Over Nord Stream Tweet." *Al Maydeen.* September 29, 2022. https://english.almayadeen.net/news/politics/polish-eu-lawmaker-deletes-thank-you-usa-over-nord-stream-tw

Aref, Anees. "The 'Great Game': Fiction and Folly in World Empire." *Responsible Statecraft.* June 19, 2023. https://responsiblestatecraft.org/2023/06/19/the-great-game-fiction-and-folly-in-world-empire/

Ash, Timothy Garton. "Postimperial Empire: How the War in Ukraine is Transforming Europe." *Foreign Affairs.* May/June 2023. https://www.foreignaffairs.com/ukraine/europe-war-russia-postimperial-empire

Baker, Peter and Eilperin, Juliet. "Clinton Impeached: House Approves Articles Alleging Perjury, Obstruction." *Washington Post.* December 20, 1998. https://www.washingtonpost.com/politics/clinton-impeachment/clinton-impeached-house-approves-articles-alleging-perjury-obstruction/

Baker, Peter and Glaser, Susan B. "Putin Threatens Attacks on Chechens in Georgia." *Washington Post.* September 13, 2002. https://www.washingtonpost.com/archive/politics/2002/09/13/putin-threatens-attacks-on-chechens-in-georgia/e68ff41b-1fac-40cc-9ea9-92c5a1f14036/

Baker, Peter. "U.S.-Russian Ties Still Fall Short of 'Reset' Goal." *New York Times.* September 2, 2013. https://www.nytimes.com/2013/09/03/world/europe/us-russian-ties-still-fall-short-of-reset-goal.html?_r=0&pagewanted=all&

Baldor, Lolita C. and Copp, Tara. "Pentagon Accounting Error Provides Extra $6.2 Billion for Ukraine Military Aid." *AP.* June 20, 2023. https://apnews.com/article/ukraine-russia-war-weapons-surplus-funding-72eeb6119439146f1939d5b1973a44ef

Beauchamp, Zack. "Donald Trump Needs to Clarify His Position on NATO Before Something Scary Happens." *Vox.* November 10, 2016. https://www.vox.com/2016/7/21/12247074/donald-trump-nato-war

Belton, Catherine. *Putin's People: How the KGB Took Back Russia and Then Took on the West* (New York: Farrar, Straus & Giroux, 2020).

Benson, Brett V. and Smith, Bradley C. "NATO's Membership Rules Invite Conflict—and Benefit Putin." *Washington Post.* February 24, 2022. https://www.washingtonpost.com/outlook/2022/02/22/natos-membership-rules-invite-conflict-benefit-putin/

Bento, John "Russia's Aggression is Really About Warm Water Ports: Guest Opinion." *The Oregonian,* March 17, 2014. https://www.oregonlive.com/opinion/2014/03/russias_aggression_is_really_a.html

Bertrand, Natasha and Cheney, Kyle. "'I'm on a Mission to Testify': Dem Ukraine Activist Eager for Impeachment Cameo." *Politico.* November 12, 2019. https://www.politico.com/news/2019/11/12/alexandra-chalupa-testify-impeachment-069817

Bertrand, Natasha. "Hunter Biden Story is Russian Disinfo, Dozens of Former Intel Officials Say." *Politico.* October 19, 2020. https://www.politico.com/news/2020/10/19/hunter-biden-story-russian-disinfo-430276

Bielieskov, Mykola. "The Russian and Ukrainian Spring 2021 War Scare." *CSIS.* September 21, 2021. https://www.csis.org/analysis/russian-and-ukrainian-spring-2021-war-scare

Bishara, Marwan. "Reckless in Kiev: Neocons, Putin, and Ukraine." *Al Jazeera.* March 10, 2014. https://www.aljazeera.com/opinions/2014/3/10/reckless-in-kiev-neocons-putin-and-Ukraine

Bishara, Marwan. "Western Media and the War on Truth in Ukraine." *Al Jazeera.* August 4, 2022. https://www.aljazeera.com/opinions/2022/8/4/western-media-and-the-war-on-truth-in

Blinken, Antony J. "Secretary Antony J. Blinken and Canadian Foreign Minister Mélanie Joly at a Joint Press Availability." *U.S. Department of State.* September 30, 2022. https://www.state.gov/secretary-antony-j-blinken-and-canadian-foreign-minister-melanie-joly-at-a-joint-press-availability/#:~:text=It's%20a%20tremendous,years%20to%20come

Boot, Max, Power, Samanth, and Garfinkle, Adam. "The Bush Doctrine." *PBS.* July 11, 2002. https://www.pbs.org/thinktank/transcript1000.html

Borger, Miriam and Taylor, Adam. "Why Poison is the Weapon of Choice in Putin's Russia." *Washington Post*. August 21, 2020. https://www.washingtonpost.com/world/2020/08/21/why-poison-is-weapon-choice-putins-russia/

Bort, Julie. "'No Drama Obama' Shares His Tricks for Staying Cool Under Pressure." *Business Insider*. March 10, 2019. https://www.businessinsider.com/obama-shares-tricks-for-cool-under-pressure-2019-3

Breaking News, Forbes. "JUST IN: Ted Cruz Confronts Top Biden Official Over Nord Stream 2 Decision," *YouTube*, January 26, 2023, 0:57-1:07, https://www.youtube.com/watch?v=VJdbMj8fStA

Brennan, David. "'A Total F***k Up': Russian Mercenaries in Syria Lament U.S. Strike That Killed Dozens." *Newsweek*. February 23, 2018. https://www.newsweek.com/total-f-russian-mercenaries-syria-lament-us-strike-killed-dozens-818073

Brychkov, A.S. and Nikonorov, G.A. "Color Revolutions in Russia: Possibility and Reality." *Journal of the Academy of Military Science*. 3, 60, 2017. https://www.armyupress.army.mil/Portals/7/Hot%20Spots/Documents/Russia/Color-Revolutions-Brychkov-Nikonorov.pdf

Bryen, Stephen. "Biden's Emerging New Ukraine Policy." *Asia Times*. February 5, 2024. https://asiatimes.com/2024/02/bidens-emerging-new-ukraine-policy/

Bryen, Stephen. "The Failed Biden-Putin Summit and Fears of War." *Asia Times*. July 2, 2021. https://asiatimes.com/2021/07/the-failed-biden-putin-summit-and-fears-of-war/

Bryen, Stephen. "Regime Change is Coming – To Kiev." *Asia Times*. February 20, 2024. https://asiatimes.com/2024/02/regime-change-is-coming-to-kiev/

Bryen, Stephen. "Zaluzhny Out, Oleksandr Syrsky In, to What Purpose?" *Asia Times*. February 9, 2024. https://asiatimes.com/2024/02/zaluzhny-out-oleksandr-syrsky-in-to-what-purpose/

Brzezinski, Mika and Schumer, Chuck. "Sen. Schumer to Speaker Johnson: Do the Right Thing on the Border Bill." *MSNBC*. February 5, 2024. 10:44. https://www.youtube.com/watch?v=QFt6Rhccg6s

Burchard, Hans von der. "Germany to Put 2 Percent NATO Spending Pledge in Writing." *Politico EU*. March 16, 2023. https://www.politico.eu/article/olaf-schlz-germany-nato-jens-stoltenberg-commits-to-2-percent-defense-spending-under-security-strategy/

Budjeryn, Mariana and Bunn, Matthew. "Budapest Memorandum at 25: Between Past and Future," *Project on Managing the Atom,* March 2020. https://www. belfercenter.org/sites/default/files/2020-03/budapest/BM25.pdf

Bumbar, Mickey. "How the Love for Drinking Drove the Kievan Rus to Christianity," *Lord of the Drinks,* December 2, 2017. https://lordsofthedrinks. org/2017/12/12/how-the-love-for-drinking-drove-the-kievan-rus-to-christianity/

Bump, Philip. "Hillary Clinton's Campaign Was Crippled by Voters Who Stayed Home." *The Washington Post.* November 9, 2016. https://www.washingtonpost. com/news/the-fix/wp/2016/11/09/hillary-clintons-campaign-was-crippled-by-voters-who-stayed-home/

Bush, George H.W. "September 11, 1990: Address Before a Joint Session of Congress." *UVA Miller Center.* https://millercenter.org/the-presidency/presidential-speeches/september-11-1990-address-joint-session-congress

"Bush on the Freedom Agenda." *Voice of America.* September 4, 2006. https://editorials.voa.gov/a/a-41-2006-09-05-voa8-83105922/1479604.html

"Bush: 'You Are Either With Us, Or With the Terrorists." *Voice of America.* October 27, 2009. https://www.voanews.com/a/a-13-a-2001-09-21-14-bush-66411197/549664.html

Butt, Usman. "The Neoconservatives Who Paved the Road to Invading Iraq." *Middle East Monitor.* March 19, 2023. https://www.middleeastmonitor. com/20230319-the-neoconservatives-who-paved-the-road-to-invading-iraq/

Cameron, David R. "Frustrated by Refusals to Give Russia Security Guarantees & Implement Minsk 2, Putin Recgonizes Pseudo-States in Donbas and Invades Ukraine." *Yale Macmillan Center.* February 24, 2022. https://macmillan. yale.edu/news/frustrated-refusals-give-russia-security-guarantees-implement-minsk-2-putin-recognizes-pseudo

Caputo, Michael R. *The Ukraine Hoax: How Decades of Corruption in the Former Soviet Republic Led to Trump's Phony Impeachment* (New York: Bombardier Books, 2020).

Carlson, Tucker and Bobulinski, Tony. "Tony Bobulinski Reveals Details on Hunter Biden Business Dealings in Exclusive Interview with Tucker Carlson." *Fox News.* October 4, 2022. https://www.foxnews.com/video/6313250859112

Carlson, Tucker and Putin, Vladimir. "The Vladimir Putin Interview." *Tucker Carlson Network.* February 5, 2024. 2:07:18. https://tuckercarlson.com/the-vladimir-putin-interview/

Carpenter, Ted Galen. "Four Western Provocations That Led to U.S.-Russia Crisis

Today." *CATO Institute*. December 28, 2021. https://www.cato.org/commentary/four-western-provocations-led-us-russia-crisis-today

Carpenter, Ted Galen. "Ignored Warnings: How NATO Expansion Led to the Current Ukraine Tragedy." *CATO Institute*. February 24, 2022. https://www.cato.org/commentary/ignored-warnings-how-nato-expansion-led-current-ukraine-tragedy

Carpenter, Ted Galen. "Many Predicted NATO Expansion Would Lead to War. Those Warnings Were Ignored." *CATO Institute*. February 28, 2022. https://www.cato.org/commentary/many-predicted-nato-expansion-would-lead-war-those-warnings-were-ignored

Cawthorne, Cameron. "Hunter Biden's Texts, Emails Contradict Lawyer's Claim That He 'Did Not Share' Money from Businesses with Dad." *Fox News*. September 18, 2023. https://www.foxnews.com/politics/hunter-bidens-texts-emails-contradict-lawyers-claim-did-not-share-money-businesses-dad

Chamberlain, Ken. "How Much Do NATO Members Spend on Defense?" *Navy Times*. March 10, 2018. https://www.navytimes.com/global/europe/2018/03/10/how-much-do-nato-member-nations-spend-on-defense/

Chang, Alvin. "How Russian Hackers Stole Information from Democrats, in 3 Simple Diagrams." *Vox*. June 16, 2018. https://www.vox.com/policy-and-politics/2018/7/16/17575940/russian-election-hack-democrats-trump-putin-diagram

Chappell, Bill. "2 Agents Carried Out Skirpal Poison Attack, U.K. Says; Arrest Warrants Issued." *NPR*. September 5, 2018. https://www.npr.org/2018/09/05/644782096/u-k-charges-2-russians-suspected-of-poison-attack-on-skripals

Chappel, Bill and Ritchie, L. Carol. "Crimea Overwhelmingly Supports Split from Ukraine to Join Russia." *NPR*. March 16, 2014. https://www.npr.org/sections/thetwo-way/2014/03/16/290525623/crimeans-vote-on-splitting-from-ukraine-to-join-russia

Chauhan, Tanvi. "Why Are Warm Water Ports Important to Russian Security?" *Journal of European, Middle Easter, and African Affairs*. Spring 2020. https://www.airuniversity.af.edu/Portals/10/JEMEAA/Journals/Volume-02_Issue-1/Chauhan.pdf

Cheng, Evelyn. "Who is Paul Manafort? A Brief Timeline of His Political Career." *CNBC*. October 30, 2017. https://www.cnbc.com/2017/10/30/who-is-paul-manafort-a-brief-timeline-of-his-political-career.html

Chen, Joyce. "Hillary Recalls Encounter with 'Manspreading' Vladimir Putin." *Rolling Stone*, September 20, 2017. https://www.rollingstone.com/tv-movies/tv-movie-news/hillary-clinton-recalls-encounter-with-manspreading-vladimir-putin-202893/

"China Stands Firm in Support of Russia on Ukraine Issue Despite US Pressure." *TASS*. January 23, 2024. https://tass.com/world/1739709

Clarke, Richard A. *Against All Enemies: Inside America's War on Terror* (New York: Free Press, 2004)

Cleave, Iona. "Living in Fear: How Putin's Biggest Fear About Being 'Killed Like Gaddafi' Almost Came True as Wagner Group Stormed Towards Moscow," *U.S. Sun*, June 25, 2023. https://www.the-sun.com/news/8451864/putin-biggest-fear-killed-gaddafi-coming-true-wagner/

Coalson, Robert. "Obama and the Russians: Moving on to the 'Post-Reset'." *Radio Free Europe/Radio Liberty*. November 7, 2012. https://www.rferl.org/a/obama-russia-moving-on-post-reset-relations/24763754.html

Codevilla, Angelo. *America's Rise and Fall Among Nations: Lessons in Statecraft from John Quincy Adams* (New York: Encounter Books, 2022)

Collinson, Stephen. "The West Must Now Consider the Possibility of a Russian Military Collapse." *CNN*. June 26, 2023. https://www.cnn.com/2023/06/26/politics/wagner-putin-us-ukraine-analysis/index.html

Colman, Zack and Lefebvre, Ben. "'Everything is Pointing to Russia': U.S., EU Officials On Edge Over Pipeline Explosions." *Politico*. September 28, 2022. https://www.politico.com/news/2022/09/28/nord-stream-pipeline-explosions-eu-00059262

"Comer Releases Third Bank Memo Detailing Payments to the Bidens from Russia, Kazakshstan, and Ukraine." *House Committee on Oversight and Accountability*. August 9, 2023. https://oversight.house.gov/release/comer-releases-third-bank-memo-detailing-payments-to-the-bidens-from-russia-kazakhstan-and-ukraine%EF%BF%BC/

Condon, Stephanie. "Hillary Clinton: The vast, Right-wing Conspiracy is 'Even Better Funded Now." *CBS News*. February 3, 2016. https://www.cbsnews.com/news/hillary-clinton-the-vast-right-wing-conspiracy-is-even-better-funded-now/

Conant, Eve. "Russia and Ukraine: The Tangled History That Connects—and Divides—Them." *National Geographic,* February 24, 2023. https://www.nationalgeographic.com/history/article/russia-and-ukraine-the-tangled-history-that-connects-and-divides-them

Conradi, Peter. *Who Lost Russia? How the World Entered a New Cold War,* (London: Oneworld Publications, 2017).

Cooper, Helene. Gibbons-Neff, Thomas, Schmitt, Eric, and Barnes, Julian E. "Ukraine War Casualties Near Half a Million, US Officials Say." *New York Times.* August 18, 2023. https://www.nytimes.com/2023/08/18/us/politics/ukraine-russia-war-casualties.html

Cordell, Jake. "Putin Uses New Year Address for Wartime Rallying Cry to Russians." *Reuters.* December 31, 2022. https://www.reuters.com/world/europe/putin-says-new-year-message-west-is-using-ukraine-destroy-russia-2022-12-31/

Cordell, Jake. "Rewriting History, Putin Pitches Russia as Defender of an Expanding Motherland." *The Moscow Times.* February 22, 2022. https://www.themoscowtimes.com/2022/02/22/rewriting-history-putin-pitches-russia-as-defender-of-an-expanding-motherland-a76518

Cramer, Andrew and Gordon, Michael R. "Ukraine Reports Russian Invasion on a New Front." *New York Times.* August 27, 2014. https://www.nytimes.com/2014/08/28/world/europe/ukraine-russia-novoazovsk-crimea.html

Cross, Samuel Hazard and Sherbowitz-Wetzor, Olgerd P. *The Russian Primary Chronicle: Laurentian Text* (Cambridge, MA: The Medieval Academy of America, 2012).

Crowley, Michael. "The Reinvention of Robert Gates." *The New Republic.* November 9, 2009. https://newrepublic.com/article/70991/the-reinvention-robert-gates

Crowley, Michael and Ioffe, Julia. "Why Putin Hates Hillary." *Politico.* 25 July 2016. https://www.politico.com/story/2016/07/clinton-putin-226153

Daalder, Ivo H. and Lindsay, James H. "The Bush Revolution: The Remaking of America's Foreign Policy." *The Brookings Institution.* April 2003. https://www.brookings.edu/wp-content/uploads/2016/06/20030425.pdf

Dannreuther, Roland. "Why the Arab Spring Set Russia on the Road to Confrontation with the West." *LSE.* January 16, 2015. https://blogs.lse.ac.uk/europpblog/2015/01/16/why-the-arab-spring-set-russia-on-the-road-to-confrontation-with-the-west/

Davenport, Christian, Nakashima, Ellen, et al. "With a Dire Warning, Concerns Rise About Conflict in Space with Russia." *Washington Post*. February 15, 2024. https://www.washingtonpost.com/technology/2024/02/15/space-weapons-russia-china-starlink/

Day, Joel. "Putin's Catherine the Great Ideology Could Hold the Key to His Future Plans." *Daily Express*. November 16, 2022. https://www.express.co.uk/news/world/1696403/putin-latest-novorossiya-new-russia-ukraine-catherine-the-great-spt

"Defence Expenditures of NATO Countries (2014-2023)." *North Atlantic Treaty Organization*. July 7, 2023. https://www.nato.int/cps/en/natohq/news_216897.htm?selectedLocale=en

Denison, Benjamin. "Where US Sees Democracy Promotion, Russia Sees Regime Change," *Russia Matters*, July 29, 2020. https://www.russiamatters.org/analysis/where-us-sees-democracy-promotion-russia-sees-regime-change

Devine, Miranda. "Hunter Biden's Biz Partner Called Joe Biden 'the Big Guy' in Panicked Message After Post's Laptop Story." *New York Post*. July 27, 2022. https://nypost.com/2022/07/27/hunter-bidens-biz-partner-called-joe-biden-the-big-guy-in-panic-over-laptop/

Devine, Miranda. *Laptop from Hell: Hunter Biden, Big Tech, and the Dirty Secrets the President Tried to Hide* (New York: Liberatio Protocol Book, 2021).

Devlin, Bradley. "The Distressing Death of Alexei Navalny." *The American Conservative*. February 16, 2024. https://www.theamericanconservative.com/the-distressing-death-of-alexei-navalny/

Diamond, Jeremy. "NATO Summit: Trump Accuses Germany of Being a 'Captive of Russia.'" *CNN*. July 11, 2018. https://www.cnn.com/2018/07/11/politics/trump-germany-russia-captive-nato/index.html

Dickinson, Peter. "How Ukraine's Orange Revolution Shaped Twenty-First Century Geopolitics." *Atlantic Council*. November 22, 2020. https://www.atlanticcouncil.org/blogs/ukrainealert/how-ukraines-orange-revolution-shaped-twenty-first-century-geopolitics/

"Did Hunter Biden Receive $3.5 Million from the Former Mayor of Moscow's Wife?" *CNN*. https://www.cnn.com/factsfirst/politics/factcheck_e879bcfe-4b2a-4b4a-a823-8c6d512c4e5e

Dilanian, Ken. "Former CIA Director: We Worried Arming Ukraine Would Hand Technology to Russian Spies." *NBC News.* November 22, 2019. https://www.nbcnews.com/politics/national-security/former-cia-director-we-worried-arming-ukraine-would-hand-technology-n1089926

Dizikes, Peter. "Foreign Policy Scholars Examine the China-Russia Relationship." *MIT News.* November 17, 2023. https://news.mit.edu/2023/foreign-policy-scholars-examine-china-russia-relationship-1117

Dogan, Cem. "Snow-White, Curvy, and Virgin: Concubinage and the Origins of White Slave Traffic in Ottoman Istanbul (1850-1920), *International Journal of Economics, Politics, Humanities, & Social Sciences,* Vol: 4, Issue: 3, Summer 2021. https://dergipark.org.tr/tr/download/article-file/1561483

Doornbos, Caitlin. "Durham Points to Clinton Crony Charles Dolan as Likely 'Pee Tape' Source from Notorious Steele Dossier Report." *New York Post.* May 16, 2023. https://nypost.com/2023/05/16/durham-points-to-clinton-crony-charles-dolan-as-likely-pee-tape-source-from-notorious-steele-dossier-report/

Dorning, Mike. "Obama Saw Too Late Putin's Return Would Undermine Reset." *Bloomberg,* February 19, 2015. https://www.bloomberg.com/news/articles/2015-02-19/obama-putin?embedded-checkout=true

Dorrien, *Imperial Designs: Neoconservatism and the New Pax Americana* (New York: Routledge, 2004).

Dougherty, Michael Brendan. "Krauthammer: Biden Holds 'American Record for Wrong on Most Issues in Foreign Affairs Ever." *Business Insider.* April 27, 2012. https://www.businessinsider.com/krauthammer-biden-holds-american-record-for-wrong-on-the-most-issues-in-foreign-affairs-ever-2012-4

Draper, Robert. "William Burns, a C.I.A. Spymaster with Unusual Powers." *New York Times.* May 9, 2023. https://www.nytimes.com/2023/05/09/us/politics/william-burns-cia-biden.html

Dresen, F. Joseph. "The Piratization of Russia: Russian Reform Goes Awry." *Wilson Center.* https://www.wilsoncenter.org/publication/the-piratization-russia-russian-reform-goes-awry

Durbin, Adam. "Ukraine War: Germany Sends Much-Awaited Leopard Tanks." *BBC.* March 28, 2023. https://www.bbc.com/news/world-europe-65095126#

"Economic Key Facts: Germany." *KPMG.* January 8, 2024. https://kpmg.com/de/en/home/insights/overview/economic-key-facts-germany.html#:~:text=Germany%20is%20the%20fourth%20largest,the%20country%27s%20gross%20domestic%20product

Edelman, Adam. "Hillary Clinton 'Convinced' Trump Associates Colluded with Russia." *NBC News*. September 12, 2017. https://www.nbcnews.com/politics/hillary-clinton/hillary-clinton-convinced-trump-associates-colluded-russia-n800566

Elder, Miriam. "Vladimir Putin Accuses Hillary Clinton of Encouraging Russian Protests." *The Guardian*. December 8, 2011. https://www.theguardian.com/world/2011/dec/08/vladimir-putin-hillary-clinton-russia

Ellyatt, Holly. "Russia is Risking All-Out War to Prevent Ukraine from Joining NATO." *CNBC*. January 12, 2022. https://www.cnbc.com/2022/01/12/russia-is-risking-all-out-war-to-prevent-ukraine-from-joining-nato.html

Emil, Payin. "Population Transfer: The Crimean Tatars Return Home." *Cultural Survival*, March 5, 2010. https://www.culturalsurvival.org/publications/cultural-survival-quarterly/population-transfer-crimean-tatars-return-home

"The Enigma of Russia." *International Churchill Society*. April 3, 2022. https://winstonchurchill.org/publications/churchill-bulletin/bulletin-166-apr-2022/the-enigma-of-russia/

"Facts and Figures on the European Union Economy." *European Union*. https://european-union.europa.eu/principles-countries-history/key-facts-and-figures/economy_en

Faiola, Anthony. "Germany Got Rich on Exports and Cheap Russian Gas. Now, It's in Trouble." *Washington Post*. October 14, 2022. https://www.washingtonpost.com/world/2022/10/14/germany-economy-recession-energy-exports/

Figes, Orlando. *The Story of Russia* (New York: Metropolitan Books, 2022).

Fisher, Max. "Everything You Need to Know About the 2014 Ukraine Crisis." *Vox*. September 3, 2014. https://www.vox.com/2014/9/3/18088560/ukraine-everything-you-need-to-know

"Former German Chancellor Gerhard Schroeder Becomes Chairman of Russian State-Controlled Nord Stream Pipeline Company Directly After Leaving Office." *Alliance for Defending Democracy*. November 2005. https://securingdemocracy.gmfus.org/incident/former-german-chancellor-gerhard-schrader-becomes-chairman-of-russian-state-controlled-nord-stream-pipeline-company-directly-after-leaving-office/

Foundation, Ronald Reagan. "Nixon Warned That This Would Happen to Russia (1992)." *YouTube*. December 7, 2023. 2:34.https://www.youtube.com/watch?v=kgG_fLNBv6A

Fredericks, Bob. "Clintons Gear Up to Cash In On the Lecture Circuit." *New York Post*. October 8, 2018. https://nypost.com/2018/10/08/clintons-gear-up-to-cash-in-on-the-lecture-circuit/

"Freedom Agenda." *The White House: President George W. Bush*. December 10, 2008. https://georgewbush-whitehouse.archives.gov/infocus/freedomagenda/

Friedman, Thomas L. "This Putin's War. But America and NATO Aren't Innocent Bystanders." *New York Times*. February 21, 2022. https://www.nytimes.com/2022/02/21/opinion/putin-ukraine-nato.html

"Funding NATO." *North Atlantic Treaty Organization*. https://www.nato.int/cps/en/natohq/topics_67655.htm#:~:text=The%202%25%20defence%20invest-ment%20guideline,ensure%20the%20Alliance%27s%20military%20readiness

Gaddis, John Lewis. *Surprise, Security, and the American Experience* (Cambridge: Harvard University Press, 2005).

Gallis, Paul. "The NATO Summit at Bucharest, 2008." *Congressional Research Service*. May 5, 2008. https://sgp.fas.org/crs/row/RS22847.pdf

Gardener, Hall. "Ukraine: A New Plan." *American Affairs Journal*. Summer 2017. Vol. 1, No. 2. https://americanaffairsjournal.org/2017/05/ukraine-new-plan/

Gaouette, Nicole. "FBI's Comey: Republicans Also Hacked by Russia." *CNN*. January 2017. https://www.cnn.com/2017/01/10/politics/comey-republi-cans-hacked-russia/index.html

Gavin, Gabrielle, Busvine, Douglas, Toosi, Nahal, et al. "Wagner Boss Prigozhin Killed in Jet Crash in Russia." *Politico EU*. August 23, 2023. https://www.polit-ico.eu/article/jet-believed-to-be-carrying-wagner-boss-prigozhin-crashes-in-russia/

Gentleman, Amelia. "Putin Dodges Ukraine Scandal." *The Guardian*. February 12, 2001. https://www.theguardian.com/world/2001/feb/12/worlddispatch.ameliagentleman

Gera, Vanessa. "AP Interview: Ex-Polish President Defends Biden and Burisma." *AP*. November 28, 2019. https://apnews.com/article/37424b8a0a994c1a-935c5831643a84e3#

Gera, Vanessa. "Poland is Done Sending Arms to Ukraine, Polish Leaders Says as Trade Dispute Escalates." *AP*. September 21, 2023. https://apnews.com/article/poland-ukraine-weapons-russia-war-trade-dispute-5e2e7a194b5238b-86c160f0f4848b4f3#

Gera, Vanessa and Scislowska, Monika. "Poland's New Prime Minister Vows to Press the West to Continue Helping Neighboring Ukraine." *AP*. October 12, 2023. https://apnews.com/article/poland-new-government-tusk-d4c7cd71e-983440b5a71e08236eaf4fc

Gertz, Bill. "China Linking with Russia, Iran and North Korea Poses Dangerous Threat to U.S., Former Leaders Warn." *Washington Times*. January 30, 2024. https://www.washingtontimes.com/news/2024/jan/30/china-linking-with-russia-iran-and-north-korea-pos/

Ghattas, Kim. "What a Decade-Old Conflict Tells Us About Putin." *The Atlantic*. March 6, 2022. https://www.theatlantic.com/international/archive/2022/03/libya-russia-ukraine-putin/626571/

Ghitis, Frida. "Why Putin Fears a Clinton Presidency." *CNN*. October 16, 2016. https://www.cnn.com/2016/10/15/opinions/putin-clinton-hate-affair-ghitis/index.html

Gibbons-Neff, Thomas. "How a 4-Hour Battle Between Russian Mercenaries and U.S. Commandos Unfolded in Syria." *New York Times*. May 24, 2018. https://www.nytimes.com/2018/05/24/world/middleeast/american-commandos-russian-mercenaries-syria.html

Glasser, Susan B. and Baker, Peter. "Inside the War Between Trump and His Generals." *New Yorker*. August 8, 2022. https://www.newyorker.com/magazine/2022/08/15/inside-the-war-between-trump-and-his-generals

Glucroft, William Noah. "NATO: Why Russia Has a Problem with Its Eastward Expansion." *DW*. February 23, 2022. https://www.dw.com/en/nato-why-russia-has-a-problem-with-its-eastward-expansion/a-60891681

Goble, Paul A. "Crimea: A New 9/11 for the United States." *Council of American Ambassadors*. Spring 2014. https://www.americanambassadors.org/publications/ambassadors-review/spring-2014/crimea-a-new-9-11-for-the-united-states

Goldenberg, Tia. "Former Israeli PM: Putin Promised Not to Kill Zelenskyy." *AP*. February 5, 2023. https://apnews.com/article/russia-ukraine-putin-politics-government-4ea6bd21cb2ac96dae731ceoe8ac2f22

Goldgeier, James. "NATO's Enlargement Didn't Cause Russian Aggression," *Carnegie Endowment for International Peace*, July 31, 2023. https://carnegieendowment.org/2023/07/31/nato-enlargement-didn-t-cause-russia-s-aggression-pub 90300#:~:text=In%20reality%2C%20it%20has%20been,it%20mischaracterizes%20the%20impetus%20for

Goldgeier, James. *Not Whether, But When* (Washington, D.C.: Brookings Institute, 1999).

Goldstein, David. "2 Clinton Supporters in '08 Reportedly Shared Obama 'Birther' Story." *McClatchy DC.* September 16, 2016. https://www.mcclatchydc.com/news/politics-government/election/article102354777.html

Gomez, Eric. "Soviet Nukes in Ukraine: A Bargaining Chip, Not a Deterrent." *CATO Institute.* March 6, 2022. https://www.cato.org/blog/soviet-nukes-ukraine-bargaining-chip-not-deterrent. February 2022

https://nucleardiner.wordpress.com/2022/02/06/could-ukraine-have-retained-soviet-nuclear-weapons/

Gramm, Jr., Thomas. "U.S. Role in Chechnya." *Carnegie Endowment for International Peace.* December 10, 1999. https://carnegieendowment.org/1999/12/10/u.s.-role-in-chechnya-pub-182

Grand, Camille. "Defence Spending: Sustaining the Effort in the Long-Term." *North Atlantic Treaty Organization.* July 3, 2023. https://www.nato.int/docu/review/articles/2023/07/03/defence-spending-sustaining-the-effort-in-the-long-term/index.html

Greenblatt, Alan. "Frenemies Forever: Why Putin and Obama Can't Get Along." *NPR.* September 12, 2013. https://www.npr.org/2013/09/12/221774010/frenemies-forever-why-putin-and-obama-cant-get-along

Greenburg, Karen J. "'The Emergency State: America's Pursuit of Absolute Security at All Costs' by David Unger and 'Permanent Emergency: Inside the TSA and the Fight for the Future of American Security' by Kip Hawley and Nathan Means." *Washington Post.* May 25, 2012. https://www.washingtonpost.com/opinions/the-emergency-state-americas-pursuit-of-absolute-security-at-all-costs-by-david-unger-and-permanent-emergency-inside-the-tsa-and-the-fight-for-the-future-of-american-security-by-kip-hawley-and-nathan-means/2012/05/25/gJQAmWzbqU_story.html

Greene, Richard. "Obama is America's Third Greatest Presidential Orator in the Modern Era." *Huffington Post.* May 25, 2011. https://www.huffpost.com/entry/obama-is-americas-3rd-gre_b_813868

Greenwald, Glenn. "Beyond Buzzfeed: The 10 Worst, Most Embarrassing U.S. Media Failures on the Trump-Russia Story." *The Intercept,* January 20, 2019. https://theintercept.com/2019/01/20/beyond-buzzfeed-the-10-worst-most-embarrassing-u-s-media-failures-on-the-trumprussia-story/

Group, Burisma. "Joseph Cofer Black: 'I Am Excited to Join Burisma's Board of Directors and to Focus on Strategic Development and Security Issues to Expand Burisma's Opportunities." *Kyiv Post*. February 15, 2017. https://www.kyivpost.com/post/7849

Guild, Blair. "David Axelrod on Hillary Clinton: 'It Takes a Lot of Work to Lose to Donald Trump." *CBS News*. May 3, 2017. https://www.cbsnews.com/news/david-axelrod-to-hillary-clinton-it-takes-a-lot-of-work-to-lose-to-donald-trump/

Gustafson, Thane. *The Bridge: Natural Gas in a Redivided Europe* (Cambridge, MA: Harvard University Press, 2020).

Hansen, Holger. "Germany Walks Back Plan to Meet NATO Spending Target on Annual Basis." *Reuters*. August 16, 2023. https://www.reuters.com/world/europe/germany-walks-back-plan-meet-nato-spending-target-annual-basis-2023-08-16/

Harding, Luke. "Alexander Litvinenko: The Man Who Solved His Own Death." *The Guardian*. January 19, 2016. https://www.theguardian.com/world/2016/jan/19/alexander-litvinenko-the-man-who-solved-his-own-murder

Harding, Luke. "Ukraine Extends Lease for Russia's Black Sea Fleet." *The Guardian*. April 21, 2010. https://www.theguardian.com/world/2010/apr/21/ukraine-black-sea-fleet-russia

Harmash, Olena. "Ukrainian Refugees: How Will the Economy Recover with a Diminished Population?" *Reuters*. July 7, 2023. https://www.reuters.com/world/europe/however-war-ends-ukraines-diminished-population-will-hit-economy-years-2023-07-07/

Harris, Carolyn. "When the Catherine the Great Invaded the Crimea and Put the Rest of the World on Edge." *Smithsonian Magazine*. March 4, 2014. https://www.smithsonianmag.com/history/when-catherine-great-invaded-crimea-and-put-rest-world-edge-180949969/

Hart, Robert. "Russia Rejects US Fears Over Russian Nuclear Weapons in Space as 'Malicious Fabrication.'" *Forbes*. February 15, 2024. https://www.forbes.com/sites/roberthart/2024/02/15/russia-rejects-us-fears-over-russian-nuclear-weapons-in-space-as-malicious-fabrication/?sh=450904e77ac3

Hassan, Oz. "Bush's Freedom Agenda: Ideology and the Democratization of the Middle East." *Democracy and Security*. Vol. 4, No. 3, September-December 2008. https://www.jstor.org/stable/48602627

Heintz, Jim. "Russian Mercenary Boss Yevgeny Prigozhin Challenged the Kremlin in a Brief Mutiny." *AP*. August 23, 2023. https://apnews.com/article/yevgeny-prigo-zhin-wagner-group-russia-crash-9982e25668efbf2863a4793fde65c03f

Hemmer, Nicole. "The 'Madman Theory' of Nuclear War Has Existed for Decades. Now, Trump is Playing the Madman." *Vox*. January 4, 2017. https://www.vox.com/the-big-idea/2017/1/4/14165670/madman-theory-nuclear-weapons-trump-nixon

Henley, Jon. "Missile That Hit Poland Likely Came from Ukraine Defences, Say Warsaw and NATO." *The Guardian*. November 16, 2022. https://www.theguardian.com/world/2022/nov/16/poland-president-missile-strike-proba-bly-ukrainian-stray

Heren, Kit. "'European Elites Have to Pitch In': Steve Bannon Says NATO has Become a 'US Protectorate, Not an Alliance.'" *LBC*. January 16, 2024. https://www.lbc.co.uk/news/steve-bannon-trump-nato-not-an-alliance/

Herszenhorn, David M. and Barry, Ellen. "Putin Contends Clinton Incited Unrest Over Vote." *New York Times*. December 8, 2011. https://www.nytimes.com/2011/12/09/world/europe/putin-accuses-clinton-of-instigating-rus-sian-protests.html

Hildebrandt, Tina and di Lorenzo, Giovanni. "Hatten Sie gedacht, ich komme mit Pferdeschwanz?" *Die Zeit*. December 7, 2022. https://www.zeit.de/2022/51/angela-merkel-russland-fluechtlingskrise-bundeskanzler/komplettansicht

Hill, Charles. *Grand Strategies: Literature, Statecraft, and World Order* (New Haven: Yale University Press, 2010).

Holden, Michael. "Britain to Send 14 of Its Main Battle Tanks to Ukraine." *Reuters*. January 15, 2023. https://www.reuters.com/world/europe/uk-has-ambition-send-tanks-ukraine-pm-sunak-tells-zelenskiy-2023-01-14/

"Hoover Fellow Victor Davis Hanson on the Type of Men Who Become Savior Generals." *Hoover Institution*. August 6, 2013. 42:45. https://www.youtube.com/watch?v=4icIzVYyhpg

Hopkirk, Peter. *The Great Game: The Struggle for Empire in Central Asia* (New York: Kodansha International, 1992).

Horvath, Robert. "Apologist of Putinism? Solzhenitsyn, the Oligarchs, and the Specter of Putinism." *The Russian Review*. Vol. 70, No. 2. April 2011. https://www.jstor.org/stable/41061849

"How 9/11 Changed the Course of the George W. Bush Presidency." *PBS Learning Media*. https://florida.pbslearningmedia.org/resource/amex32gwb-soc-911bush/how-911-changed-the-course-of-the-george-w-bush-presidency-george-w-bush/

Hulse, Carl, Peters, Jeremy W., and Shear, Michael D. "Obama is Seen as Frustrating His Own Party." *New York Times*. August 18, 2014. https://www.nytimes.com/2014/08/19/us/aloof-obama-is-frustrating-his-own-party.html

Hyrtsak, Yaroslav. *A Brief History of Ukraine: The Forging of a Nation* (New York, NY: Public Affairs, 2024).

Illiarionov, Andrei. "Reading Russia: The Siloviki In Charge." *Journal of Democracy*. April 2009,. Vol. 20, Issue 2. https://www.journalofdemocracy.org/articles/reading-russia-the-siloviki-in-charge/

"Iraq War was Unjustified, Putin Says." *Australian Broadcasting Corporation*. December 18, 2003. https://www.abc.net.au/news/2003-12-19/iraq-war-was-unjustified-putin-says/108124?utm_campaign=abc_news_web&utm_content=link&utm_medium=content _shared&utm_source=abc_news_web

Jacobson, Gary C. "George W. Bush, the Iraq War, and the Election of Barack Obama." *Presidential Studies Quarterly*, Vol. 40, No. 2, 2010, pp. 207-24. http://www.jstor.org/stable/23044817

Johnson, Rebecca J. "Russian Responses to Crisis Management in the Balkans." *Demokratizatsiya: The Journal of Post-Soviet Democratization*. "Joint Statement on the U.S.-Ukraine Strategic Partnership." *The White House*. September 1,2021. https://www.whitehouse.gov/briefing-room/statements-releases/2021/09/01/joint-statement-on-the-u-s-ukraine-strategic-partnership/

Jo-Morris, Emma. "Ukraine Says U.S. Money Not Going to Ukraine, 'Benefiting American Interests.'" *Breitbart*. January 29, 2024. https://www.breitbart.com/politics/2024/01/29/ukraine-says-u-s-money-not-going-ukraine-benefiting-american-interests/

"Judicial Watch: White House Visitor Logs Detail Meetings of Eric Ciaramella." *Judicial Watch*. November 8, 2019. https://www.judicialwatch.org/judicial-watch-white-house-visitor-logs-detail-meetings-of-eric-ciaramella/

Myroniuk, Emma. "Investigation: Poroshenko's Administration Conceals $600,000 Payment to Lobby Firm That Employs Volker." *Kyiv Post*. November 8, 2019. https://www.kyivpost.com/post/10754

Jones, Jeffrey M. "Public Gives Clinton Best Odds of Being Elected President." *Gallup*. November 1, 2007. https://news.gallup.com/poll/102481/public-gives-clinton-best-odds-being-elected-president.aspx

Kagan, Frederick W. "The Problem with a Neutral Ukraine: Putin is as Bad as His Word." *The Hill*. April 4, 2022. https://thehill.com/opinion/international-al/3258072-the-problem-with-a-neutral-ukraine-putin-is-as-bad-as-his-word/

Kaldor, Mary. *Human Security: Reflections on Globalization and Intervention* (Malden, MA: Polity Press, 2007).

Kasturi, Charu Sudan. "Food Security: One Area Where Putin's Plans Are Bearing Fruit." *G Zero*. April 19, 2022. https://www.gzeromedia.com/climate/food-se-curity-one-area-where-putins-plans-are-bearing-fruit

Kennan, George F. "A Letter on Germany." *The New York Review*. December 3, 1998. https://www.nybooks.com/articles/1998/12/03/a-letter-on-germany/

Kettle, Martin. "Cold Warriors Keep Control of Republican Defence Agenda." *The Guardian*. September 3, 2000. https://www.theguardian.com/world/2000/sep/04/uselections2000.usa4

Kilmeade, Brian and Shokin, Viktor. "Viktor Shokin to Kilmeade: I Believe Biden and Hunter Were Bribed." *Fox News*. August 26, 2023. https://www.foxnews.com/video/6335654002112

Kimmage, Michael and Lété, Bruno. "Is the Minsk Process for Eastern Ukraine Dead or Deadlocked?" *German Marshall Fund*. https://www.gmfus.org/down-load/article/14875

Kipp, Jacob W. "Vostok 2010 and the Very Curious Hypothetical Opponent." *Eurasia Daily Monitor*. Vol. 7. Issue 133, July 12, 2010. https://jamestown.org/program/vostok-2010-and-the-very-curious-hypothetical-opponent/

Kirkpatrick, Jeanne. "A Normal Country In a Normal Time." *National Interest*. No. 21. Fall 1990.

Kizilov, Mikhail B. "The Black Sea and the Slave Trade: The Role of Crimean Maritime Towns in the Trade in Slaves and Captives in the Fifteenth to Eighteenth Centuries." *Critical Readings on Global Slavery*, pp. 958-82. https://doi.org/10.1163/9789004346611_032

Klarenberg, Kit. "FOI Raises Further Questions About Bellingcat Coordination with Western Intelligence." *The Gray Zone*. November 30, 2023. https://thegray-zone.com/2023/11/30/bellingcat-collusion-western-intelligence/

Kochubey, Bogdan. "Ukraine's Zelenskiy Blames Russian Missiles for Deadly Poland Explosion." *Reuters*. November 15, 2022. https://www.reuters.com/world/europe/ukraines-zelenskiy-says-russian-missiles-hit-poland-signif-icant-escalation-2022-11-15/#:~:text=Ukraine%27s%20Zelenskiy%20blames%20Russian%20missiles%20for%20deadly%20Poland%20explo-sion,-By%20Bogdan%20Kochubey&text=KYIV%2C%20Nov%2015%20(Reuters),significant%20escalation%22%20of%20the%20conflict

Koffler, Rebekah. *Putin's Playbook: Russia's Secret Plan to Defeat America* (New York: Regnery Gateway, 2021).

Kramer, Mark. "Why Did Russia Give Away Crimea Sixty Years Ago?" *Wilson Center*. CWIHP. No. 47. https://www.wilsoncenter.org/publication/why-did-russia-give-away-crimea-sixty-years-ago

Krauthammer, Charles. "The Unipolar Moment." *Foreign Affairs*. Vol. 70, No. 1, 1990/91. https://www.foreignaffairs.com/articles/1990-01-01/unipolar-moment

Krueger, Anne E. "Why the Russia Sanctions are Failing." *Project Syndicate*. January 18, 2024. https://www.project-syndicate.org/commentary/how-russia-cir-cumvented-western-sanctions-by-anne-o-krueger-2024-01

Kuzio, Taras. "Leaked Cables Show U.S. Was Wrong on Ukraine's Yanukovych." *Radio Free Europe/Radio Liberty*. March 31, 2011. https://www.rferl.org/a/com-mentary_us_was_wrong_on_ukraine_yanukovych/3542980.html.

Kuzio, Taras. "The Orange Revolution." *Elections Today*. Vol. 12, No. 4,.2005. chrome-extension://efaidnbmnnnibpcajpcglclefindmkaj/https://ciaotest. cc.columbia.edu/olj/et/et_v12n4/et_v12n4_003.pdf

Kuzio, Taras. "Ukrainian Kleptocrats and America's Real Life House of Cards: Corruption, Lobbyism, and the Rule of Law." *Communist and Post-Communist Studies*. 50, No.1. (2017). https://www.jstor.org/stable/48609771

Kuzio, Taras. "Yanukovych and Oligarchs: A Short or Long-Term Relationship?" *Jamestown Foundation*. Eurasia Daily Monitor: Vol. 7, Issue 203. November 9, 2010. https://www.refworld.org/docid/4cdba2132.html

Lange, Jeva. "Hillary Clinton Also Got Foreign Help in the Election—From Ukraine." *The Week*. January 11, 2017. https://theweek.com/speedreads/672549/hillary-clin-ton-also-got-foreign-help-election-from-ukraine

Laruelle, Marlene. "Putin's War and the Dangers of Russian Disintegration." *Foreign Affairs*. December 9, 2022. https://www.foreignaffairs.com/russian-federation/putins-war-and-dangers-russian-disintegration

Latschan, Thomas. "The Black Sea's Role in Russia's War on Ukraine." *DW*. August 13, 2023. https://www.dw.com/en/the-black-sea-plays-a-key-role-in-russias-war-on-ukraine/a-66517223.

Lauria, Joe. "Tangled Tale of NATO Expansion at the Heart of Ukraine Crisis." *Consortium News*. January 28, 2022. https://consortiumnews.com/2022/01/28/the-tangled-tale-of-nato-expansion-at-the-heart-of-ukraine-crisis/

Lee, Carole E., Kube, Courtney, and Welker, Kristen. "Trump Tells Aides Not to Talk About Russia Policy Moves." *NBC News*. March 29, 2018. https://www.nbcnews.com/politics/donald-trump/trump-tells-aides-not-talk-publicly-about-russia-policy-moves-n861256

Left, Sarah. "France, Germany and Russia Condemn War Threat." *The Guardian*. March 19, 2003. https://www.theguardian.com/world/2003/mar/19/iraq.russia

Lillis, Katie Bo, Sciutto, Jim, et al. "Exclusive: Russia Attempting to Develop Nuclear Space Weapon to Destroy Satellites with Massive Energy Wave, Sources Familiar with Intel Say." *CNN*. February 17, 2024. https://www.cnn.com/2024/02/16/politics/russia-nuclear-space-weapon-intelligence/index.html

Lind, Michael. "The Debunked 'Russian Interference' Nonsense is Infantilizing Liberals." *Salon*. January 26, 2020. https://www.salon.com/2020/01/26/the-debunked-russian-influence-nonsense-is-infantilizing-liberals/

Lister, Tim, John, Tara, et al., "World Leaders Hold Emergency Meeting as 'Russian-Made' Missile Kills Two in Poland," *CNN*, November 16, 2022. https://www.cnn.com/2022/11/15/europe/poland-missile-rocket-nato-prze-wodow-ukraine-intl/index.html

Little, Becky. "JFK Was Completely Unprepared for His Summit with Khrushchev." *History Channel*. October 12, 2023. https://www.history.com/news/kennedy-krushchev-vienna-summit-meeting-1961

Longley, Robert. "What is Retributive Justice?" *Thought Co*. June 29, 2022. https://www.thoughtco.com/what-is-retributive-justice-5323923

Lubold, Gordon, Youssef, Nancy A., and Kesling, Ben. "Ukraine War is Depleting U.S. Ammunition Stockpiles, Sparking Pentagon Concern." *Wall Street Journal*. August 29, 2022. https://www.wsj.com/articles/ukraine-war-depleting-u-s-ammunition-stockpiles-sparking-pentagon-concern-11661792188

Luce, Dan De. "China Helps Russia Evade Sanctions and Likely Most Supplies Tech Used in Ukraine, U.S. Report Says." *NBC News.* July 27, 2023. https://www.nbcnews.com/news/investigations/china-helps-russia-evade-sanctions-tech-used-ukraine-war-rcna96693

MacFarquhar, Neil. "Putin Opens New Mosque Amid Lingering Intolerance." *New York Times.* September 23, 2015. https://www.nytimes.com/2015/09/24/world/europe/putin-opens-moscows-most-elaborate-mosque.html

Maguire, Gavin. "U.S. LNG Exports Both a Lifeline and a Drain for Europe in 2023." *Reuters.* December 21, 2022. https://www.reuters.com/business/energy/us-lng-exports-both-lifeline-drain-europe-2023-maguire-2022-12-20/

Magruder, Allan B. "The Will of Peter the Great, and the Eastern Question." *The Atlantic.* July 1878. https://www.theatlantic.com/magazine/archive/1878/07/the-will-of-peter-the-great-and-the-eastern-question/631948/

Maitra, Sumantra. "Policy Brief: Pivoting the US Away from Europe to a Dormant NATO." *Center for Renewing America.* February 16, 2023. https://americarenewing.com/issues/policy-brief-pivoting-the-us-away-from-europe-to-a-dormant-nato/

Marcetic, Branko. "A US-Backed, Far Right-Led Revolution in Ukraine Helped Bring Us to the Brink of War." *Jacobin.* July 2, 2022. https://jacobin.com/2022/02/maidan-protests-neo-nazis-russia-nato-crimea

Marcetic, Branko. "Did the West Deliberately Prolong the Ukraine War?" *Responsible Statecraft.* December 4, 2023. https://responsiblestatecraft.org/ukraine-russia-talks/

Marshall, Andrew. "Russia Warns of a 'Cold Peace.'" *The Independent.* December 6, 1994. https://www.independent.co.uk/news/russia-warns-nato-of-a-cold-peace-1386966.html

Marson James and Grytsenko, Oksana. "Ukraine's War Effort is Stuck. This Heroic Battlefield Failure Shows Why." *Wall Street Journal.* January 10. 2024. https://www.wsj.com/world/europe/ukraine-russia-war-counteroffensive-5b309595

Martin, Jonathan and Landler, Mark. "Bob Corker Says Trump's Recklessness Threatens 'World War III.'" *New York Times.* October 8, 2017. https://www.nytimes.com/2017/10/08/us/politics/trump-corker.html

Maté, Aaron. "Hidden Over Two Years: Dem Cyber-Firm's Sworn Testimony It Had No Proof of Russian Hack of DNC." *Real Clear Investigations*. May 13, 2020. https://www.realclearinvestigations.com/articles/2020/05/13/hidden_over_2_years_dem_cyber-firms_sworn_testimony_it_had_no_proof_of_russian_hack_of_dnc_123596.html

McCallion, Christopher. "Russian Disintegration is a Dangerously Dumb Delusion." *The Hill*. February 3, 2023. https://thehill.com/opinion/national-security/3837672-russian-disintegration-is-a-dangerously-dumb-delusion/

McCarthy, Daniel. "When the Neocons Wanted to 'Go All the Way' to Baghdad' After 1991 War." *Responsible Statecraft*. May 6, 2022. https://responsiblestatecraft.org/2022/05/06/when-the-neocons-wanted-to-go-all-the-way-to-baghdad-after-1991-war/

McFate, Sean. *The New Rules of War: Victory in the Age of Durable Disorder* (New York: William Murrow, 2019).

McFaul, Michael. "U.S.-Russia Relations After September 11, 2001." *Carnegie Endowment for International Peace*. October 24, 2001. https://carnegieendowment.org/2001/10/24/u.s.-russia-relations-after-september-11-2001-pub-840

McKernan, Bethan. "Putin Promised Me He Would Not Kill Zelenskiy, Says Former Israeli PM." *The Guardian*. February 5, 2023. https://www.theguardian.com/world/2023/feb/05/putin-promised-me-he-would-not-kill-zelenskiy-says-former-israeli-pm-naftali-bennett

Mearsheimer, John J. "The Case for a Ukrainian Nuclear Deterrent." *Foreign Affairs*. Vol. 72, No. 3, Summer 1993. https://www.mearsheimer.com/wp-content/uploads/2019/07/Mearsheimer-Case-for-Ukrainian-Nuclear-Deterrent.pdf

Meredith, Sam. "Trump Meets Putin Behind Closed Doors After Scolding US Policy on Russia." *CNBC*. July 16, 2018. https://www.cnbc.com/2018/07/16/trump-putin-summit-us-president-arrives-in-helsinki-to-meet-russian-c.html

Meyer, David. "Trump Has Long Wanted to Kill a Russia-Germany Natural Gas Pipeline. Navalny's Poisoning Could Do It for Him." *Fortune*. September 8, 2020. https://fortune.com/2020/09/08/trump-pipeline-russia-germany-natural-gas-merkel-navalny-poisoned-nord-stream-2/

Michel, Casey. "Alexei Navalny Has a Crimea Problem." *The New Republic*. October 4, 2022. https://newrepublic.com/article/167944/alexei-navalny-crimea-problem-putin

Milligan, Susan. "Biden: Help Ukraine Now or Send Americans to Fight Russia with NATO Later." *U.S. News & World Report.* December 6, 2023. https://www. usnews.com/news/national-news/articles/2023-12-06/biden-help-ukraine-now-or-send-americans-to-fight-russia-with-nato-later

Milne, Seumas. "Now the Truth Emerges: How the US Fuelled the Rise of Isis in Syria and Iraq." *The Guardian.* June 3, 2015. https://www.theguardian.com/commentisfree/2015/jun/03/us-isis-syria-iraq

Mizokami, Kyle. "Germany's Entire Submarine Fleet is Out of Commission." *Popular Mechanics.* December 21, 2017. https://www.popularmechan-ics.com/military/navy-ships/a14480191/germanys-entire-subma-rine-fleet-is-out-of-commission/

Montefiore, Simon Sebag. *Potemkin: Catherine the Great's Imperial Partner* (New York: Vintage Books, 2005)

Moore, David W. "Bush Job Approval Highest in Gallup History." *Gallup.* September 24, 2001. https://news.gallup.com/poll/4924/bush-job-approv-al-highest-gallup-history.aspx

Moore, James. "Trump Would Have Easily Won a Second Term If It Weren't for the Coronavirus." *The Independent.* November 7, 2020. https://www.indepen-dent.co.uk/voices/trump-us-election-coronavirus-second-term-b1667035.html

Morris, Nicholas. "Humanitarian Intervention in the Balkans." *Humanitarian Intervention and International Relations.* December 2003. https://doi.org/10.1093/0199267219.003.0006

"Mueller Finds No Collusion with Russia, Leaves Obstruction Question Open." *American Bar Association.* March 25, 2019. https://www.americanbar.org/news/abanews/aba-news-archives/2019/03/mueller-concludes-investigation/

Myre, Greg. "Who is Lt. Col. Alexander Vindman." *NPR.* October 29, 2019. https://www.npr.org/2019/10/29/774507048/who-is-lt-col-alexander-vind-man

Nakashima, Ellen and Harris, Shane. "U.S. Spies Learned in Mid-June was Planning Armed Action in Russia." *Washington Post.* June 24, 2023. https://www.washingtonpost.com/national-security/2023/06/24/us-intelligence-pri-gozhin-putin/

"NATO Expansion – The Budapest Blow Up 1994." *National Security Archive.* November 24, 2021. https://nsarchive.gwu.edu/briefing-book/russia-pro-grams/2021-11-24/nato-expansion-budapest-blow-1994#_edn1

"NATO Expansion: What Yeltsin Heard." *National Security Archive*. March 16, 2018. https://nsarchive.gwu.edu/briefing-book/russia-programs/2018-03-16/nato-expansion-what-yeltsin-heard

Nelson, Louis. "With Putin By His Side, Trump Calls Mueller Probe a 'Disaster for Our Country.'" *Politico*. July 16, 2018. https://www.politico.com/story/2018/07/16/trump-putin-meeting-mueller-investigation-722685

Nelson, Steve. "Biden $10M Bribe File Released: Burisma Chief Said He was 'Coerced' to Pay Joe, 'Stupid' Hunter in Bombshell Allegations." *New York Post*. August 9, 2023. https://nypost.com/2023/07/20/biden-bribe-file-released-burisma-chief-said-both-joe-and-hunter-involved/

Nelson, Steven. "Biden Tells US Troops They'll Be in Ukraine in War Gaffe." *New York Post*. March 25, 2022. https://nypost.com/2022/03/25/joe-biden-says-us-troops-will-be-in-ukraine-in-apparent-gaffe/

Nemec, Paul. "The Missile Defense Systems of George W. Bush: A Critical Assessment." *Air University Press*. February 8, 2012. https://www.airuniversity.af.edu/AUPress/Book-Reviews/Display/Article/1192392/the-missile-defense-systems-of-george-w-bush-a-critical-assessment/

Neoliberal. "A Brief Tale of Two Neos: Neoconservatism and Neoliberalism." *Medium*. April 29, 2018. https://medium.com/@neoliberal/a-brief-tale-of-two-neos-neoconservatism-and-neoliberalism-efc7ee6add15

Network, Euractiv. "Poland 'Key' in Western Weapons Supplies to Ukraine." *Euractiv*. March 1, 2022. https://www.euractiv.com/section/politics/news/poland-key-in-western-weapons-supplies-to-ukraine/

Nichols, Hans. "Biden's Hardline Russia Reset." *Axios*. September 18, 2020. https://www.axios.com/2020/09/18/biden-russia-policy-putin

Norton, Tom. "The Year Putin Didn't Die." *Newsweek*. February 24, 2023. https://www.newsweek.com/putin-health-cancer-parkinsons-rumors-1783665

O'Connor, Tom. "West's Libya Bombing 10 Years Ago Drove Vladimir Putin to Middle East Showdown with U.S." *Newsweek*. March 19, 2021. https://www.newsweek.com/west-libya-bombing-ten-years-ago-putin-showdown-mideast-1577266

O'Hanlon, Michael E. "Beyond Missile Defense: Countering Terrorism and Weapons of Mass Destruction." *Brookings Institute*. August 1, 2001. https://www.brookings.edu/articles/beyond-missile-defense-countering-terrorism-and-weapons-of-mass-destruction/

O'Neill, Kelly. *Imperiia: A Spatial History of the Russian Empire.* "1783: The Founding of Sevastopol." https://scalar.fas.harvard.edu/imperiia/1783-the-founding-of-sevastopol#_ftnref2

O'Reilly, Bill and Trump, Donald J. "Bill O'Reilly Interviews President Donald Trump Before Super Bowl LI." *Fox Sports.* February 5, 2017. 09:50. https://www.youtube.com/watch?v=74DAI2hr9Kk

Oliynyk, Kateryna. "The Destruction of Ukraine's Nuclear Arsenal." *Radio Free Europe/Radio Liberty.* January 9, 2019. https://www.rferl.org/a/the-destruction-of-ukraines-nuclear-arsenal/29699706.html

Ormiston, Susan. "Remembering the 2014 Ukraine Revolution, which Set the Stage for the 2022 Russian Invasion." *CBC.* February 23, 2023. https://www.cbc.ca/news/ukraine-2014-euromaidan-1.6756384

Osburn, Madeline. "Anti-Trump 'Whistleblower' Worked with DNC Operative Who Sought Dirt on Trump from Ukrainian Officials." *The Federalist.* October 30, 2019. https://thefederalist.com/2019/10/30/anti-trump-whistleblower-worked-with-dnc-operative-who-sought-dirt-on-trump-from-ukrainian-officials/

Page, Clarence. "Putin Tames Savage Trump by Feeding His Monster Ego." *Las Vegas Sun.* December 28, 2015. https://lasvegassun.com/news/2015/dec/28/putin-tames-savage-trump-by-feeding-his-monster-eg//

Parks, Michael. "Moscow Asks West's Help on Baltics: Soviet Union: The Kremlin Wants U.S., Other Nations to Discourage the Region from Succeeding. A Break Could Lead to a 'Catastrophe', A Party Official Said." *Los Angeles Times.* January 15, 1990. https://www.latimes.com/archives/la-xpm-1990-01-15-mn-210-story.html

Parks, Miles and Lucas, Ryan. "Paul Manafort, Former Trump Campaign Chairman, Sentenced to Just Under 4 Years." March 7, 2019. https://www.npr.org/2019/03/07/701045248/paul-manafort-former-trump-campaign-chairman-sentenced-to-just-under-4-years

Patteson, Callie. "Hillary Clinton Pushed Trump-Russia Theory at Center of Durham Case." *New York Post.* February 14, 2022. https://nypost.com/2022/02/14/hillary-clinton-pushed-trump-russia-theory-in-2016/

Paul, Jimmy. "Column: Biden's Comments Favor GOP Charges of Obama's Inexperience." *CBS News.* October 28, 2008. https://www.cbsnews.com/news/column-bidens-comments-favor-gop-charges-of-obamas-inexperience/

Perrigo, Billy. "How Putin's Denial of Ukraine's Statehood Rewrites History." *Time*. February 22, 2022. https://time.com/6150046/ukraine-statehood-russia-history-putin/

Person, Robert and McFaul, Michael. "What Putin Fears Most." *Journal of Democracy*. Vol. 3, Issue 2, April 2022. https://www.journalofdemocracy.org/articles/what-putin-fears-most/

Petit, Stephanie. "'Horrified' Ivanka Trump May Have Influenced Her Father's Decision to Bomb Syria, President's Son Eric Says." *People*. April 11, 2017. https://people.com/politics/ivanka-trump-influenced-decision-bomb-syria-eric-trump-says/

Picheta, Rob. "Germany is 'Wasting Time' on Sending Tanks to Ukraine, Its Allies Say. Here's Why the Leopard 2 is So Important." *CNN*. January 23, 2023. https://www.cnn.com/2023/01/20/europe/germany-leopard-2-tank-ukraine-explainer-intl/index.html

Picket, Kerry. "'Bro-Like': Schiff Aide was White House Friend of Alleged Whistleblower Eric Ciaramella." *Washington Examiner*. November 19, 2019. https://www.washingtonexaminer.com/news/628108/bro-like-schiff-aide-was-white-house-friend-of-alleged-whistleblower-eric-ciaramella/

Pifer, Steven. "Why Care About Ukraine and the Budapest Memorandum?" *Brookings Institute*. December 5, 2019. https://www.brookings.edu/blog/order-from-chaos/2019/12/05/why-care-about-ukraine-and-the-budapest-memorandum/

Pikayev, Alexander A. "Post-Soviet Russia and Ukraine: Who Can Push the Button?" *The Nonproliferation Review*. Spring-Summer 1994. https://www.nonproliferation.org/wp-content/uploads/npr/pikaye13.pdf

Plokhy, Sergii. *The Gates of Europe: A History of Ukraine* (New York, NY: Basic Books, 2021).

Plokhy, Sergii. *The Russo-Ukrainian War: The Return of History* (New York, NY: W.W. Norton & Company, 2023).

Podcast, Tommy's. "Ukraine, Israel, Taiwan." *Rumble*. February 5, 2024. 58:14. https://rumble.com/v4bdj4x-ukraine-israel-taiwan-brandon-weichert-and-lee-slusher-tpc-1410.html

"Poland's New PM Promises to Push for Full Western Support of Ukraine." *Al Jazeera*. December 12, 2023. https://www.aljazeera.com/news/2023/12/12/polands-donald-tusk-says-hell-push-for-western-support-for-ukraine

Post, Re. "Марионетки Майдана." *YouTube*. February 4, 2014. https://www.you-tube.com/watch?v=MSxaa-67yGM#t=89

Post, Washington. "Biden: 'Russia Will Be Held Accountable' If It Invades Ukraine." *YouTube*. January 19, 2022. https://www.youtube.com/watch?v=7C-oqHmKshb4

Preble, Christopher A. and Logan, Justin. "Neocons Forced to Face Reality." *CATO Institute*. July 26, 2004. https://www.cato.org/commentary/neo-cons-forced-face-reality

"Putin Accuses the West of Trying to 'Dismember and Plunder' Russia in a Ranting Speech." *AP*. November 28, 2023. https://apnews.com/article/russia-pu-tin-speech-ukraine-world-order-747d4cb0b899cf5c76f2f5ae80df376c

"Putin and the Presidents." January 24, 2023. *PBS*. 52:47. https://www.youtube.com/watch?v=aJI8XTa_DII

"Putin Seems to Be Winning the War in Ukraine—For Now." *The Economist*. November 30, 2023. https://www.economist.com/leaders/2023/11/30/putin-seems-to-be-winning-the-war-in-ukraine-for-now

Putin, Vladimir. "Speech and the Following Discussion at the Munich Conference on Security Policy." *President of Russia*. February 10, 2007. http://en.kremlin.ru/events/president/transcripts/24034

Putin, Vladimir. (@RussianEmbassy). "President #Putin: The so-called collective West does not need a strong and sovereign #Russia, and will not forgive us our independent policy and standing up." *Twitter*. March 23, 2022. https://twitter.com/RussianEmbassy/status/1506685581866278922?s=20&t=u7Znbe_87T7BLSJ_Qp9GIw

Qena, Nebi and Karmanau, Yuras. "Russia Says It Will Reduce Military Operations Near Kyiv as Peace Talks Continue." *PBS News Hour*. March 29, 2022. https://www.pbs.org/newshour/world/russia-says-it-will-reduce-mili-tary-operations-near-kyiv-as-peace-talks-continue

Rankin, Jennifer. "Ex-NATO Head Says Putin Wanted to Join Alliance Early On In His Rule." *The Guardian*. November 4, 2021. https://www.theguardian.com/world/2021/nov/04/ex-nato-head-says-putin-wanted-to-join-alliance-early-on-in-his-rule

"Rebuilding America's Defenses: Strategy, Forces, and Resources for a New Century." *Project for a New American Century*, September 2000. https://resistir.info/livros/rebuilding_americas_defenses.pdf

"Remarks by the President to Students and Faculty at National Defense University." *The White House: President George W. Bush.* May 2001. https://georgew-bush-whitehouse.archives.gov/news/releases/2001/05/20010501-10.html

Research Department, Statista. "Arms Imports Into Ukraine from 2018-2022, By Country." *Statista.* https://www.statista.com/statistics/1294196/ukraine-arms-imports-by-country/#:~:text=The%20United%20States%20was%20the,of%20arms%20imports%20into%20Ukraine

"Resilience, Civil Preparedness, and Article 3." *North Atlantic Treaty Organization.* August 2, 2023, https://www.nato.int/cps/en/natohq/topics_132722.htm

Reuters. "Poland Says Russian Rocket Entered Its Airspace, Summons Diplomat." *Reuters.* December 29, 2023. https://www.reuters.com/world/europe/uniden-tified-object-entered-poland-direction-ukraine-says-polish-army-2023-12-29/

Reuters. "Russia's Prigozhin Posts First Video Since Mutiny, Hints He is In Africa." *AP.* August 22, 2023. https://www.reuters.com/world/africa/russias-prigo-zhin-posts-first-video-since-mutiny-hints-hes-africa-2023-08-21/

Reynolds, Maura. "Bush Says U.S. Must Spread Democracy." *Baltimore Sun.* 7 November 2003. https://www.baltimoresun.com/2003/11/07/bush-says-us-must-spread-democracy/

Riddell, Kelly. "Hillary Clinton Haunted by Efforts to 'Destroy' Bill Clinton Accusers." *Washington Times.* January 14, 2016. https://www.washingtontimes.com/news/2016/jan/14/hillary-clinton-haunted-by-efforts-to-destroy-bill/

Robertson, Nic. "Why Prigozhin's Short-Lived Russian Rebellion Failed." *CNN.* June 27, 2023. https://www.cnn.com/2023/06/26/europe/prigozhin-pu-tin-wagner-rebellion-analysis-intl/index.html

Robinson, Emerald and Weichert, Brandon J. "Is Zelensky About to Be Overthrown?" *The Absolute Truth with Emerald Robinson.* February 1, 2024. *Rumble.* https://rumble.com/v4as3ai-the-absolute-truth-with-emerald-robin-son-february-1-2024.html

Robinson, Emerald. and Weichert, Brandon J. "Zelensky Wants to Play Make a Deal with Putin." January 18, 2024. *Frank TV.* https://rumble.com/v47us1o-zelensky-wants-to-play-lets-make-a-deal-with-putin.html

Rofer, Cherly. "Could Ukraine Have Retained Soviet Nuclear Weapons?" *Nuclear Diner.* February 6, 2022. https://nucleardiner.wordpress.com/2022/02/06/could-ukraine-have-retained-soviet-nuclear-weapons/

"Ronald Reagan Address to the British Parliament." *The History Place.* https://www. historyplace.com/speeches/reagan-parliament.htm.

Rumer, Eugene and Sokolsky, Richard. "Thirty Years of U.S. Policy Toward Russia: Can the Vicious Circle Be Broken?" *Carnegie Endowment for International Peace.* June 20, 2019. https://carnegieendowment.org/2019/06/20/thirty-years-of-u.s.-policy-toward-russia-can-vicious-circle-be-broken-pub-79323

Rummler, Orion. "Alexander Vindman Calls Trump a 'Useful Idiot' for Putin." *Axios.* September 14, 2020. https://www.axios.com/2020/09/14/vind-man-trump-russia-putin

"Russia Claims Capture of Avdiivka After Ukraine Withdraws from Key City." *Al Jazeera.* February 17, 2024. https://www.aljazeera.com/news/2024/2/17/ukraine-troops-withdraw-from-frontline-city-of-avdiivka-army-chief-says

Rosentiel, Tim. "Inside Obama's Sweeping Victory." *Pew Research Center.* November 5, 2008. https://www.pewresearch.org/2008/11/05/inside-obamas-sweep-ing-victory/

Roth, Andrew. "Prigozhin Calls Off March on Moscow to Avert 'Russian Bloodshed.'" *The Guardian.* June 24, 2023. https://www.theguardian.com/world/2023/jun/24/wagner-troops-may-reach-moscow-by-evening-as-krem-lin-hurries-to-intercept

Ryan, Danielle. "Dictator vs. Democrat? Not Quite: Russian Opposition Leader Alexey Navalny is No Progressive Hero." *Salon.* April 2, 2017. https://www.salon.com/2017/04/02/dictator-vs-democrat-not-quite-russian-opposi-tion-leader-alexey-navalny-is-no-progressive-hero/

Sadovskaya, Paolina and Pfeilschifter, Veronika. "From Stalin to Putin: The Crimean Tatars Face a New Era of Persecution." *Atlantic Council.* May 17, 2020. https://www.atlanticcouncil.org/blogs/ukrainealert/from-stalin-to-putin-the-crimean-tatars-face-a-new-era-of-kremlin-persecution/

Sainato, Michael "Ukraine Tried to Tip the Election in Clinton's Favor." *Observer.* January 12, 2017. https://observer.com/2017/01/ukraine-hillary-clinton-don-ald-trump-election/

Sakwa, Richard. *Frontline Ukraine: Crisis in the Borderlands* (London: I.B. Taurus, 2022).

Sakwa, Richard. *The Lost Peace: How the West Failed to Prevent a Second Cold War* (New Haven: Yale University Press, 2023).

Salem, Harriet. "Beware of the Russian Bear in the Balkans." *Atlantic Council.* December 7, 2016. https://www.atlanticcouncil.org/blogs/ukrainealert/beware-of-the-russian-bear-in-the-balkans/

Salem, Harriet, Walker, Shaun, and Grytsenko, Oksana. "Russia Puts Military on High Alert as Crimea Protests Leave One Man Dead." *The Guardian.* February 26, 2014. https://www.theguardian.com/world/2014/feb/26/ukraine-new-leader-disbands-riot-police-crimea-separatism

Sanchez, Yvonne Wingett. "Sen. John McCain's Role in Trump Dossier Intrigue Detailed in Deposition." *AZ Central.* March 18, 2019. https://www.azcentral.com/story/news/politics/arizona/2019/03/18/new-details-senator-john-mccain-role-trump-dossier-detailed-deposition-david-kramer/3205658002/

Sanger, David E. "Bush Outlines Vision for Expanding Democracy in Mideast." *New York Times.* November 6, 2003. https://www.nytimes.com/2003/11/06/international/middleeast/bush-outlines-vision-for-expanding-democracy-in.html

Sarotte, M.E. *Not One Inch: America, Russia, and the Making of Post-Cold War Stalemate* (New Haven: Yale University Press, 2021).

Satter, David. "The Mystery of Russia's 1999 Apartment Bombings Lingers—the CIA Could Clear It Up." *National Review Online.* February 2, 2017. https://www.hudson.org/national-security-defense/the-mystery-of-russia-s-1999-apartment-bombings-lingers-the-cia-could-clear-it-up

Savranskaya, Svetlana and Blanton, Tom. "NATO Expansion: What Gorbachev Heard." *National Security Archive.* Briefing Book No.: 613, December 12, 2017. https://nsarchive.gwu.edu/briefing-book/russia-programs/2017-12-12/nato-expansion-what-gorbachev-heard-western-leaders-early

Schemann, Serge. "The Day the Soviet Flag Came Down." *New York Times.* December 31, 2021. https://www.nytimes.com/2021/12/31/opinion/ussr-memorial-shutdown-ukraine.html

Schweizer, Peter. *Secret Empires* (New York: Harper-Collins, 2018).

Sciolino, Elaine. "Why Russia Still Bangs Its Shoe." *New York Times.* December 11, 1994. https://www.nytimes.com/1994/12/11/weekinreview/the-world-why-russia-still-bangs-its-shoe.html

Sciolino, Elaine. "Yeltsin Says NATO is Trying to Split Continent Again." *New York Times.* December 6, 1994. https://www.nytimes.com/1994/12/06/world/yeltsin-says-nato-is-trying-to-split-continent-again.html

Sebestyen, Victor. *Revolution 1989: The Fall of the Soviet Empire* (New York, NY: Vintage Books, 2010).

"Senior US Official in Ukraine Confident Congress Will Back Aid Package." *Reuters.* January 31, 2024/ https://www.reuters.com/world/us/senior-us-official-ukraine-talks-amid-uncertainty-over-aid-2024-01-31/#:~:text=Nuland%20said%20she%20was%20leaving,nice%20surprises%20on%20the%20battle-field%22

Serhan, Yasmeen. "Why Germany Agonized Over Sending Tanks to Ukraine." *Time.* January 24, 2023. https://time.com/6249710/germany-leopard-2-tanks-ukraine/

Shalal, Andrea, Rinke, Andreas and Mason, Jeff. "Biden Pledges End to Nord Stream 2 if Russia Invades Ukraine." *Reuters.* February 8, 2022. https://www.reuters.com/world/biden-germanys-scholz-stress-unified-front-against-any-russian-aggression-toward-2022-02-07/

Shelbourne, Mallory. "U.S., Ukraine Begin Sea Breeze 2021 Exercise with 30 Other Countries." *USNI News.* June 28, 2021. https://news.usni.org/2021/06/28/u-s-ukraine-begin-sea-breeze-2021-exercise-with-30-other-countries

Shemmel, Alec. "NATO Slammed for Comparing War in Ukraine to Star Wars, Other Pop Culture Movie References." *KTXS-12-ABC.* February 24, 2023. https://ktxs.com/news/nation-world/nato-criticized-for-comparing-war-in-ukraine-to-star-wars-other-pop-culture-movie-references

Shumylo-Tapiola, Ogla. "Viktor Yanukovych: A Man of the Oligarchs." *Carnegie Endowment for International Peace.* March 10, 2011. https://carnegieeurope.eu/2011/03/10/viktor-yanukovych-man-of-oligarchs-pub-42942

Shuster, Simon. "How Paul Manafort Helped Elect Russia's Man in Ukraine." *Time.* October 31, 2017, https://time.com/5003623/paul-manafort-mueller-in-dictment-ukraine-russia/

Simon, Roger. "Obama Off and Running." *Politico.* February 7, 2007. https://www.politico.com/story/2007/02/obama-off-and-running-002687

Sinar, Chaim. "Vladimir Putin's Aspiration to Restore the Lost Russian Empire." *SSRN.* November 15, 2016. http://dx.doi.org/10.2139/ssrn.2869863

Sindelar, Daisy. "Ukraine: Kyiv Poised Between Russia and the West?" *Radio Free Europe/Radio Liberty.* March 24, 2006. https://www.rferl.org/a/1067059.html

Sixsmith, Martin and Sixsmith, Daniel. *Putin and the Return of History: How the Kremlin Rekindled the Cold War* (London: Bloomsbury Continuum Press, 2024).

Sixsmith, Martin. *Russia: A 1,000-Year Chronicle of the Wild East* (New York, NY: Henry N. Adams, 2013).

Skorkin, Konstantin. "Ukraine's Oligarchs are a Dying Breed. The Country Will Never Be the Same." *Carnegie Endowment for International Peace.* September 14, 2022. https://carnegieendowment.org/politika/87914#:~:text=all%20be%20positive.-,It%27s%20true%20that%20Ukraine%27s%20oligarchs%20corrupted%20the%20Ukrainian%20state%20and,as%20effectively%20as%20civil%20society

Smith, Alex Duval. "Is Trade, Not Aid, the Answer for Africa?" *The Guardian.* May 25, 2009. https://www.theguardian.com/business/2009/may/25/africa-entrepreneurs-charity

Smith, Ben. "Hillary: Putin 'Doesn't Have a Soul.'" *Politico.* January 6, 2008. https://www.politico.com/blogs/ben-smith/2008/01/hillary-putin-doesnt-have-a-soul-005126

Soldatenko, Mykhailo. "Constructive Ambiguity of the Budapest Memorandum at 28: Making Sense of the Controversial Agreement." *Lawfare.* February 7, 2023. https://www.lawfaremedia.org/article/constructive-ambiguity-of-the-budapest-memorandum-at-28-making-sense-of-the-controversial-agreement

Soldatkin, Vladimir and Holland, Steve. "Far Apart at First Summit, Biden and Putin Agree to Steps on Cybersecurity, Arms Control." *Reuters.* June 16, 2021. https://www.reuters.com/world/wide-disagreements-low-expectations-biden-putin-meet-2021-06-15/

Sokolov, Mikhail and Kirilenko, Anastasia. "20 Years Ago, Russia Had its Biggest Political Crisis Since the Bolshevik Revolution." *The Atlantic.* October 4, 2013. https://www.theatlantic.com/international/archive/2013/10/20-years-ago-russia-had-its-biggest-political-crisis-since-the-bolshevik-revolution/280237/

Solomon, John. "Ukrainian Embassy Confirms DNC Contractor Solicited Trump Dirt in 2016." *The Hill.* May 2, 2019. https://thehill.com/opinion/whitehouse/441892-ukrainian-embassy-confirms-dnc-contractor-solicited-trump-dirt-in-2016/

Solzhenitsyn, Alexander. *Rebuilding Russia: Reflections and Tentative Proposals* (Vintage/Ebury: New York, 1991).

Sonne, Paul, Coker, Margaret, and Kolandyr, Alexander. "After Flight 17 Crash, Debris and Heartbreak in Ukraine Villages." *Wall Street Journal.* July 25, 2014. https://www.wsj.com/articles/after-flight-17-crash-agony-debris-and-heartbreak-in-ukraine-villages-1406335532

Sperry, Paul. "The Beltway's Whistleblower Furor Obsesses Over One Name." *Real Clear Investigations*. October 30, 2019. https://www.realclearinvestigations. com/articles/2019/10/30/whistleblower_exposed_close_to_biden_brennan_ dnc_oppo_researcher_120996.html

Staff, RM. "From Accepting NATO Aspirations to 'Denazifying': 20+ Years of Putin's Changing Views on Ukraine." *Russia Matters*. June 16, 2022. https:// www.russiamatters.org/analysis/accepting-nato-aspirations-denazify- ing-20-years-putins-changing-views-ukraine

Stahl, Leslie and Clinton, Hillary. "Clinton on Qaddafi: We Came, We Saw, He Died." *YouTube*. October 20, 2011. 0:11. https://www.youtube.com/ watch?v=6DXDU48RHLU

Stallard, Katie. *Dancing on Bones: History and Power in China, Russia, and North Korea* (New York: Oxford University Press, 2022).

Stefan-Grady. "Thucydides' Ignored Lesson." *The Diplomat*. August 11, 2017. https://thediplomat.com/2017/08/thucydides-ignored-lesson/

Stern, David. "Ukrainian MP Seeks Probe of Ukraine-Clinton Ties." *Politico*. August 16, 2017. https://www.politico.eu/article/ukraine-mp-derkach-seeks- probe-of-ukraine-hillary-clinton-ties/

Stracqualursi, Veronica. "DNC Chair Slams 'Distracting Donald' for Focusing on Server at Putin Press Conference." *CNN*. July 21, 2018. https://www.cnn. com/2018/07/21/politics/tom-perez-trump-dnc-servers-ozy-fest/index.html

Studies, Neutrality. "Neocon Hate for Russia Makes a European Settlement with Moscow Impossible Dr. Anatol Lieven (1/2)." *YouTube*. September 9, 2023. 2:55. https://www.youtube.com/watch?v=oHXiasGAzmg

Subramanian, Courtney. "Explainer: Biden, Allies Pushed Out Ukrainian Prosecutor Because He Didn't Pursue Corruption Cases." *USA Today*. November 15, 2019. https://www.usatoday.com/story/news/poli- tics/2019/10/03/what-really-happened-when-biden-forced-out-ukraines-top- prosecutor/3785620002/

Suny, Ronald. "Ukraine War Follows Decades of Warnings That NATO Expansion Into Eastern Europe Could Provoke Russia." *The Conversation*. February 28, 2022. https://theconversation.com/ukraine-war-follows-decades-of-warn- ings-that-nato-expansion-into-eastern-europe-could-provoke-russia-177999.

Tan, Huileng. "How Russia Has Avoided Bankrupting Itself After 2 Years of Waging War in Ukraine." *Business Insider.* February 18, 2024. https://www.businessinsider.com/russia-economy-how-moscow-pays-war-economy-afloat-sanctions-ukraine-2024-2

Tatum, Sophie. "Trump Seems to Question US Commitment to Defending All NATO Allies." *CNN.* July 18, 2018. https://www.cnn.com/2018/07/17/politics/trump-nato-fox/index.html

Tavernise, Sabrina. "Why Russians Hate America. Again." *New York Times.* September 12, 2015. https://www.nytimes.com/2015/09/13/sunday-review/why-russians-hate-america-again.html

Taylor, Adam. "That Time Ukraine Tried to Join NATO—and NATO Said No." *Washington Post.* September 4, 2014. https://www.washingtonpost.com/news/worldviews/wp/2014/09/04/that-time-ukraine-tried-to-join-nato-and-nato-said-no/

Taylor, Jessica. "Clinton Says She was 'Right' About 'Vast Russia Conspiracy'; Investigations Ongoing." *NPR.* June 1, 2017. https://www.npr.org/2017/06/01/530941011/clinton-says-she-was-right-about-vast-russia-conspiracy-investigations-ongoing

Tétrault-Farber, Gabrielle and Balmforth, Tom. "Russia Demands NATO roll back from Eastern Europe and Stay Out of Ukraine." *Reuters.* December 17, 2021. https://www.reuters.com/world/russia-unveils-security-guarantees-says-western-response-not-encouraging-2021-12-17/#:~:text=Russia%20demands%20NATO%20roll%20back%20from%20East%20Europe%20and%20stay%20out%20of%20Ukraine,-By%20Gabrielle%20Tétrault&text=MOSCOW%2C%20Dec%2017%20(Reuters),to%20negotiate%20with%20the%20West

"The Berlin Airlift, 1948-49." *Milestones in the History of U.S. Foreign Relations.* Accessed On: December 14, 2023. https://history.state.gov/milestones/1945-1952/berlin-airlift#:~:text=The%20Berlin%20Crisis%20of%201948,the%20creation%20of%20East%20Germany

"The Bush Doctrine." *Carnegie Endowment for International Peace.* October 7, 2002. https://carnegieendowment.org/2002/10/07/bush-doctrine-pub-1088

"The Embassy of Ukraine to the United States Has Launched 'House of Ukraine.'" *Embassy of Ukraine in the United States of America.* June 9, 2016. https://usa.mfa.gov.ua/en/news/48302-v-posolystvi-ukrajini-v-ssha-vidkrivsya-dim-ukrajini

"The Enigma of Russia." *International Churchill Society*. April 3, 2022. https://winstonchurchill.org/publications/churchill-bulletin/bulletin-166-apr-2022/the-enigma-of-russia/

"The Period of Mongol Invasion and Rule, 1237-1480." *New York Public Library Online Exhibition Archive*. http://web-static.nypl.org/exhibitions/russia/history/mongol.html

"The Politico 50: Robert Kagan and Victoria Nuland." *Brookings Institute*. September 4, 2014. https://www.brookings.edu/articles/the-politico-50-robert-kagan-and-victoria-nuland/

"The Ukrainian-Russian War: Which Countries are Fighting Side by Side with Ukraine?" *Visit Ukraine*. June 22, 2023. https://visitukraine.today/blog/2122/the-ukrainian-russian-war-which-countries-are-fighting-side-by-side-with-ukraine

"The Will of Peter the Great/Testament of Peter the Great," *Global Security,* March 8, 2012. https://www.globalsecurity.org/military/world/russia/czar-peter-i-will.htm

"'Thin-Armored' French Tanks Impractical for Attacks, Ukraine Commander." *France 24*. February 7, 2023. https://www.france24.com/en/live-news/20230702-thin-armoured-french-tanks-impractical-for-attacks-says-ukraine-commander

Tiezzi, Shannon. "China, Russia Recommit to Close Partnership in the Shadow of the Ukraine War." *The Diplomat*. March 22, 2023. https://thediplomat.com/2023/03/china-russia-recommit-to-close-partnership-in-the-shadow-of-ukraine-war/

Thompson, Loren. "Love Him or Hate Him, President Trump's Defense Legacy is Profound." *Forbes*. December 15, 2020. https://www.forbes.com/sites/lorenthompson/2020/12/15/love-him-or-hate-him-president-trumps-defense-legacy-is-profound/?sh=7dccbf1a795a

Tirpak, John A. "NATO Details Leap in Member Defense Spending Ahead of Summit." *Air & Space Forces Magazine*. July 8, 2023. https://www.airandspace-forces.com/nato-member-defense-spending-summit/

TOC. "2017: US Launched Tomahawks in Syria, but Russia Didn't Use the S-400 Defense." *BULGARIANMILITARY.COM*. April 9, 2021. https://bulgarianmilitary.com/2021/04/09/2017-us-launched-tomahawks-in-syria-but-russia-didnt-use-the-s-400-defense/

Toosi, Nahal. "Biden Disliked Putin Before It was Cool." *Politico*. June 9, 2021. https://www.politico.com/news/2021/06/09/biden-russia-putin-love-story-492195

Toosi, Nahal. "Trump Demands Other NATO Members Pay Their Fair Share." *Politico*. February 28, 2017. https://www.politico.com/story/2017/02/donald-trump-congress-speech-nnato-235543

"Top U.S. Official Visits Protesters in Kiev as Obama admin. Ups Pressure on Ukraine president Yanukovych." *CBS News*. December 11, 2013. https://www.cbsnews.com/news/us-victoria-nuland-wades-into-ukraine-turmoil-over-yanukovich/

Trevithick, Joseph. "It's Official, Russia and Syria Have Linked Their Air Defense Networks." *The Drive*. June 29, 2019. https://www.thedrive.com/the-warzone/13836/its-official-russia-and-syria-have-linked-their-air-defense-networks

Trifkovic, Srdja. "Neoconservatism—Where Trotsky Meets Stalin and Hitler." *Chronicles Magazine*. April 2, 2015. https://chroniclesmagazine.org/web/neoconservatism-where-trotsky-meets-stalin-and-hitler/

"Trump Sides with Russia Against FBI at Helsinki Summit." *BBC*. July 16, 2018. https://www.bbc.com/news/world-europe-44852812

Tselichtchev, Ivan. "Chinese in the Russian Far East: A Geopolitical Time Bomb?" *South China Morning Post*. July 8, 2017. https://www.scmp.com/week-asia/geopolitics/article/2100228/chinese-russian-far-east-geopolitical-time-bomb

Tucker, Eric and Merchant, Nomaan. "Durham Report Takeaways: A 'Seriously Flawed' Russia Investigation and Its Lasting Impact on the FBI." *AP*. May 16, 2023. https://apnews.com/article/durham-report-fbi-trump-clinton-2016-campaign-f3039e651eeb35a09091c363419e6766

Tucker, Eric. "US Says Russia was Given Trump Campaign Polling Data in 2016." *AP*. April 16, 2021. https://apnews.com/article/donald-trump-paul-manafort-russia-campaigns-konstantin-kilimnik-d2fdefdb37077e28eba135e21fce6ebf

Turner, Susan. "Russia, China, and a Multipolar World Order: The Danger in the Undefined." *Asian Perspective*. 33, No. 1. (2009): 159-184. https://doi.org/10.1353/apr.2009.0029

"Ukraine Crisis: Transcript of Leaked Nuland-Pratt Call." *BBC*. February 7, 2014. https://www.bbc.com/news/world-europe-26079957

Ukraine, Interfax. "Poll: Yanukovych Most Trusted Politician in Ukraine." *Kyiv Post.* May 28, 2009. https://www.kyivpost.com/post/7911

"Ukraine-Russia Crisis: What is the Minsk Agreement." *Al Jazeera.* February 9, 2022. https://www.aljazeera.com/news/2022/2/9/what-is-the-minsk-agreement-and-why-is-it-relevant-now

Ukrainian Service, RFE/RL's. "Switzerland Agrees to Zelenskiy's Request to Host Peace Summit." *Radio Free Europe/Radio Liberty.* January 25, 2024. https://www.rferl.org/a/ukraine-zelenskiy-switzerland-davos/32775285.html

Vinograd, Cassandra. "Donald Trump Remarks on NATO Trigger Alarm Bells in Europe." *NBC News.* July 21, 2016. https://www.nbcnews.com/politics/2016-election/donald-trump-remarks-nato-trigger-alarm-bells-europe-n613911

"Vladimir Putin's Interview with Le Figaro." *President of Russia.* May 31, 2017. http://www.en.kremlin.ru/events/president/news/54638

Vogel, Kenneth P. and Stern, David. "Ukrainian Efforts to Sabotage Trump Backfire." *Politico.* January 11, 2017. https://www.politico.com/story/2017/01/ukraine-sabotage-trump-backfire-233446

Volker, Kurt. "Don't Let Russia Fool You About the Minsk Agreements." *CEPA.* December 16, 2021. https://cepa.org/article/dont-let-russia-fool-you-about-the-minsk-agreements/

Wade, Robert H. "Why the US and NATO Have Long Wanted Russia to Attack Ukraine." *LSE Blogs.* March 30, 2022. https://blogs.lse.ac.uk/europpblog/2022/03/30/why-the-us-and-nato-have-long-wanted-russia-to-attack-ukraine/

Walsh, Kenneth T. "The 10 Youngest Presidents." *U.S. News.* December 3, 2009. https://www.usnews.com/news/politics/slideshows/the-10-youngest-presidents

Walsh, Michael. "The Permanent Bipartisan Fusion Party Prepares for War." *PJ Media.* August 26, 2013. https://pjmedia.com/michaelwalsh/2013/08/26/the-permanent-bipartisan-fusion-party-prepares-for-war-n1119986

"War and Peace in the Nuclear Age; Missile Experimental; Interview with Edward Teller, 1987." December 15, 1987. GBH Archives, accessed December 19, 2023. http://openvault.wgbh.org/catalog/V_67DE2EAC03504AE4ADEB-78A27C71A11dD.

Weber, Peter. "Obama's 'Reset' with Russia: What Went Wrong?" *The Week*. January 8, 2015. https://theweek.com/articles/460485/obamas-reset-russia-what-went-wrong

Weichert, Brandon J. "A China-Russia Alliance is Neither Permanent nor Strong." *The Weichert Report*. January 30, 2017. https://theweichertreport.wordpress.com/2017/01/30/a-china-russia-alliance-is-neither-permanent-nor-strong/

Weichert, Brandon J. "A Deep Cleansing of the Deep State." *American Spectator*. October 2, 2019. https://spectator.org/a-deep-cleansing-of-the-deep-state-is-coming/

Weichert, Brandon J. "Biden Came to Make a Mess and Eat Ice Cream." *American Greatness*. February 16, 2022. https://amgreatness.com/2022/02/16/biden-came-to-make-a-mess-and-eat-ice-cream/

Weichert, Brandon J. "Biden's Mission from God Taking NATO Straight to Hell." *Asia Times*. February 27, 2023. https://asiatimes.com/2023/02/bidens-mission-from-god-taking-nato-straight-to-hell/

Weichert, Brandon J. "Breaking Russia? More Like Breaking Ourselves." *Asia Times*. February 11, 2023. https://asiatimes.com/2023/02/breaking-russia-more-like-breaking-ourselves/

Weichert, Brandon J. "Cheney's One-Percent Doctrine Lives On." *The American Spectator*. April 10, 2019. https://spectator.org/cheneys-one-percent-doctrine-lives-on/

Weichert, Brandon J. "End of the Line for Hunter Biden." *MSN*. May 30, 2023. https://www.msn.com/en-us/news/politics/the-end-of-the-line-for-hunter-biden/ar-AA188VQK

Weichert, Brandon J. "European Energy Politics, Nationalism, and Russia." *The Weichert Report*. May 30, 2018. https://theweichertreport.wordpress.com/2018/05/30/european-energy-politics-nationalism-and-russia/

Weichert, Brandon J. "Has America Almost Depleted Its Supply of Essential Weapons for Ukraine?" *The Washington Times*. May 3, 2022. https://www.washingtontimes.com/news/2022/may/3/has-america-almost-depleted-its-supply-of-essentia/

Weichert, Brandon J. "Is Russia About to Checkmate US in Europe?" *Asia Times*. November 22, 2021. https://asiatimes.com/2021/11/is-russia-about-to-checkmate-us-in-europe/

Weichert, Brandon J. "Much More Than a Trade War with China." *New English Review*. June 2019. https://www.newenglishreview.org/articles/much-more-than-a-trade-war-with-china/

Weichert, Brandon J. "NATO Must Pay." *The American Spectator*. July 13, 2018. https://spectator.org/nato-must-pay/

Weichert, Brandon J. "Neocons Empower America's Enemies." *American Greatness*. July 2, 2018. https://amgreatness.com/2018/07/02/neocons-empower-americas-enemies/

Weichert, Brandon J. "Putin Has Already Beaten America in Eastern Ukraine." *Asia Times*. February 22, 2022. https://asiatimes.com/2022/02/putin-has-already-beaten-america-in-eastern-ukraine/

Weichert, Brandon J. "Putin is Here to Stay, and the Russian State Will Die with Him." *American Thinker*. September 9, 2018. https://www.americanthinker.com/articles/2018/09/putin_is_here_to_stay_and_the_russian_state_will_die_with_him.html

Weichert, Brandon J. "Russia Becomes an Asian Nation." *Asia Times*. April 25, 2022. https://asiatimes.com/2022/04/russia-becomes-an-asian-nation/

Weichert, Brandon J. "Russia is Not Going to Change." *New English Review*. September 2018. https://www.newenglishreview.org/articles/russia-is-not-going-to-change/

Weichert, Brandon J. "The Eurasian Steel Trap is Closing." *Real Clear World*. September 7, 2021. https://www.realclearworld.com/articles/2021/09/07/the_eurasian_steel_trap_is_closing_793416.html

Weichert, Brandon J. "The Hunter Biden Laptop Is a Scandal Like No Other." *19FortyFive*.   May 31, 2023. https://www.19fortyfive.com/2023/05/the-hunter-biden-laptop-is-a-scandal-like-no-other/

Weichert, Brandon J. "The Hunter Biden Laptop 'Letter' Just Blew Up." *19FortyFive*. May 18, 2023. https://www.19fortyfive.com/2023/05/the-hunter-biden-laptop-letter-scandal-just-blew-up/

Weichert, Brandon J. "The Joe Biden Corruption Disaster Has Finally Exploded." *MSN*. August 27, 2023. https://www.msn.com/en-us/news/politics/the-joe-biden-corruption-disaster-has-finally-exploded/ar-AA1fQdpH

Weichert, Brandon J. "Trump's Transactional Worldview is a Benefit." *American Greatness*. August 1, 2018, https://amgreatness.com/2018/08/01/trumps-transactional-worldview-is-a-benefit/

Weichert, Brandon J. *Winning Space: How America Remains a Superpower* (Alexandria: Republic Book Publishers, 2020).

Whitmore, Brian. "Did Russia Plan Its War in Georgia?" *Radio Free Europe/Radio Liberty*. August 15, 2008. https://www.rferl.org/a/Did_Russia_Plan_Its_War_In_Georgia__/1191460.html

Williams, Brian Glyn. "From 'Seccessionist Rebels' to 'Al Qaeda Shock Brigades': Assessing Russia's Efforts to Extend the Post-September 11th War on Terror to Chechnya." *Comparative Studies of Asia, Africa, and the Middle East*, 24, No.1, 2004. muse.jhu.edu/article/181226

Williams, Brian Glyn. "The Sultan's Raiders: The Military Role of the Crimean Tatars in the Ottoman Empire." (Jamestown Foundation: Washington, D.C., 2013).

Williams, Daniel. "Yeltsin, Clinton Clash Over NATO's Role." *Washington Post*. December 6, 1994. https://www.washingtonpost.com/archive/politics/1994/12/06/yeltsin-clinton-clash-over-natos-role/19b7b3a1-abd1-4b1e-b4b2-362f1a236ce9/

Williams, Michael John. "How Putin's Fear of Democracy Convinced Him to Invade Ukraine." *Atlantic Council*. March 6, 2023. https://www.atlanticcouncil.org/blogs/ukrainealert/how-putins-fear-of-democracy-convinced-him-to-invade-ukraine/

Wintour, Patrick. "Helsinki Summit: What Did Trump and Russia Agree?" *The Guardian*. July 17, 2018. https://www.theguardian.com/world/2018/jul/17/helsinki-summit-what-did-trump-and-putin-agree

Wintour, Patrick. "Russia's Belief in NATO 'Betrayal'—and Why It Matters Today." *The Guardian*. January 12, 2022. https://www.theguardian.com/world/2022/jan/12/russias-belief-in-nato-betrayal-and-why-it-matters-today

Wintour, Patrick and Traynor, Ian. "Russian and British Troops in Tense Pristina Stand-Off," *The Guardian*, June 12, 1999. https://www.theguardian.com/world/1999/jun/13/balkans5

Wolff, Joesphine. "The FBI Relied on a Private Firm's Investigation of the DNC Hack—Which Makes the Agency Harder to Trust." *Slate*. May 9, 2017. https://slate.com/technology/2017/05/the-fbi-is-harder-to-trust-on-the-dnc-hack-because-it-relied-on-crowdstrikes-analysis.html

Wood, Dakota. "Joe Biden's 'Minor Incursion' Russia Remark: History Proves It was a Mistake." *Heritage Foundation.* January 26, 2022. https://www.heritage. org/global-politics/commentary/joe-bidens-minor-incursion-russia-remark-history-proves-it-was-mistake

Worland, Justin. "President Trump's Pick for Secretary of State Just Confirmed 'Hundreds' of Russians Were Killed in a U.S. Attack in Syria." *Time.* April 12, 2018. https://time.com/5237922/mike-pompeo-russia-confirmation

"Xi Hails 'Deepening Trust' Between China and Russia as He Meets Putin." *Al Jazeera.* October 18, 2023. https://www.aljazeera.com/news/2023/10/18/xi-hails-deepening-trust-between-china-and-russia-as-he-meets-putin

Zimin, Igor and Grzybowski, Andrzej. "Peter the Great and Sexually Transmitted Diseases." *Clinics in Dermatology.* Volume 38, Issue 5. September-October 2020. https://doi.org/10.1016/j.clindermatol.2019.09.002

Zwoliński, Krzysztof. "Moscow is the Largest Muslim City in Europe. Islam Grows Under Putin's Watch." *TVP World.* September 13, 2023. https://weekly. tvp.pl/72661513/moscow-is-the-largest-muslim-city-in-europe-islam-grows-under-putins-watch

[A DISASTER OF OUR OWN MAKING

ENDNOTES

Introduction

1   Robert Longley, "What is Retributive Justice?" *Thought Co.*, June 29, 2022. https://www.thoughtco.com/what-is-retributive-justice-5323923

2   Thucydides, *The Peloponnesian War* (London: J.M. Dent, 1919).

3   Alec Shemmel, "NATO Slammed for Comparing War in Ukraine to Star Wars, Other Pop Culture Movie References," *KTXS-12-ABC*, February 24, 2023. https://ktxs.com/news/nation-world/nato-criticized-for-comparing-war-in-ukraine-to-star-wars-other-pop-culture-movie-references

4   Marwan Bishara, "Western Media and the War on Truth in Ukraine," *Al Jazeera*, August 4, 2022. https://www.aljazeera.com/opinions/2022/8/4/western-media-and-the-war-on-truth-in

5   Franz Stefan-Grady, "Thucydides' Ignored Lesson," *The Diplomat*, August 11, 2017. https://thediplomat.com/2017/08/thucydides-ignored-lesson/

6   Charles Hill, *Grand Strategies: Literature, Statecraft, and World Order* (New Haven: Yale University Press, 2010), pp. 1-48.

7   Ted Galen Carpenter, "Four Western Provocations That Led to U.S.-Russia Crisis Today," *CATO Institute*, December 28, 2021. https://www.cato.org/commentary/four-western-provocations-led-us-russia-crisis-today

8   Angelo Codevilla, *America's Rise and Fall Among Nations: Lessons in Statecraft from John Quincy Adams* (New York: Encounter Books, 2022), pp. 212-13.

9   Neil MacFarquhar, "Putin Opens New Mosque Amid Lingering Intolerance," *New York Times*, September 23, 2015. https://www.nytimes.com/2015/09/24/world/europe/putin-opens-moscows-most-elaborate-mosque.html

10 Ivan Tselichtchev, "Chinese in the Russian Far East: A Geopolitical Time Bomb?" *South China Morning Post,* July 8, 2017. https://www.scmp.com/week-asia/geopolitics/article/2100228/chinese-russian-far-east-geopolitical-time-bomb

11 Codevilla, *America's Rise and Fall Among Nations,* 211.

12 Tommy's Podcast, "Ukraine, Israel, Taiwan," *Rumble,* February 5, 2024, 27:00-30:01, https://rumble.com/v4bdj4x-ukraine-israel-taiwan-brandon-weichert-and-lee-slusher-tpc-1410.html

13 Codevilla, *America's Rise and Fall Among Nations,* 213.

14 Tucker Carlson and Vladimir Putin, "The Vladimir Putin Interview," *Tucker Carlson Network,* February 8, 2024, 17:13-30:00, https://tuckercarlson.com/the-vladimir-putin-interview/

15 Gary Dorrien, *Imperial Designs: Neoconservatism and the New Pax Americana* (New York: Routledge, 2004), pp. 125-80.

16 Neutrality Studies, "Neocon Hate for Russia Makes a European Settlement with Moscow Impossible Dr. Anatol Lieven (1/2)," *YouTube,* September 9, 2023. https://www.youtube.com/watch?v=oHXiasGAzmg

17 Brandon J. Weichert, "Cheney's One-Percent Doctrine Lives On," *The American Spectator,* April 10, 2019. https://spectator.org/cheneys-one-percent-doctrine-lives-on/

18 George H.W. Bush, "September 11, 1990: Address Before a Joint Session of Congress," *UVA Miller Center,* https://millercenter.org/the-presidency/presidential-speeches/september-11-1990-address-joint-session-congress

19 "Rebuilding America's Defenses: Strategy, Forces, and Resources for a New Century," *Project for a New American Century,* September 2000, https://resistir.info/livros/rebuilding_americas_defenses.pdf

20 Jeanne Kirkpatrick, "A Normal Country In a Normal Time," *National Interest,* No. 21, Fall 1990, pp. 40-44.

21 Charles Krauthammer, "The Unipolar Moment," *Foreign Affairs,* Vol. 70, No. 1, 1990/91, pp. 23-33. https://www.foreignaffairs.com/articles/1990-01-01/unipolar-moment

22 Brandon J. Weichert, "Much More Than a Trade War with China," *New English Review,* June 2019. https://www.newenglishreview.org/articles/much-more-than-a-trade-war-with-china/

23 Robert H. Wade, "Why the US and NATO Have Long Wanted Russia to Attack Ukraine," *LSE Blogs,* March 30, 2022. https://blogs.lse.ac.uk/europpblog/2022/03/30/why-the-us-and-nato-have-long-wanted-russia-to-attack-ukraine/

24 Brandon J. Weichert, "Putin is Here to Stay, and the Russian State Will Die with Him," *American Thinker*, September 9, 2018. https://www.americanthinker.com/articles/2018/09/putin_is_here_to_stay_and_the_russian_state_will_die_with_him.html

25 Brandon J. Weichert, "Neocons Empower America's Enemies," *American Greatness*, July 2, 2018. https://amgreatness.com/2018/07/02/neocons-empower-americas-enemies/

Chapter 1

1 W. Mark Hamilton, "The Enigma of Russia," *International Churchill Society*, April 3, 2022. https://winstonchurchill.org/publications/churchill-bulletin/bulletin-166-apr-2022/the-enigma-of-russia/

2 "NATO Expansion – The Budapest Blow Up 1994," *National Security Archive*, November 24, 2021. https://nsarchive.gwu.edu/briefing-book/russia-programs/2021-11-24/nato-expansion-budapest-blow-1994#_edn1

3 Andrew Marshall, "Russia Warns of a 'Cold Peace'," *The Independent*, December 6, 1994. https://www.independent.co.uk/news/russia-warns-nato-of-a-cold-peace-1386966.html

4 Elaine Sciolino, "Yeltsin Says NATO is Trying to Split Continent Again," *The New York Times*, December 6, 1994. https://www.nytimes.com/1994/12/06/world/yeltsin-says-nato-is-trying-to-split-continent-again.html

5 Elaine Sciolino, "Why Russia Still Bangs Its Shoe," *The New York Times*, December 11, 1994. https://www.nytimes.com/1994/12/11/weekinreview/the-world-why-russia-still-bangs-its-shoe.html

6 Mikhail Sokolov and Anastasia Kirilenko, "20 Years Ago, Russia Had its Biggest Political Crisis Since the Bolshevik Revolution," *The Atlantic*, October 4, 2013. https://www.theatlantic.com/international/archive/2013/10/20-years-ago-russia-had-its-biggest-political-crisis-since-the-bolshevik-revolution/280237/

7 Daniel Williams, "Yeltsin, Clinton Clash Over NATO's Role," *Washington Post*, December 6, 1994. https://www.washingtonpost.com/archive/politics/1994/12/06/yeltsin-clinton-clash-over-natos-role/19b7b3a1-abd1-4b1e-b4b2-362f1a236ce9/

8 "NATO Expansion: What Yeltsin Heard," *National Security Archive*, March 16, 2018. https://nsarchive.gwu.edu/briefing-book/russia-programs/2018-03-16/nato-expansion-what-yeltsin-heard

9 James Goldgeier, *Not Whether, But When* (Washington, D.C.: Brookings Institute, 1999), pp. 69-76.

10 Michael Walsh, "The Permanent Bipartisan Fusion Party Prepares for War," *PJ Media*, August 26, 2013. https://pjmedia.com/michaelwalsh/2013/08/26/the-permanent-bipartisan-fusion-party-prepares-for-war-n119986

11 Christopher A. Preble and Justin Logan, "Neocons Forced to Face Reality," *CATO Institute*, July 26, 2004. https://www.cato.org/commentary/neocons-forced-face-reality

12 Eugene Rumer and Richard Sokolsky, "Thirty Years of U.S. Policy Toward Russia: Can the Vicious Circle Be Broken?" *Carnegie Endowment for International Peace*, June 20, 2019. https://carnegieendowment.org/2019/06/20/thirty-years-of-u.s.-policy-toward-russia-can-vicious-circle-be-broken-pub-79323

13 Thomas L. Friedman, "This Putin's War. But America and NATO Aren't Innocent Bystanders," *The New York Times*, February 21, 2022. https://www.nytimes.com/2022/02/21/opinion/putin-ukraine-nato.html

14 Nicholas Morris, "Humanitarian Intervention in the Balkans," *Humanitarian Intervention and International Relations*, December 2003, pp. 98-119. https://doi.org/10.1093/0199267219.003.0006

15 Mary Kaldor, *Human Security: Reflections on Globalization and Intervention* (Malden, MA: Polity Press, 2007), pp. 122-33.

16 Harriet Salem, "Beware of the Russian Bear in the Balkans," *Atlantic Council*, December 7, 2016. https://www.atlanticcouncil.org/blogs/ukrainealert/beware-of-the-russian-bear-in-the-balkans/

17 Rebecca J. Johnson, "Russian Responses to Crisis Management in the Balkans," *Demokratizatsiya: The Journal of Post-Soviet Democratization*, January 2001, pp. 292-309..

18 Patrick Wintour and Ian Traynor, "Russian and British Troops in Tense Pristina Stand-Off," *The Guardian*, June 12, 1999. https://www.theguardian.com/world/1999/jun/13/balkans5

19 Michael McFaul, "U.S.-Russia Relations After September 11, 2001," *Carnegie Endowment for International Peace*, October 24, 2001. https://carnegieendowment.org/2001/10/24/u.s.-russia-relations-after-september-11-2001-pub-840

20 Thomas Gramm, Jr., "U.S. Role in Chechnya," *Carnegie Endowment for International Peace*, December 10, 1999. https://carnegieendowment.org/1999/12/10/u.s.-role-in-chechnya-pub-182

21 Brian Glyn Williams, "From 'Seccessionist Rebels' to 'Al Qaeda Shock Brigades': Assessing Russia's Efforts to Extend the Post-September 11th War on Terror to Chechnya," *Comparative Studies of Asia, Africa, and the Middle East*, 24, No. 1, 2004, pp. 197-209. muse.jhu.edu/article/181226.

22 David Satter, "The Mystery of Russia's 1999 Apartment Bombings Lingers—the CIA Could Clear It Up," *National Review Online*, February 2, 2017. https://www.hudson.org/national-security-defense/the-mystery-of-russia-s-1999-apartment-bombings-lingers-the-cia-could-clear-it-up

23 Susan Turner, "Russia, China, and a Multipolar World Order: The Danger in the Undefined," *Asian Perspective*, 33, No. 1, (2009): 159-184. https://doi.org/10.1353/apr.2009.0029

24 "Iraq War was Unjustified, Putin Says," *Australian Broadcasting Corporation*, December 18, 2003. https://www.abc.net.au/news/2003-12-19/iraq-war-was-unjustified-putin-says/108124?utm_campaign=abc_news_web&utm_content=link&utm_medium=content_shared&utm_source=abc_news_web

25 David E. Sanger, "Bush Outlines Vision for Expanding Democracy in Mideast," *New York Times*, November 6, 2003. https://www.nytimes.com/2003/11/06/international/middleeast/bush-outlines-vision-for-expanding-democracy-in.html

26 Benjamin Denison, "Where US Sees Democracy Promotion, Russia Sees Regime Change," *Russia Matters*, July 29, 2020. https://www.russiamatters.org/analysis/where-us-sees-democracy-promotion-russia-sees-regime-change

27 Sarah Left, "France, Germany and Russia Condemn War Threat," *The Guardian*, March 19, 2003. https://www.theguardian.com/world/2003/mar/19/iraq.russia

28 James Goldgeier, "NATO's Enlargement Didn't Cause Russian Aggression," *Carnegie Endowment for International Peace*, July 31, 2023. https://carnegieendowment.org/2023/07/31/nato-enlargement-didn-t-cause-russia-s-aggression-pub-90300#:~:text=In%20reality%2C%20it%20has%20been,it%20mischaracterizes%20the%20impetus%20for

29 Ted Galen Carpenter, "Ignored Warnings: How NATO Expansion Led to the Current Ukraine Tragedy," *CATO Institute*, February 24, 2022. https://www.cato.org/commentary/ignored-warnings-how-nato-expansion-led-current-ukraine-tragedy

30 Ted Galen Carpenter, "Many Predicted NATO Expansion Would Lead to War. Those Warnings Were Ignored," *CATO Institute*, February 28, 2022. https://www.cato.org/commentary/many-predicted-nato-expansion-would-lead-war-those-warnings-were-ignored

31 Vladimir Putin, "Speech and the Following Discussion at the Munich Conference on Security Policy," *President of Russia*, February 10, 2007. http://en.kremlin.ru/events/president/transcripts/24034

32 Ibid.

33 Ibid.

34 Peter Baker and Susan B. Glaser, "Putin Threatens Attacks on Chechens in Georgia," *Washington Post,* September 13, 2002. https://www.washingtonpost. com/archive/politics/2002/09/13/putin-threatens-attacks-on-chechens-in-georgia/e68ff41b-1fac-40cc-9ea9-92c5a1f14036/

35 "15 Years Ago, Russia Invaded Georgia Under the Pretext of Supporting Separatists," *The New Voice of Ukraine,* August 8, 2023. https://english.nv.ua/ nation/15-years-ago-russia-invaded-georgia-under-the-pretext-of-support-ing-separatists-50344641.html

36 Brian Whitmore, "Did Russia Plan Its War in Georgia?" *Radio Free Europe/Radio Liberty,* August 15, 2008. https://www.rferl.org/a/Did_Russia_Plan_Its_War_In_Georgia__/1191460.html

37 Seumas Milne, "Now the Truth Emerges: How the US Fuelled the Rise of Isis in Syria and Iraq," *The Guardian,* June 3, 2015. https://www.theguardian.com/ commentisfree/2015/jun/03/us-isis-syria-iraq

38 Krzysztof Zwoliński, "Moscow is the Largest Muslim City in Europe. Islam Grows Under Putin's Watch," *TVP World,* September 13, 2023. https://weekly. tvp.pl/72661513/moscow-is-the-largest-muslim-city-in-europe-islam-grows-under-putins-watch

39 Iona Cleave, "Living in Fear: How Putin's Biggest Fear About Being 'Killed Like Gaddafi' Almost Came True as Wagner Group Stormed Towards Moscow," *U.S. Sun,* June 25, 2023. https://www.the-sun.com/news/8451864/ putin-biggest-fear-killed-gaddafi-coming-true-wagner/

Chapter 2

1 Mickey Bumbar, "How the Love for Drinking Drove the Kievan Rus to Christianity," *Lord of the Drinks,* December 2, 2017. https://lordsofthedrinks. org/2017/12/12/how-the-love-for-drinking-drove-the-kievan-rus-to-christi-anity/

2 (1985) The Battle at Kulikovo Field, Soviet Studies in History, 24:1-2, 11-44, DOI: 10.2753/RSH1061-198324010211

3 "The Period of Mongol Invasion and Rule, 1237-1480," *New York Public Library Online Exhibition Archive.* http://web-static.nypl.org/exhibitions/russia/ history/mongol.html

4 Eve Conant, "Russia and Ukraine: The Tangled History That Connects—and Divides—Them," *National Geographic,* February 24, 2023. https://www.nation-algeographic.com/history/article/russia-and-ukraine-the-tangled-history-that-connects-and-divides-them

5   Thomas Latschan, "The Black Sea's Role in Russia's War on Ukraine," *DW*, August 13, 2023. https://www.dw.com/en/the-black-sea-plays-a-key-role-in-russias-war-on-ukraine/a-66517223

6   Brandon J. Weichert, "Russia is Not Going to Change," *New English Review*, September 2018. https://www.newenglishreview.org/articles/russia-is-not-going-to-change/

7   Brian Glyn Williams, "The Sultan's Raiders: The Military Role of the Crimean Tatars in the Ottoman Empire" (Jamestown Foundation: Washington, D.C., 2013), pp. 15-21. https://jamestown.org/wp-content/uploads/2013/05/Crimean_Tatar_-_complete_report_01.pdf

8   Mikhail B. Kizilov, "The Black Sea and the Slave Trade: The Role of Crimean Maritime Towns in the Trade in Slaves and Captives in the Fifteenth to Eighteenth Centuries," *Critical Readings on Global Slavery*, pp. 958-82. https://doi.org/10.1163/9789004346611_032

9   Cem Dogan, "Snow-White, Curvy, and Virgin: Concubinage and the Origins of White Slave Traffic in Ottoman Istanbul (1850-1920), *International Journal of Economics, Politics, Humanities, & Social Sciences*, Vol: 4, Issue: 3, Summer 2021. https://dergipark.org.tr/tr/download/article-file/1561483

10 Carolyn Harris, "When the Catherine the Great Invaded the Crimea and Put the Rest of the World on Edge," *Smithsonian Magazine*, March 4, 2014. https://www.smithsonianmag.com/history/when-catherine-great-invaded-crimea-and-put-rest-world-edge-180949969/

11 Joel Day, "Putin's Catherine the Great Ideology Could Hold the Key to His Future Plans," *Daily Express*, November 16, 2022. https://www.express.co.uk/news/world/1696403/putin-latest-novorossiya-new-russia-ukraine-catherine-the-great-spt

12 Payin Emil, "Population Transfer: The Crimean Tatars Return Home," *Cultural Survival*, 5 March 2010. https://www.culturalsurvival.org/publications/cultural-survival-quarterly/population-transfer-crimean-tatars-return-home

13 Polina Sadovskaya and Veronika Pfeilschifter, "From Stalin to Putin: The Crimean Tatars Face a New Era of Persecution," *Atlantic Council*, May 17, 2020. https://www.atlanticcouncil.org/blogs/ukrainealert/from-stalin-to-putin-the-crimean-tatars-face-a-new-era-of-kremlin-persecution/

14 Mark Kramer, "Why Did Russia Give Away Crimea Sixty Years Ago?" *Wilson Center*, CWIHP, No. 47. https://www.wilsoncenter.org/publication/why-did-russia-give-away-crimea-sixty-years-ago

15 Paul A. Goble, "Crimea: A New 9/11 for the United States," *Council of American Ambassadors*, Spring 2014. https://www.americanambassadors.org/publications/ambassadors-review/spring-2014/crimea-a-new-9-11-for-the-united-states

16 Chaim Sinar, "Vladimir Putin's Aspiration to Restore the Lost Russian Empire," *SSRN*, 15 November 2016. http://dx.doi.org/10.2139/ssrn.2869863

17 Timothy Garton Ash, "Postimperial Empire: How the War in Ukraine is Transforming Europe," *Foreign Affairs*, May/June 2023. https://www.foreignaffairs.com/ukraine/europe-war-russia-postimperial-empire

18 Alexander Solzhenitsyn, *Rebuilding Russia: Reflections and Tentative Proposals* (Vintage/Ebury: New York, 1991).

19 Robert Horvath, "Apologist of Putinism? Solzhenitsyn, the Oligarchs, and the Specter of Putinism," *The Russian Review*, Vol. 70, No. 2, April 2011, pp. 300-18. https://www.jstor.org/stable/41061849

20 Casey Michel, "Alexei Navalny Has a Crimea Problem," *The New Republic*, October 4, 2022. https://newrepublic.com/article/167944/alexei-navalny-crimea-problem-putin

21 Patrick Wintour, "Russia's Belief in NATO 'Betrayal' – and Why It Matters Today," *The Guardian*, January 12, 2022. https://www.theguardian.com/world/2022/jan/12/russias-belief-in-nato-betrayal-and-why-it-matters-today

Chapter 3

1 "Ronald Reagan Address to the British Parliament," *The History Place*, https://www.historyplace.com/speeches/reagan-parliament.htm

2 Catherine Belton, *Putin's People: How the KGB Took Back Russia and Then Took on the West* (Farrar, Strauss, & Giroux: New York, 2020), pp. 54-55.

3 Ibid.

4 M.E. Sarotte, *Not One Inch: America, Russia, and the Making of Post-Cold War Stalemate* (Yale University Press: New Haven, 2021), p. 11.

5 "The Berlin Airlift, 1948-49," *Milestones in the History of U.S. Foreign Relations*. https://history.state.gov/milestones/1945-1952/berlin-airlift#:~:text=The%20Berlin%20Crisis%20of%201948,the%20creation%20of%20East%20Germany.

6 Sarotte, *Not One Inch*.

7 Svetlana Savranskaya and Tom Blanton, "NATO Expansion: What Gorbachev Heard," *National Security Archive*, Briefing Book No.: 613, December 12, 2017. https://nsarchive.gwu.edu/briefing-book/russia-programs/2017-12-12/nato-expansion-what-gorbachev-heard-western-leaders-early

8   "Putin Accuses the West of Trying to 'Dismember and Plunder' Russia in a
     Ranting Speech," *AP*, November 28, 2023. https://apnews.com/article/rus-
     sia-putin-speech-ukraine-world-order-747d4cb0b899cf5c76f2f5ae80df376c

9   Jake Cordell, "Rewriting History, Putin Pitches Russia as Defender of an
     Expanding Motherland," *The Moscow Times*, February 22, 2022. https://www.
     themoscowtimes.com/2022/02/22/rewriting-history-putin-pitches-rus-
     sia-as-defender-of-an-expanding-motherland-a76518

10   Stephen Collinson, "The West Must Now Consider the Possibility of a Russian
     Military Collapse," *CNN*, June 26, 2023. https://www.cnn.com/2023/06/26/
     politics/wagner-putin-us-ukraine-analysis/index.html

11   Marlene Laruelle, "Putin's War and the Dangers of Russian Disintegration,"
     Foreign Affairs, 9 December 2022. https://www.foreignaffairs.com/rus-
     sian-federation/putins-war-and-dangers-russian-disintegration

12   Robert Person and Michael McFaul, "What Putin Fears Most," *Journal of De-
     mocracy*, Vol. 3, Issue 2, April 2022, pp. 18-27. https://www.journalofdemocra-
     cy.org/articles/what-putin-fears-most/

13   Ibid.

14   Michael John Williams, "How Putin's Fear of Democracy Convinced Him to
     Invade Ukraine," *Atlantic Council*, March 6, 2023. https://www.atlanticcouncil.
     org/blogs/ukrainealert/how-putins-fear-of-democracy-convinced-him-to-in-
     vade-ukraine/

15   RM Staff, "From Accepting NATO Aspirations to 'Denazifying': 20+ Years of
     Putin's Changing Views on Ukraine," *Russia Matters*, June 16, 2022. https://
     www.russiamatters.org/analysis/accepting-nato-aspirations-denazify-
     ing-20-years-putins-changing-views-ukraine

16   Richard Nixon Foundation, "Nixon Warned That This Would Happen to
     Russia (1992)," *YouTube*, December 7, 2023, 2:34. https://www.youtube.com/
     watch?v=kgG_fLNBv6A

Chapter 4

1   Srdja Trifkovic, "Neoconservatism—Where Trotsky Meets Stalin and Hitler,"
     Chronicles Magazine, April 2, 2015. https://chroniclesmagazine.org/web/neo-
     conservatism-where-trotsky-meets-stalin-and-hitler/

2   Joe Lauria, "Tangled Tale of NATO Expansion at the Heart of Ukraine
     Crisis," *Consortium News*, January 28, 2022. https://consortiumnews.
     com/2022/01/28/the-tangled-tale-of-nato-expansion-at-the-heart-of-
     ukraine-crisis/

3   Daniel McCarthy, "When the Neocons Wanted to 'Go All the Way' to Baghdad' After 1991 War," *Responsible Statecraft,* May 6, 2022. https://responsiblestatecraft.org/2022/05/06/when-the-neocons-wanted-to-go-all-the-way-to-baghdad-after-1991-war/

4   Usman Butt, "The Neoconservatives Who Paved the Road to Invading Iraq," *Middle East Monitor,* March 19, 2023. https://www.middleeastmonitor.com/20230319-the-neoconservatives-who-paved-the-road-to-invading-iraq/

5   Ken Adelman, "Cakewalk in Iraq," *Washington Post,* February 12, 2002. https://www.washingtonpost.com/archive/opinions/2002/02/13/cakewalk-in-iraq/cf09301c-c6c4-4f2e-8268-7c93017f5e93/

6   Neoliberal, "A Brief Tale of Two Neos: Neoconservatism and Neoliberalism," *Medium, April 29, 2018.* https://medium.com/@neoliberal/a-brief-tale-of-two-neos-neoconservatism-and-neoliberalism-efc7ee-6add15

Chapter 5

1   Kateryna Oliynyk, "The Destruction of Ukraine's Nuclear Arsenal," *Radio Free Europe/Radio Liberty,* January 9, 2019. https://www.rferl.org/a/the-destruction-of-ukraines-nuclear-arsenal/29699706.html

2   Alexander A. Pikayev, "Post-Soviet Russia and Ukraine: Who Can Push the Button?" *The Nonproliferation Review,* Spring-Summer 1994, pp. 31-46. https://www.nonproliferation.org/wp-content/uploads/npr/pikaye13.pdf

3   Eric Gomez, "Soviet Nukes in Ukraine: A Bargaining Chip, Not a Deterrent," *CATO Institute,* March 6, 2022. https://www.cato.org/blog/soviet-nukes-ukraine-bargaining-chip-not-deterrent

4   Cheryl Rofer, "Could Ukraine Have Retained Soviet Nuclear Weapons?" *Nuclear Diner,* February 6, 2022. https://nucleardiner.wordpress.com/2022/02/06/could-ukraine-have-retained-soviet-nuclear-weapons/

5   John J. Mearsheimer, "The Case for a Ukrainian Nuclear Deterrent," *Foreign Affairs,* Vol. 72, No. 3, Summer 1993, pp. 50-66. https://www.mearsheimer.com/wp-content/uploads/2019/07/Mearsheimer-Case-for-Ukrainian-Nuclear-Deterrent.pdf

6   Ibid.

7   Brandon J. Weichert, "Is Russia About to Checkmate US in Europe?" *Asia Times,* November 22, 2021. https://asiatimes.com/2021/11/is-russia-about-to-checkmate-us-in-europe/

8   Mariana Budjeryn and Matthew Bunn, "Budapest Memorandum at 25: Between Past and Future," *Project on Managing the Atom,* March 2020. https://www.belfercenter.org/sites/default/files/2020-03/budapest/BM25.pdf

9   Mykhailo Soldatenko, "Constructive Ambiguity of the Budapest Memorandum at 28: Making Sense of the Controversial Agreement," *Lawfare*, February
    7, 2023. https://www.lawfaremedia.org/article/constructive-ambiguity-of-the-budapest-memorandum-at-28-making-sense-of-the-controversial-agreement

10 Frederick W. Kagan, "The Problem with a Neutral Ukraine: Putin is as Bad
    as His Word," *The Hill*, April 4, 2022. https://thehill.com/opinion/international/3258072-the-problem-with-a-neutral-ukraine-putin-is-as-bad-as-his-
    word/

11 "The Politico 50: Robert Kagan and Victoria Nuland," *Brookings Institute*,
    September 4, 2014. https://www.brookings.edu/articles/the-politico-50-robert-kagan-and-victoria-nuland/

12 "A Fatal Friendship?" *Wall Street Journal*, December 17, 2010. https://www.wsj.
    com/articles/SB10001424052748704828104576021823816289798

13 Karen J. Greenburg, "'The Emergency State: America's Pursuit of Absolute
    Security at All Costs' by David Unger and 'Permanent Emergency: Inside the
    TSA and the Fight for the Future of American Security' by Kip Hawley and
    Nathan Means," *Washington Post*, May 25, 2012. https://www.washingtonpost.
    com/opinions/the-emergency-state-americas-pursuit-of-absolute-security-
    at-all-costs-by-david-unger-and-permanent-emergency-inside-the-tsa-and-
    the-fight-for-the-future-of-american-security-by-kip-hawley-and-nathan-
    means/2012/05/25/gJQAmWzbqU_story.html.

14 Ronald Suny, "Ukraine War Follows Decades of Warnings That NATO Expansion Into Eastern Europe Could Provoke Russia," *The Conversation*, February
    28, 2022. https://theconversation.com/ukraine-war-follows-decades-of-
    warnings-that-nato-expansion-into-eastern-europe-could-provoke-russia-177999

15 Brandon J. Weichert, "Putin Has Already Beaten America in Eastern Ukraine,"
    Asia Times, February 22, 2022. https://asiatimes.com/2022/02/putin-has-already-beaten-america-in-eastern-ukraine/

16 "Putin Seems to Be Winning the War in Ukraine—For Now," *The Economist*,
    November 30, 2023. https://www.economist.com/leaders/2023/11/30/putin-seems-to-be-winning-the-war-in-ukraine-for-now

Chapter 6

1   "How 9/11 Changed the Course of the George W. Bush Presidency," *PBS
    Learning Media*. https://florida.pbslearningmedia.org/resource/amex32gwb-
    soc-911bush/how-911-changed-the-course-of-the-george-w-bush-presidency-george-w-bush/

2   David W. Moore, "Bush Job Approval Highest in Gallup History," *Gallup*, September 24, 2001. https://news.gallup.com/poll/4924/bush-job-approval-highest-gallup-history.aspx

3   Gary C. Jacobson, "George W. Bush, the Iraq War, and the Election of Barack Obama," *Presidential Studies Quarterly*, Vol. 40, No. 2, 2010, pp. 207-24. http://www.jstor.org/stable/23044817

4   Maura Reynolds, "Bush Says U.S. Must Spread Democracy," *Baltimore Sun*, November 7, 2003. https://www.baltimoresun.com/2003/11/07/bush-says-us-must-spread-democracy/

5   "The Bush Doctrine," *Carnegie Endowment for International Peace*, October 7, 2002. https://carnegieendowment.org/2002/10/07/bush-doctrine-pub-1088

6   "Bush on the Freedom Agenda," *Voice of America*, September 4, 2006. https://editorials.voa.gov/a/a-41-2006-09-05-voa8-83105922/1479604.html

7   Oz Hassan, "Bush's Freedom Agenda: Ideology and the Democratization of the Middle East," *Democracy and Security*, Vol. 4, No. 3, September-December 2008, pp. 268-89. https://www.jstor.org/stable/48602627

8   "Freedom Agenda," *The White House: President George W. Bush*, December 10, 2008. https://georgewbush-whitehouse.archives.gov/infocus/freedomagenda/

9   Ivo H. Daalder and James M. Lindsay, "The Bush Revolution: The Remaking of America's Foreign Policy," *The Brookings Institution*, April 2003. https://www.brookings.edu/wp-content/uploads/2016/06/20030425.pdf

10 Max Boot, Samantha Power, and Adam Garfinkle, "The Bush Doctrine," *PBS*, July 11, 2002. https://www.pbs.org/thinktank/transcript1000.html

11 John Lewis Gaddis, *Surprise, Security, and the American Experience* (Cambridge: Harvard University Press, 2005), pp. 7-35.

12 Martin Kettle, "Cold Warriors Keep Control of Republican Defence Agenda," *The Guardian*, September 3, 2000. https://www.theguardian.com/world/2000/sep/04/uselections2000.usa4

13 "Remarks by the President to Students and Faculty at National Defense University," *The White House: President George W. Bush*, May 2001. https://georgewbush-whitehouse.archives.gov/news/releases/2001/05/20010501-10.html

14 Richard A. Clarke, *Against All Enemies: Inside America's War on Terror* (New York: Free Press, 2004), pp. 227-246.

15 Michael E. O'Hanlon, "Beyond Missile Defense: Countering Terrorism and Weapons of Mass Destruction," *Brookings Institute*, August 1, 2001. https://www.brookings.edu/articles/beyond-missile-defense-countering-terrorism-and-weapons-of-mass-destruction/

16 Joshua Daviscourt, "COTS and Space-Based Missile Defense," *Wild Blue Yonder*, June 28, 2021. https://www.airuniversity.af.edu/Wild-Blue-Yonder/Article-Display/Article/2673038/cots-and-space-based-missile-defense/#:~:text=Current%20monolithic%20architectures%20are%20unable,effective%20than%20traditional%20terrestrial%20interdiction.

17 "War and Peace in the Nuclear Age; Missile Experimental; Interview with Edward Teller, 1987," December 15, 1987, GBH Archives. http://openvault.wgbh.org/catalog/V_67DE2EAC03504AE4ADEB78A27C71A11D.

18 Paul Nemec, "The Missile Defense Systems of George W. Bush: A Critical Assessment," *Air University Press*, February 8, 2012. https://www.airuniversity.af.edu/AUPress/Book-Reviews/Display/Article/1192392/the-missile-defense-systems-of-george-w-bush-a-critical-assessment/

19 Paul Gallis, "The NATO Summit at Bucharest, 2008," *Congressional Research Service*, 5 May 2008. https://sgp.fas.org/crs/row/RS22847.pdf

20 Adam Taylor, "That Time Ukraine Tried to Join NATO—and NATO Said No," *Washington Post*, September 4, 2014. https://www.washingtonpost.com/news/worldviews/wp/2014/09/04/that-time-ukraine-tried-to-join-nato-and-nato-said-no/

21 Sabrina Tavernise, "Why Russians Hate America. Again." The *New York Times*, September 12, 2015. https://www.nytimes.com/2015/09/13/sunday-review/why-russians-hate-america-again.html

22 Taras Kuzio, "The Orange Revolution," *Elections Today*, Vol. 12, No. 4, 2005, chrome-extension://efaidnbmnnnibpcajpcglclefindmkaj/https://ciaotest.cc.columbia.edu/olj/et/et_v12n4/et_v12n4_003.pdf

23 Amelia Gentleman, "Putin Dodges Ukraine Scandal," *The Guardian*, February 12, 2001. https://www.theguardian.com/world/2001/feb/12/worlddispatch.ameliagentleman

24 Roman Kupchinsky, "Ukraine: Mystery Behind Yuschenko's Poisoning Continues," *Radio Free Europe/Radio Liberty*, September 18, 2006. https://www.rferl.org/a/1071434.html

25 Spengler, "Americans Play Monopoly, Russians Play Chess," *Asia Times*, August 19, 2008. https://asiatimes.com/2008/08/americans-play-monopoly-russians-chess/

26 Miriam Borger and Adam Taylor, "Why Poison is the Weapon of Choice in Putin's Russia," *Washington Post*, August 21, 2020. https://www.washingtonpost.com/world/2020/08/21/why-poison-is-weapon-choice-putins-russia/

27 Luke Harding, "Alexander Litvinenko: The Man Who Solved His Own Death," *The Guardian*, January 19, 2016. https://www.theguardian.com/world/2016/jan/19/alexander-litvinenko-the-man-who-solved-his-own-murder

28 Bill Chappell, "2 Agents Carried Out Skirpal Poison Attack, U.K. Says; Arrest Warrants Issued," *NPR*, September 5, 2018. https://www.npr.org/2018/09/05/644782096/u-k-charges-2-russians-suspected-of-poison-attack-on-skripals

29 Kit Klarenberg, "FOI Raises Further Questions About Bellingcat Coordination with Western Intelligence," *The Gray Zone*, November 30, 2023. https://thegrayzone.com/2023/11/30/bellingcat-collusion-western-intelligence/

30 Spengler, "Americans Play Monopoly, Russians Play Chess," *Asia Times*, August 19, 2008. https://asiatimes.com/2008/08/americans-play-monopoly-russians-chess/

31 Vladimir Putin (@RussianEmbassy), "President #Putin: The so-called collective West does not need a strong and sovereign #Russia, and will not forgive us our independent policy and standing up," Twitter. March 23, 2022. https://twitter.com/RussianEmbassy/status/1506685581866278922?s=20&t=u7Znbe_87T7BLSJ_Qp9GIw

Chapter 7

1 John Bento, "Russia's Aggression is Really About Warm Water Ports: Guest Opinion," *The Oregonian*, March 17, 2014. https://www.oregonlive.com/opinion/2014/03/russias_aggression_is_really_a.html

2 Igor Zimin and Andrzej Grzybowski, "Peter the Great and Sexually Transmitted Diseases," *Clinics in Dermatology*, Volume 38, Issue 5, September-October 2020, pp. 598-603. https://doi.org/10.1016/j.clindermatol.2019.09.002

3 Anees Aref, "The 'Great Game': Fiction and Folly in World Empire," *Responsible Statecraft*, June 19, 2023. https://responsiblestatecraft.org/2023/06/19/the-great-game-fiction-and-folly-in-world-empire/

4 Peter Hopkirk, *The Great Game: The Struggle for Empire in Central Asia* (New York: Kodansha International, 1992), pp. 11-22.

5 Allan B. Magruder, "The Will of Peter the Great, and the Eastern Question," *The Atlantic*, July 1878. https://www.theatlantic.com/magazine/archive/1878/07/the-will-of-peter-the-great-and-the-eastern-question/631948/

6   "The Will of Peter the Great/Testament of Peter the Great," *Global Security*,
     March 8, 2012. https://www.globalsecurity.org/military/world/russia/czar-
     peter-i-will.htm

7   Tanvi Chauhan, "Why Are Warm Water Ports Important to Russian Security?"
     Journal of European, Middle Eastern, and African Affairs, Spring 2020. https://
     www.airuniversity.af.edu/Portals/10/JEMEAA/Journals/Volume-02_Is-
     sue-1/Chauhan.pdf

8   Mary Dejevsky, "Putin's Rationale for Syria," *World Today*, 74, no. 1, (2018), 44.
     https://www.chathamhouse.org/publications/the-world-today/2018-02/
     putins-rationale-syria

9   Simon Sebag Montefiore, *Potemkin: Catherine the Great's Imperial Partner* (New
     York: Vintage Books, 2005).

10   Kelly O'Neill, *Imperiia: A Spatial History of the Russian Empire*, "1783:
     The Founding of Sevastopol." https://scalar.fas.harvard.edu/imperi-
     ia/1783-the-founding-of-sevastopol#_ftnref2

11   Luke Harding, "Ukraine Extends Lease for Russia's Black Sea Fleet," *The
     Guardian*, April 21, 2010. https://www.theguardian.com/world/2010/
     apr/21/ukraine-black-sea-fleet-russia

Chapter 8

1   Tim Rosentiel, "Inside Obama's Sweeping Victory," *Pew Research Cen-
     ter*, November 5, 2008. https://www.pewresearch.org/2008/11/05/in-
     side-obamas-sweeping-victory/

2   Kenneth T. Walsh, "The 10 Youngest Presidents," *U.S. News*, December 3,
     2009. https://www.usnews.com/news/politics/slideshows/the-10-young-
     est-presidents

3   Roger Simon, "Obama Off and Running," *Politico*, February 7, 2007. https://
     www.politico.com/story/2007/02/obama-off-and-running-002687

4   Richard Greene, "Obama is America's Third Greatest Presidential Orator in
     the Modern Era," *Huffington Post*, May 25, 2011. https://www.huffpost.com/
     entry/obama-is-americas-3rd-gre_b_813868

5   Julie Bort, "'No Drama Obama' Shares His Tricks for Staying Cool Under
     Pressure," *Business Insider*, March 10, 2019. https://www.businessinsider.com/
     obama-shares-tricks-for-cool-under-pressure-2019-3

6   Jimmy Paul, "Column: Biden's Comments Favor GOP Charges of Obama's In-
     experience," *CBS News*, October 28, 2008. https://www.cbsnews.com/news/
     column-bidens-comments-favor-gop-charges-of-obamas-inexperience/

7   "Hoover Fellow Victor Davis Hanson On the Type of Men Who Become Savior Generals," *Hoover Institution*, August 6, 2013. 42:45. https://www.youtube.com/watch?v=4icIzVYyhpg

8   Chris McGreal and Luke Harding, "Barack Obama: Putin Has One Foot in the Past," *The Guardian*, July 2, 2009. https://www.theguardian.com/world/2009/jul/02/obama-putin-us-russia-relations

9   Mike Dorning, "Obama Saw Too Late Putin's Return Would Undermine Reset," *Bloomberg*, February 19, 2015. https://www.bloomberg.com/news/articles/2015-02-19/obama-putin?embedded-checkout=true

10 Robert Draper, "William Burns, a C.I.A. Spymaster with Unusual Powers," *New York Times*, May 9, 2023. https://www.nytimes.com/2023/05/09/us/politics/william-burns-cia-biden.html

11 "Putin and the Presidents," PBS. January 24, 2023. 52:47. https://www.youtube.com/watch?v=aJI8XTa_DII

12 Becky Little, "JFK Was Completely Unprepared for His Summit with Khrushchev," *History Channel*, October 12, 2023. https://www.history.com/news/kennedy-krushchev-vienna-summit-meeting-1961

13 Michael Brendan Dougherty, "Krauthammer: Biden Holds 'American Record for Wrong on Most Issues in Foreign Affairs Ever," *Business Insider*, April 27, 2012. https://www.businessinsider.com/krauthammer-biden-holds-american-record-for-wrong-on-the-most-issues-in-foreign-affairs-ever-2012-4

14 Carl Hulse, Jeremy W. Peters, and Michael D. Shear, "Obama is Seen as Frustrating His Own Party," The *New York Times*, August 18, 2014. https://www.nytimes.com/2014/08/19/us/aloof-obama-is-frustrating-his-own-party.html

15 Peter Weber, "Obama's 'Reset' with Russia: What Went Wrong?" *The Week*, January 8, 2015. https://theweek.com/articles/460485/obamas-reset-russia-what-went-wrong

16 Peter Baker, "U.S.-Russian Ties Still Fall Short of 'Reset' Goal," The *New York Times*, September 2, 2013. https://www.nytimes.com/2013/09/03/world/europe/us-russian-ties-still-fall-short-of-reset-goal.html?_r=0&pagewanted=all&

17 Marwan Bishara, "Reckless in Kiev: Neocons, Putin, and Ukraine," *Al Jazeera*, March 10, 2014. https://www.aljazeera.com/opinions/2014/3/10/reckless-in-kiev-neocons-putin-and-ukraine

18 Robert Coalson, "Obama and the Russians: Moving on to the 'Post-Reset'," *Radio Free Europe/Radio Liberty*, November 7, 2012. https://www.rferl.org/a/obama-russia-moving-on-post-reset-relations/24763754.html

19 Helene Cooper, Thomas Gibbons-Neff, Eric Schmitt, and Julian E. Barnes, "Ukraine War Casualties Near Half a Million, US Officials Say," The *New York Times*, August 18, 2023. https://www.nytimes.com/2023/08/18/us/politics/ ukraine-russia-war-casualties.html

Chapter 9

1 Interfax-Ukraine, "Poll: Yanukovych Most Trusted Politician in Ukraine," *Kyiv Post*, May 28, 2009. https://www.kyivpost.com/post/7911

2 Taras Kuzio, "Leaked Cables Show U.S. Was Wrong on Ukraine's Yanukovych," *Radio Free Europe/Radio Liberty*, March 31, 2011. https://www.rferl.org/a/ commentary_us_was_wrong_on_ukraine_yanukovych/3542980.html

3 Daisy Sindelar, "Ukraine: Kyiv Poised Between Russia and the West?" *Radio Free Europe/Radio Liberty*, March 24, 2006. https://www.rferl.org/a/1067059. html

4 Konstantin Skorkin, "Ukraine's Oligarchs are a Dying Breed. The Country Will Never Be the Same," *Carnegie Endowment for International Peace*, September 14, 2022. https://carnegieendowment.org/politika/87914#:~:text=all%20 be%20positive.-,It%27s%20true%20that%20Ukraine%27s%20oligarchs%20 corrupted%20the%20Ukrainian%20state%20and,as%20effectively%20 as%20civil%20society.

5 Ogla Shumylo-Tapiola, "Viktor Yanukovych: A Man of the Oligarchs," *Carnegie Endowment for International Peace*, March 10, 2011. https://carnegieeurope. eu/2011/03/10/viktor-yanukovych-man-of-oligarchs-pub-42942

6 Taras Kuzio, "Yanukovych and Oligarchs: A Short or Long-Term Relationship?" Jamestown Foundation, Eurasia Daily Monitor: Vol. 7, Issue 203, November 9, 2010. https://www.refworld.org/docid/4cdba2132.html

7 Branko Marcetic, "A US-Backed, Far Right-Led Revolution in Ukraine Helped Bring Us to the Brink of War," *Jacobin*, July 2, 2022. https://jacobin. com/2022/02/maidan-protests-neo-nazis-russia-nato-crimea

8 Brandon J. Weichert, "European Energy Politics, Nationalism, and Russia," *The Weichert Report*, May 30, 2018. https://theweichertreport.wordpress. com/2018/05/30/european-energy-politics-nationalism-and-russia/

9 "Bush: 'You Are Either With Us, Or With the Terrorists," *Voice of America*, October 27, 2009. https://www.voanews.com/a/a-13-a-2001-09-21-14- bush-66411197/549664.html

10 Alex Duval Smith, "Is Trade, Not Aid, the Answer for Africa?" *The Guardian*, May 25, 2009. https://www.theguardian.com/business/2009/may/25/afri- ca-entrepreneurs-charity

11 "Top U.S. Official Visits Protesters in Kiev as Obama admin. Ups Pressure on Ukraine president Yanukovych," *CBS* News, December 11, 2013. https://www.cbsnews.com/news/us-victoria-nuland-wades-into-ukraine-turmoil-over-yanukovich/

12 Re Post, "Марионетки Майдана," *YouTube*, February 4, 2014. https://www.youtube.com/watch?v=MSxaa-67yGM#t=89

13 "Ukraine Crisis: Transcript of Leaked Nuland-Pratt Call," *BBC*, February 7, 2014. https://www.bbc.com/news/world-europe-26079957

14 Susan Ormiston, "Remembering the 2014 Ukraine Revolution, which Set the Stage for the 2022 Russian Invasion," CBC, February 23, 2023. https://www.cbc.ca/news/ukraine-2014-euromaidan-1.6756384

Chapter 10

1 Harriet Salem, Shaun Walker, and Oksana Grytsenko, "Russia Puts Military on High Alert as Crimea Protests Leave One Man Dead," *The Guardian*, February 26, 2014. https://www.theguardian.com/world/2014/feb/26/ukraine-new-leader-disbands-riot-police-crimea-separatism

2 Bill Chappel and L. Carol Ritchie, "Crimea Overwhelmingly Supports Split from Ukraine to Join Russia," NPR, March 16, 2014. https://www.npr.org/sections/thetwo-way/2014/03/16/290525623/crimeans-vote-on-splitting-from-ukraine-to-join-russia

3 Max Fisher, "Everything You Need to Know About the 2014 Ukraine Crisis," *Vox*, 3 September 2014. https://www.vox.com/2014/9/3/18088560/ukraine-everything-you-need-to-know

4 Paul Sonne, Margaret Coker, and Alexander Kolandyr, "After Flight 17 Crash, Debris and Heartbreak in Ukraine Villages," *Wall Street Journal*, July 25, 2014. https://www.wsj.com/articles/after-flight-17-crash-agony-debris-and-heartbreak-in-ukraine-villages-1406335532

5 Andrew Cramer and Michael R. Gordon, "Ukraine Reports Russian Invasion on a New Front," *New York Times*, August 27, 2014. https://www.nytimes.com/2014/08/28/world/europe/ukraine-russia-novoazovsk-crimea.html

6 Tina Hildebrandt and Giovanni di Lorenzo, "Hatten Sie gedacht, ich komme mit Pferdeschwanz?" *Die Zeit*, December 7, 2022. https://www.zeit.de/2022/51/angela-merkel-russland-fluechtlingskrise-bundeskanzler/komplettansicht

7 "Ukraine-Russia Crisis: What is the Minsk Agreement," *Al Jazeera*, February 9, 2022. https://www.aljazeera.com/news/2022/2/9/what-is-the-minsk-agreement-and-why-is-it-relevant-now

8   Michael Kimmage and Bruno Lété, "Is the Minsk Process for Eastern Ukraine Dead or Deadlocked?" *German Marshall Fund*. https://www.gmfus.org/download/article/14875

9   Kurt Volker, "Don't Let Russia Fool You About the Minsk Agreements," *CEPA*, December 16, 2021. https://cepa.org/article/dont-let-russia-fool-you-about-the-minsk-agreements/

10   David R. Cameron, "Frustrated by Refusals to Give Russia Security Guarantees & Implement Minsk 2, Putin Recgonizes Pseudo-States in Donbas and Invades Ukraine," *Yale Macmillan Center*, February 24, 2022. https://macmillan.yale.edu/news/frustrated-refusals-give-russia-security-guarantees-implement-minsk-2-putin-recognizes-pseudo

11   Gabrielle Tétrault-Farber and Tom Balmforth, "Russia Demands NATO roll back from Eastern Europe and Stay Out of Ukraine," *Reuters*, December 17, 2021. https://www.reuters.com/world/russia-unveils-security-guarantees-says-western-response-not-encouraging-2021-12-17/#:~:text=Russia%20demands%20NATO%20roll%20back%20from%20East%20Europe%20and%20stay%20out%20of%20Ukraine,-By%20Gabrielle%20Tétrault&text=MOSCOW%2C%20Dec%2017%20(Reuters),to%20negotiate%20with%20othe%20West.

12   Hall Gardener, "Ukraine: A New Plan," *American Affairs Journal*, Summer 2017, Vol. 1, No. 2. https://americanaffairsjournal.org/2017/05/ukraine-new-plan/

13   Ibid.

14   Ibid.

15   George F. Kennan, "A Letter on Germany," *The New York Review*, December 3, 1998. https://www.nybooks.com/articles/1998/12/03/a-letter-on-germany/

16   RFE/RL's Ukrainian Service, "Switzerland Agrees to Zelenskiy's Request to Host Peace Summit," *Radio Free Europe/Radio Liberty*, January 25, 2024. https://www.rferl.org/a/ukraine-zelenskiy-switzerland-davos/32775285.html

17   Emerald Robinson and Brandon J. Weichert, "Zelensky Wants to Play Make a Deal with Putin," January 18, 2024, *Frank TV*, https://rumble.com/v47us1o-zelensky-wants-to-play-lets-make-a-deal-with-putin.html

Chapter 11

1   Callie Patteson, "Hillary Clinton Pushed Trump-Russia Theory at Center of Durham Case," *New York Post*, February 14, 2022. https://nypost.com/2022/02/14/hillary-clinton-pushed-trump-russia-theory-in-2016/

2   Jessica Taylor, "Clinton Says She was 'Right' About 'Vast Russia Con-
    spiracy'; Investigations Ongoing," NPR, June 1, 2017. https://www.npr.
    org/2017/06/01/530941011/clinton-says-she-was-right-about-vast-rus-
    sia-conspiracy-investigations-ongoing

3   Bob Fredericks, "Clintons Gear Up to Cash In On the Lecture Circuit," New
    York Post, October 8, 2018. https://nypost.com/2018/10/08/clintons-gear-
    up-to-cash-in-on-the-lecture-circuit/

4   Michael Lind, "The Debunked 'Russian Interference' Nonsense is Infantiliz-
    ing Liberals," Salon, January 26, 2020. https://www.salon.com/2020/01/26/
    the-debunked-russian-influence-nonsense-is-infantilizing-liberals/

5   Stephanie Condon, "Hillary Clinton: The vast, Right-wing Conspiracy is 'Even
    Better Funded Now,'" CBS News, February 3, 2016. https://www.cbsnews.
    com/news/hillary-clinton-the-vast-right-wing-conspiracy-is-even-better-
    funded-now/

6   Kelly Riddell, "Hillary Clinton Haunted by Efforts to 'Destroy' Bill Clinton
    Accusers," Washington Times, January 14, 2016. https://www.washingtontimes.
    com/news/2016/jan/14/hillary-clinton-haunted-by-efforts-to-destroy-bill/

7   Peter Baker and Juliet Eilperin, "Clinton Impeached: House Approves Articles
    Alleging Perjury, Obstruction," Washington Post, December 20, 1998. https://
    www.washingtonpost.com/politics/clinton-impeachment/clinton-im-
    peached-house-approves-articles-alleging-perjury-obstruction/

8   Jeffrey M. Jones, "Public Gives Clinton Best Odds of Being Elected President,"
    Gallup, November 1, 2007. https://news.gallup.com/poll/102481/public-
    gives-clinton-best-odds-being-elected-president.aspx

9   David Goldstein, "2 Clinton Supporters in '08 Reportedly Shared Obama
    'Birther' Story," McClatchy DC, September 16, 2016. https://www.mcclatchydc.
    com/news/politics-government/election/article102354777.html

10 Philip Bump, "Hillary Clinton's Campaign Was Crippled by Voters Who
    Stayed Home," Washington Post, November 9, 2016, https://www.washing-
    tonpost.com/news/the-fix/wp/2016/11/09/hillary-clintons-campaign-was-
    crippled-by-voters-who-stayed-home/

11 Blair Guild, "David Axelrod on Hillary Clinton: 'It Takes a Lot of Work to
    Lose to Donald Trump," CBS News, May 3, 2017. https://www.cbsnews.com/
    news/david-axelrod-to-hillary-clinton-it-takes-a-lot-of-work-to-lose-to-don-
    ald-trump/

12 Joyce Chen, "Hillary Recalls Encounter with 'Manspreading' Vladimir Putin,"
    Rolling Stone, September 20, 2017, https://www.rollingstone.com/tv-movies/
    tv-movie-news/hillary-clinton-recalls-encounter-with-manspreading-vladi-
    mir-putin-202893/

13 Frida Ghitis, "Why Putin Fears a Clinton Presidency," CNN, October 16, 2016. https://www.cnn.com/2016/10/15/opinions/putin-clinton-hate-affair-ghitis/index.html

14 Yvonne Wingett Sanchez, "Sen. John McCain's Role in Trump Dossier Intrigue Detailed in Deposition," *AZ Central*, March 18, 2019. https://www.azcentral.com/story/news/politics/arizona/2019/03/18/new-details-senator-john-mccain-role-trump-dossier-detailed-deposition-david-kramer/3205658002/

15 Caitlin Doornbos, "Durham Points to Clinton Crony Charles Dolan as Likely 'Pee Tape' Source from Notorious Steele Dossier Report," *New York Post*, May 16, 2023. https://nypost.com/2023/05/16/durham-points-to-clinton-crony-charles-dolan-as-likely-pee-tape-source-from-notorious-steele-dossier-report/

16 Glenn Greenwald, "Beyond Buzzfeed: The 10 Worst, Most Embarrassing U.S. Media Failures on the Trump-Russia Story," *The Intercept*, January 20, 2019, https://theintercept.com/2019/01/20/beyond-buzzfeed-the-10-worst-most-embarrassing-u-s-media-failures-on-the-trumprussia-story/

17 Carole E. Lee, Courtney Kube, and Kristen Welker, "Trump Tells Aides Not to Talk About Russia Policy Moves," NBC News, March 29, 2018. https://www.nbcnews.com/politics/donald-trump/trump-tells-aides-not-talk-publicly-about-russia-policy-moves-n861256

18 Ben Smith, "Hillary: Putin 'Doesn't Have a Soul,'" *Politico*, January 6, 2008. https://www.politico.com/blogs/ben-smith/2008/01/hillary-putin-doesnt-have-a-soul-005126

19 Michael Crowley and Julia Ioffe, "Why Putin Hates Hillary," *Politico*, July 25, 2016, https://www.politico.com/story/2016/07/clinton-putin-226153

20 Roland Dannreuther, "Why the Arab Spring Set Russia on the Road to Confrontation with the West," *LSE*, January 16, 2015. https://blogs.lse.ac.uk/europpblog/2015/01/16/why-the-arab-spring-set-russia-on-the-road-to-confrontation-with-the-west/

21 Kim Ghattas, "What a Decade-Old Conflict Tells Us About Putin," *The Atlantic*, March 6, 2022. https://www.theatlantic.com/international/archive/2022/03/libya-russia-ukraine-putin/626571/

22 Tom O'Connor, "West's Libya Bombing 10 Years Ago Drove Vladimir Putin to Middle East Showdown with U.S.," *Newsweek*, March 19, 2021. https://www.newsweek.com/west-libya-bombing-ten-years-ago-putin-showdown-mideast-1577266

23 Leslie Stahl and Hillary Clinton, "Clinton on Qaddafi: We Came, We Saw, He Died," *YouTube*, October 20, 2011, 0:11, https://www.youtube.com/watch?v=6DXDU48RHLU

24 Miriam Elder, "Vladimir Putin Accuses Hillary Clinton of Encouraging Russian Protests," *The Guardian,* December 8, 2011. https://www.theguardian.com/world/2011/dec/08/vladimir-putin-hillary-clinton-russia

25 David M. Herszenhorn and Ellen Barry, "Putin Contends Clinton Incited Unrest Over Vote," *New York Times,* December 8, 2011. https://www.nytimes.com/2011/12/09/world/europe/putin-accuses-clinton-of-instigating-russian-protests.html

26 A.S. Brychkov and G.A. Nikonorov, "Color Revolutions in Russia: Possibility and Reality," *Journal of the Academy of Military Science,* 3, 60, 2017, pp. 4-9. https://www.armyupress.army.mil/Portals/7/Hot%20Spots/Documents/Russia/Color-Revolutions-Brychkov-Nikonorov.pdf

27 Ibid.

28 Ibid.

29 Alvin Chang, "How Russian Hackers Stole Information from Democrats, in 3 Simple Diagrams," *Vox,* June 16, 2018. https://www.vox.com/policy-and-politics/2018/7/16/17575940/russian-election-hack-democrats-trump-putin-diagram

30 Eric Tucker and Nomaan Merchant, "Durham Report Takeaways: A 'Seriously Flawed' Russia Investigation and Its Lasting Impact on the FBI," Associated Press, May 16, 2023, https://apnews.com/article/durham-report-fbi-trump-clinton-2016-campaign-f3039e651eeb35a09091c363419e6766

31 Nicole Gaouette, "FBI's Comey: Republicans Also Hacked by Russia," CNN, January 10, 2017, https://www.cnn.com/2017/01/10/politics/comey-republicans-hacked-russia/index.html

32 Michael Crowley and Julia Ioffe, "Why Putin Hates Hillary," *Politico,* July 25, 2016, https://www.politico.com/story/2016/07/clinton-putin-226153.

33 "Mueller Finds No Collusion with Russia, Leaves Obstruction Question Open," *American Bar Association,* March 25, 2019. https://www.americanbar.org/news/abanews/aba-news-archives/2019/03/mueller-concludes-investigation/

Chapter 12

1 Taras Kuzio, "Ukrainian Kleptocrats and America's Real Life House of Cards: Corruption, Lobbyism, and the Rule of Law," *Communist and Post-Communist Studies,* 50, No.1, (2017), p. 29. https://www.jstor.org/stable/48609771.

2 Evelyn Cheng, "Who is Paul Manafort? A Brief Timeline of His Political Career," CNBC, October 30, 2017. https://www.cnbc.com/2017/10/30/who-is-paul-manafort-a-brief-timeline-of-his-political-career.html

3 Simon Shuster, "How Paul Manafort Helped Elect Russia's Man in Ukraine," *Time,* October 31, 2017. https://time.com/5003623/paul-manafort-mueller-indictment-ukraine-russia/

4 Miles Parks and Ryan Lucas, "Paul Manafort, Former Trump Campaign Chairman, Sentenced to Just Under 4 Years," March 7, 2019. https://www.npr.org/2019/03/07/701045248/paul-manafort-former-trump-campaign-chairman-sentenced-to-just-under-4-years

5 Eric Tucker, "US Says Russia was Given Trump Campaign Polling Data in 2016," Associated Press, April 16, 2021. https://apnews.com/article/don-ald-trump-paul-manafort-russia-campaigns-konstantin-kilimnik-d2fdefd-b37077e28eba135e21fce6ebf

6 Kenneth P. Vogel and David Stern, "Ukrainian Efforts to Sabotage Trump Backfire," *Politico,* January 11, 2017. https://www.politico.com/sto-ry/2017/01/ukraine-sabotage-trump-backfire-233446

7 Natasha Bertrand and Kyle Cheney, "'I'm on a Mission to Testify': Dem Ukraine Activist Eager for Impeachment Cameo," *Politico,* November 12, 2019. https://www.politico.com/news/2019/11/12/alexandra-chalupa-testi-fy-impeachment-069817

8 Kenneth P. Vogel and David Stern, "Ukrainian Efforts to Sabotage Trump Backfire," *Politico,* January 11, 2017. https://www.politico.com/sto-ry/2017/01/ukraine-sabotage-trump-backfire-233446

9 John Solomon, "Ukrainian Embassy Confirms DNC Contractor Solicited Trump Dirt in 2016," *The Hill,* May 2, 2019. https://thehill.com/opinion/white-house/441892-ukrainian-embassy-confirms-dnc-contractor-solicited-trump-dirt-in-2016/

10 Kenneth P. Vogel and David Stern, "Ukrainian Efforts to Sabotage Trump Backfire," *Politico,* January 11, 2017. https://www.politico.com/sto-ry/2017/01/ukraine-sabotage-trump-backfire-233446

11 Jeva Lange, "Hillary Clinton Also Got Foreign Help in the Election—From Ukraine," *The Week,* January 11, 2017. https://theweek.com/speedreads/672549/hillary-clinton-also-got-foreign-help-election--from-ukraine

12 Kenneth P. Vogel and David Stern, "Ukrainian Efforts to Sabotage Trump Backfire," *Politico,* January 11, 2017. https://www.politico.com/sto-ry/2017/01/ukraine-sabotage-trump-backfire-233446

13 Michael Sainato, "Ukraine Tried to Tip the Election in Clinton's Favor," *Observer,* January 12, 2017. https://observer.com/2017/01/ukraine-hillary-clin-ton-donald-trump-election/

14 Kenneth P. Vogel and David Stern, "Ukrainian Efforts to Sabotage Trump Backfire," *Politico*, January 11, 2017. https://www.politico.com/story/2017/01/ukraine-sabotage-trump-backfire-233446

15 "The Embassy of Ukraine to the United States Has Launched 'House of Ukraine,'" *Embassy of Ukraine in the United States of America*, June 9, 2016. https://usa.mfa.gov.ua/en/news/48302-v-posolystvi-ukrajini-v-ssha-vid-krivsya-dim-ukrajini

16 Kenneth P. Vogel and David Stern, "Ukrainian Efforts to Sabotage Trump Backfire," *Politico*, January 11, 2017. https://www.politico.com/story/2017/01/ukraine-sabotage-trump-backfire-233446

17 John Solomon, "Ukrainian Embassy Confirms DNC Contractor Solicited Trump Dirt in 2016," *The Hill*, May 2, 2019. https://thehill.com/opinion/white-house/441892-ukrainian-embassy-confirms-dnc-contractor-solicited-trump-dirt-in-2016/

18 David Stern, "Ukrainian MP Seeks Probe of Ukraine-Clinton Ties," *Politico*, August 16, 2017. https://www.politico.eu/article/ukraine-mp-derkach-seeks-probe-of-ukraine-hillary-clinton-ties/

Chapter 13

1 Brandon J. Weichert, "NATO Must Pay," *The American Spectator*, July 13, 2018. https://spectator.org/nato-must-pay/

2 Brandon J. Weichert, "Biden's Mission from God Taking NATO Straight to Hell," *Asia Times*, February 27, 2023. https://asiatimes.com/2023/02/bidens-mission-from-god-taking-nato-straight-to-hell/

3 Sophie Tatum, "Trump Seems to Question US Commitment to Defending All NATO Allies," CNN, July 18, 2018. https://www.cnn.com/2018/07/17/politics/trump-nato-fox/index.html

4 Susan B. Glasser and Peter Baker, "Inside the War Between Trump and His Generals," *New Yorker*, August 8, 2022. https://www.newyorker.com/magazine/2022/08/15/inside-the-war-between-trump-and-his-generals

5 Nahal Toosi, "Trump Demands Other NATO Members Pay Their Fair Share," *Politico*, February 28, 2017. https://www.politico.com/story/2017/02/donald-trump-congress-speech-nato-235543

6 "Funding NATO," *North Atlantic Treaty Organization*.https://www.nato.int/cps/en/natohq/topics_67655.htm#:~:text=The%202%25%20defence%20investment%20guideline,ensure%20the%20Alliance%27s%20military%20readiness.

7   "Facts and Figures on the European Union Economy," *European Union*. https://european-union.europa.eu/principles-countries-history/key-facts-and-figures/economy_en

8   Camille Grand, "Defence Spending: Sustaining the Effort in the Long-Term," *North Atlantic Treaty Organization*, July 3, 2023, https://www.nato.int/docu/review/articles/2023/07/03/defence-spending-sustaining-the-effort-in-the-long-term/index.html

9   Cassandra Vinograd, "Donald Trump Remarks on NATO Trigger Alarm Bells in Europe," NBC News, July 21, 2016, https://www.nbcnews.com/politics/2016-election/donald-trump-remarks-nato-trigger-alarm-bells-europe-n613911

10 George Allison, "German Military Short on Tanks and Combat Aircraft for NATO Mission," *UK Defence Journal*, February 19, 2018. https://ukdefence-journal.org.uk/german-military-short-tanks-combat-aircraft-nato-mission/

11 Kyle Mizokami, "Germany's Entire Submarine Fleet is Out of Commission," *Popular Mechanics*, December 21, 2017. https://www.popularme-chanics.com/military/navy-ships/a14480191/germanys-entire-subma-rine-fleet-is-out-of-commission/

12 George Allison, "Less Than a Third of German Military Assets are Operational, Says Report," *UK Defence Journal*, June 21, 2018. https://ukdefencejournal.org.uk/less-third-german-military-assets-operational-says-report/

13 Ken Chamberlain, "How Much Do NATO Members Spend on Defense?" *Navy Times*, March 10, 2018. https://www.navytimes.com/global/eu-rope/2018/03/10/how-much-do-nato-member-nations-spend-on-defense/

14 "Economic Key Facts: Germany," *KPMG*, January 8, 2024. https://kpmg.com/de/en/home/insights/overview/economic-key-facts-germany.ht-ml#:~:text=Germany%20is%20the%20fourth%20largest,the%20coun-try%27s%20gross%20domestic%20product.

15 Hans von der Burchard, "Germany to Put 2 Percent NATO Spending Pledge in Writing," *Politico EU*, March 16, 2023. https://www.politico.eu/article/olaf-schlz-germany-nato-jens-stoltenberg-commits-to-2-percent-de-fense-spending-under-security-strategy/

16 Holger Hansen, "Germany Walks Back Plan to Meet NATO Spending Target on Annual Basis," *Reuters*, August 16, 2023. https://www.reuters.com/world/europe/germany-walks-back-plan-meet-nato-spending-target-annual-ba-sis-2023-08-16/

17 "Defence Expenditures of NATO Countries (2014-2023)," *North Atlantic Treaty Organization*, July 7, 2023. https://www.nato.int/cps/en/natohq/news_216897.htm?selectedLocale=en

18 John A. Tirpak, "NATO Details Leap in Member Defense Spending Ahead of Summit," *Air & Space Forces Magazine*, July 8, 2023. https://www.airandspace-forces.com/nato-member-defense-spending-summit/

19 Zack Beauchamp, "Donald Trump Needs to Clarify His Position on NATO Before Something Scary Happens," *Vox*, November 10, 2016. https://www.vox.com/2016/7/21/12247074/donald-trump-nato-war

20 Jonathan Martin and Mark Landler, "Bob Corker Says Trump's Recklessness Threatens 'World War III,'" *New York Times*, October 8, 2017. https://www.nytimes.com/2017/10/08/us/politics/trump-corker.html

21 Adam Edelman, "Hillary Clinton 'Convinced' Trump Associates Colluded with Russia," *NBC News*, September 12, 2017. https://www.nbcnews.com/politics/hillary-clinton/hillary-clinton-convinced-trump-associates-colluded-russia-n800566

22 Loren Thompson, "Love Him or Hate Him, President Trump's Defense Legacy is Profound," *Forbes*, December 15, 2020. https://www.forbes.com/sites/lorenthompson/2020/12/15/love-him-or-hate-him-president-trumps-defense-legacy-is-profound/?sh=7dccbf1a795a

23 John Ainger, "NATO Members Ramp Up Defense Spending After Pressure from Trump," *Bloomberg*, March 16, 2021. https://www.bloomberg.com/news/articles/2021-03-16/nato-members-ramp-up-defense-spending-after-pressure-from-trump?embedded-checkout=true

24 Kit Heren, "'European Elites Have to Pitch In': Steve Bannon Says NATO has Become a 'US Protectorate, Not an Alliance,'" *LBC*, January 16, 2024. https://www.lbc.co.uk/news/steve-bannon-trump-nato-not-an-alliance/

25 "Resilience, Civil Preparedness, and Article 3," *North Atlantic Treaty Organization*, August 2, 2023. https://www.nato.int/cps/en/natohq/topics_132722.htm

26 Brandon J. Weichert, "Trump's Transactional Worldview is a Benefit," *American Greatness*, August 1, 2018. https://amgreatness.com/2018/08/01/trumps-transactional-worldview-is-a-benefit/

27 Gary Dorrien, *Imperial Designs: Neoconservatism and the New Pax Americana* (New York: Routledge, 2004), pp. 125-80.

28 Alan Greenblatt, "Frenemies Forever: Why Putin and Obama Can't Get Along," *NPR*, September 12, 2013. https://www.npr.org/2013/09/12/221774010/frenemies-forever-why-putin-and-obama-cant-get-along

29 Nicole Hemmer, "The 'Madman Theory' of Nuclear War Has Existed for Decades. Now, Trump is Playing the Madman," *Vox*, January 4, 2017. https://www.vox.com/the-big-idea/2017/1/4/14165670/madman-theory-nuclear-weapons-trump-nixon

30 Clarence Page, "Putin Tames Savage Trump by Feeding His Monster Ego," *Las Vegas Sun*, December 28, 2015. https://lasvegassun.com/news/2015/dec/28/putin-tames-savage-trump-by-feeding-his-monster-eg//

31 Stephanie Petit, "'Horrified' Ivanka Trump May Have Influenced Her Father's Decision to Bomb Syria, President's Son Eric Says," *People*, April 11, 2017. https://people.com/politics/ivanka-trump-influenced-decision-bomb-syria-eric-trump-says/

32 TOC, "2017: US Launched Tomahawks in Syria, but Russia Didn't Use the S-400 Defense," *BULGARIANMILITARY.COM*, April 9, 2021. https://bulgarianmilitary.com/2021/04/09/2017-us-launched-tomahawks-in-syria-but-russia-didnt-use-the-s-400-defense/

33 Joseph Trevithick, "It's Official, Russia and Syria Have Linked Their Air Defense Networks," *The Drive*, June 29, 2019. https://www.thedrive.com/the-war-zone/13836/its-official-russia-and-syria-have-linked-their-air-defense-networks

34 Thomas Gibbons-Neff, "How a 4-Hour Battle Between Russian Mercenaries and U.S. Commandos Unfolded in Syria," *New York Times*, May 24, 2018. https://www.nytimes.com/2018/05/24/world/middleeast/american-commandos-russian-mercenaries-syria.html

35 Justin Worland, "President Trump's Pick for Secretary of State Just Confirmed 'Hundreds' of Russians Were Killed in a U.S. Attack in Syria," *Time*, April 12, 2018. https://time.com/5237922/mike-pompeo-russia-confirmation/

36 Sean McFate, *The New Rules of War: Victory in the Age of Durable Disorder* (New York: William Murrow, 2019), pp. 132-33.

37 David Brennan, "'A Total F***k Up': Russian Mercenaries in Syria Lament U.S. Strike That Killed Dozens," *Newsweek*, February 23, 2018. https://www.newsweek.com/total-f-russian-mercenaries-syria-lament-us-strike-killed-dozens-818073

38 Bill O'Reilly and Donald J. Trump, "Bill O'Reilly Interviews President Donald Trump Before Super Bowl LI," *Fox Sports*, February 5, 2017. 09:50, https://www.youtube.com/watch?v=74DAI2hr9Kk

39 "Vladimir Putin's Interview with Le Figaro," *President of Russia*, May 31, 2017. http://www.en.kremlin.ru/events/president/news/54638

40 Sam Meredith, "Trump Meets Putin Behind Closed Doors After Scolding US Policy on Russia," CNBC, July 16, 2018. https://www.cnbc.com/2018/07/16/trump-putin-summit-us-president-arrives-in-helsinki-to-meet-russian-c.html

41 Louis Nelson, "With Putin By His Side, Trump Calls Mueller Probe a 'Disaster for Our Country,'" *Politico*, July 16, 2018. https://www.politico.com/story/2018/07/16/trump-putin-meeting-mueller-investigation-722685

42 "Trump Sides with Russia Against FBI at Helsinki Summit," BBC, July 16, 2018. https://www.bbc.com/news/world-europe-44852812

43 Veronica Stracqualursi, "DNC Chair Slams 'Distracting Donald' for Focusing on Server at Putin Press Conference," CNN, July 21, 2018. https://www.cnn.com/2018/07/21/politics/tom-perez-trump-dnc-servers-ozy-fest/index.html

44 Joesphine Wolff, "The FBI Relied on a Private Firm's Investigation of the DNC Hack—Which Makes the Agency Harder to Trust," *Slate*, May 9, 2017. https://slate.com/technology/2017/05/the-fbi-is-harder-to-trust-on-the-dnc-hack-because-it-relied-on-crowdstrikes-analysis.html

45 Aaron Maté, "Hidden Over Two Years: Dem Cyber-Firm's Sworn Testimony It Had No Proof of Russian Hack of DNC," *Real Clear Investigations*, May 13, 2020. https://www.realclearinvestigations.com/articles/2020/05/13/hidden_over_2_years_dem_cyber-firms_sworn_testimony_it_had_no_proof_of_russian_hack_of_dnc_123596.html

46 Jeremy Diamond, "NATO Summit: Trump Accuses Germany of Being a 'Captive of Russia,'" CNN, July 11, 2018. https://www.cnn.com/2018/07/11/politics/trump-germany-russia-captive-nato/index.html

47 Patrick Wintour, "Helsinki Summit: What Did Trump and Russia Agree?" *The Guardian*, July 17, 2018. https://www.theguardian.com/world/2018/jul/17/helsinki-summit-what-did-trump-and-putin-agree

Chapter 14

1 Courtney Subramanian, "Explainer: Biden, Allies Pushed Out Ukrainian Prosecutor Because He Didn't Pursue Corruption Cases," *USA Today*, November 15, 2019. https://www.usatoday.com/story/news/politics/2019/10/03/what-really-happened-when-biden-forced-out-ukraines-top-prosecutor/3785620002/

2 Brian Kilmeade and Viktor Shokin, "Viktor Shokin to Kilmeade: I Believe Biden and Hunter Were Bribed," *Fox News*, August 26, 2023. https://www.foxnews.com/video/6335654002112

3 Steve Nelson, "Biden $10M Bribe File Released: Burisma Chief Said He was 'Coerced' to Pay Joe, 'Stupid' Hunter in Bombshell Allegations," *New York Post*, August 9, 2023. https://nypost.com/2023/07/20/biden-bribe-file-released-burisma-chief-said-both-joe-and-hunter-involved/

4   Brandon J. Weichert, "The Joe Biden Corruption Disaster Has Finally Exploded," MSN, August 27, 2023. https://www.msn.com/en-us/news/politics/the-joe-biden-corruption-disaster-has-finally-exploded/ar-AA1fQdpH

5   Tucker Carlson and Tony Bobulinski, "Tony Bobulinski Reveals Details on Hunter Biden Business Dealings in Exclusive Interview with Tucker Carlson," Fox News, October 4, 2022. https://www.foxnews.com/video/6313250859112

6   Miranda Devine, "Hunter Biden's Biz Partner Called Joe Biden 'the Big Guy' in Panicked Message After Post's Laptop Story," New York Post, July 27, 2022. https://nypost.com/2022/07/27/hunter-bidens-biz-partner-called-joe-biden-the-big-guy-in-panic-over-laptop/

7   Cameron Cawthorne, "Hunter Biden's Texts, Emails Contradict Lawyer's Claim That He 'Did Not Share' Money from Businesses with Dad," Fox News, September 18, 2023. https://www.foxnews.com/politics/hunter-bidens-texts-emails-contradict-lawyers-claim-did-not-share-money-businesses-dad

8   Burisma Group, "Joseph Cofer Black: 'I Am Excited to Join Burisma's Board of Directors and to Focus on Strategic Development and Security Issues to Expand Burisma's Opportunities," Kyiv Post, February 15, 2017. https://www.kyivpost.com/post/7849

9   Vanessa Gera, "AP Interview: Ex-Polish President Defends Biden and Burisma," Associated Press, November 28, 2019. https://apnews.com/article/37424b8a0a994c1a935c5831643a84e3#

10 Bruce Golding, "Washington Post Joins New York Times in Finally Admitting Emails from Hunter Biden Laptop are Real," New York Post, March 30, 2022. https://nypost.com/2022/03/30/washington-post-admits-hunter-biden-laptop-is-real/

11 Miranda Devine, Laptop From Hell: Hunter Biden, Big Tech, and the Dirty Secrets the President Tried to Hide (New York: Liberatio Protocol, 2021), pp. ix-xiii

12 Natasha Bertrand, "Hunter Biden Story is Russian Disinfo, Dozens of Former Intel Officials Say," Politico, October 19, 2020. https://www.politico.com/news/2020/10/19/hunter-biden-story-russian-disinfo-430276

13 Brandon J. Weichert, "The Hunter Biden Laptop Is a Scandal Like No Other," 19FortyFive, May 31, 2023. https://www.19fortyfive.com/2023/05/the-hunter-biden-laptop-is-a-scandal-like-no-other/

14 Brandon J. Weichert, "The Hunter Biden Laptop 'Letter' Just Blew Up," 19FortyFive, May 18, 2023, https://www.19fortyfive.com/2023/05/the-hunter-biden-laptop-letter-scandal-just-blew-up/

15 James Moore, "Trump Would Have Easily Won a Second Term If It Weren't for the Coronavirus," *The Independent,* November 7, 2020. https://www.independent.co.uk/voices/trump-us-election-coronavirus-second-term-b1667035.html

16 Emma Jo-Morris, "Ukraine Says U.S. Money Not Going to Ukraine, 'Benefiting American Interests,'" *Breitbart,* January 29, 2024. https://www.breitbart.com/politics/2024/01/29/ukraine-says-u-s-money-not-going-ukraine-benefiting-american-interests/

17 Emma Myroniuk, "Investigation: Poroshenko's Administration Conceals $600,000 Payment to Lobby Firm That Employs Volker," *Kyiv Post,* November 8, 2019. https://www.kyivpost.com/post/10754

18 Brandon J. Weichert, "Biden Came to Make a Mess and Eat Ice Cream," *American Greatness,* February 16, 2022. https://amgreatness.com/2022/02/16/biden-came-to-make-a-mess-and-eat-ice-cream/

19 Ken Dilanian, "Former CIA Director: We Worried Arming Ukraine Would Hand Technology to Russian Spies," NBC News, November 22, 2019, https://www.nbcnews.com/politics/national-security/former-cia-director-we-worried-arming-ukraine-would-hand-technology-n1089926

20 Paul Sperry, "The Beltway's Whistleblower Furor Obsesses Over One Name," *Real Clear Investigations,* October 30, 2019. https://www.realclearinvestigations.com/articles/2019/10/30/whistleblower_exposed_close_to_biden_brennan_dnc_oppo_researcher_120996.html

21 Kerry Picket, "'Bro-Like': Schiff Aide was White House Friend of Alleged Whistleblower Eric Ciaramella," *Washington Examiner,* November 19, 2019. https://www.washingtonexaminer.com/news/628108/bro-like-schiff-aide-was-white-house-friend-of-alleged-whistleblower-eric-ciaramella/

22 Brandon J. Weichert, "A Deep Cleansing of the Deep State," *American Spectator,* October 2, 2019. https://spectator.org/a-deep-cleansing-of-the-deep-state-is-coming/

23 Madeline Osburn, "Anti-Trump 'Whistleblower' Worked with DNC Operative Who Sought Dirt on Trump from Ukrainian Officials," *The Federalist,* October 30, 2019. https://thefederalist.com/2019/10/30/anti-trump-whistleblower-worked-with-dnc-operative-who-sought-dirt-on-trump-from-ukrainian-officials/

24 "Judicial Watch: White House Visitor Logs Detail Meetings of Eric Ciaramella," *Judicial Watch,* November 8, 2019. https://www.judicialwatch.org/judicial-watch-white-house-visitor-logs-detail-meetings-of-eric-ciaramella/

25 Greg Myre, "Who is Lt. Col. Alexander Vindman," NPR, October 29, 2019. https://www.npr.org/2019/10/29/774507048/who-is-lt-col-alexander-vindman

26 Ibid.

27 Orion Rummler, "Alexander Vindman Calls Trump a 'Useful Idiot' for Putin," *Axios*, September 14, 2020, https://www.axios.com/2020/09/14/vind-man-trump-russia-putin

Chapter 15

1   Hans Nichols, "Biden's Hardline Russia Reset," *Axios*, September 18, 2020. https://www.axios.com/2020/09/18/biden-russia-policy-putin

2   Brandon J. Weichert, "End of the Line for Hunter Biden," *MSN*, May 30, 2023. https://www.msn.com/en-us/news/politics/the-end-of-the-line-for-hunter-biden/ar-AA188VQK

3   "Did Hunter Biden Receive $3.5 Million from the Former Mayor of Moscow's Wife?" CNN. https://www.cnn.com/factsfirst/politics/factcheck_e879bcfe-4b2a-4b4a-a823-8c6d512c4e5e

4   "Comer Releases Third Bank Memo Detailing Payments to the Bidens from Russia, Kazakshstan, and Ukraine," *House Committee on Oversight and Account-ability*, August 9, 2023. https://oversight.house.gov/release/comer-releases-third-bank-memo-detailing-payments-to-the-bidens-from-russia-kazakh-stan-and-ukraine%EF%BF%BC/

5   Brandon J. Weichert, "Russia Becomes an Asian Nation," *Asia Times*, April 25, 2022. https://asiatimes.com/2022/04/russia-becomes-an-asian-nation/

6   Shannon Tiezzi, "China, Russia Recommit to Close Partnership in the Shad-ow of the Ukraine War," *The Diplomat*, March 22, 2023. https://thediplomat.com/2023/03/china-russia-recommit-to-close-partnership-in-the-shadow-of-ukraine-war/

7   "Xi Hails 'Deepening Trust' Between China and Russia as He Meets Putin," *Al Jazeera*, October 18, 2023. https://www.aljazeera.com/news/2023/10/18/xi-hails-deepening-trust-between-china-and-russia-as-he-meets-putin

8   "China Stands Firm in Support of Russia on Ukraine Issue Despite US Pres-sure," *TASS*, January 23, 2024. https://tass.com/world/1739709

9   Bill Gertz, "China Linking with Russia, Iran and North Korea Poses Danger-ous Threat to U.S., Former Leaders Warn," *Washington Times*, January 30, 2024. https://www.washingtontimes.com/news/2024/jan/30/china-linking-with-russia-iran-and-north-korea-pos/

10 Peter Dizikes, "Foreign Policy Scholars Examine the China-Russia Relationship," *MIT News*, November 17, 2023. https://news.mit.edu/2023/for-
eign-policy-scholars-examine-china-russia-relationship-1117

11 Brandon J. Weichert, "A China-Russia Alliance is Neither Permanent nor
Strong," *The Weichert Report*, January 30, 2017. https://theweichertreport.
wordpress.com/2017/01/30/a-china-russia-alliance-is-neither-permanent-
nor-strong/

12 Jacob W. Kipp, "Vostok 2010 and the Very Curious Hypothetical Opponent,"
Eurasia Daily Monitor, Vol. 7, Issue 133, July 12, 2010. https://jamestown.org/
program/vostok-2010-and-the-very-curious-hypothetical-opponent/

13 Brandon J. Weichert, "The Eurasian Steel Trap is Closing," *Real Clear World*,
September 7, 2021.https://www.realclearworld.com/articles/2021/09/07/
the_eurasian_steel_trap_is_closing_793416.html

14 Nahal Toosi, "Biden Disliked Putin Before It was Cool," *Politico*, June 9, 2021.
https://www.politico.com/news/2021/06/09/biden-russia-putin-love-sto-
ry-492195

15 Vladimir Soldatkin and Steve Holland, "Far Apart at First Summit, Biden
and Putin Agree to Steps on Cybersecurity, Arms Control," *Reuters*, June 16,
2021. https://www.reuters.com/world/wide-disagreements-low-expecta-
tions-biden-putin-meet-2021-06-15/

16 Mykola Bielieskov, "The Russian and Ukrainian Spring 2021 War Scare," *CSIS*,
September 21, 2021. https://www.csis.org/analysis/russian-and-ukrainian-
spring-2021-war-scare

17 Paul Adams, "Classified Ministry of Defence Documents Found at Bus Stop,"
BBC, June 27, 2021, https://www.bbc.com/news/uk-57624942

18 Stephen Bryen, "The Failed Biden-Putin Summit and Fears of War," *Asia Times*,
July 2, 2021. https://asiatimes.com/2021/07/the-failed-biden-putin-sum-
mit-and-fears-of-war/

19 Mallory Shelbourne, "U.S., Ukraine Begin Sea Breeze 2021 Exercise
with 30 Other Countries," *USNI News*, June 28, 2021. https://news.usni.
org/2021/06/28/u-s-ukraine-begin-sea-breeze-2021-exercise-with-30-oth-
er-countries

20 Stephen Bryen, "The Failed Biden-Putin Summit and Fears of War," *Asia Times*,
July 2, 2021. https://asiatimes.com/2021/07/the-failed-biden-putin-sum-
mit-and-fears-of-war/

21 Brett V. Benson and Bradley C. Smith, "NATO's Membership Rules Invite Conflict—and Benefit Putin," *Washington Post*, February 24, 2022.
https://www.washingtonpost.com/outlook/2022/02/22/natos-member-
ship-rules-invite-conflict-benefit-putin/

22 "Joint Statement on the U.S.-Ukraine Strategic Partnership," *The White House*, September 1, 2021. https://www.whitehouse.gov/briefing-room/statements-releases/2021/09/01/joint-statement-on-the-u-s-ukraine-strategic-partnership/

23 *Washington Post*, "Biden: 'Russia Will Be Held Accountable' If It Invades Ukraine," YouTube, January 19, 2022. https://www.youtube.com/watch?v=7CoqHmKshb4

24 Dakota Wood, "Joe Biden's 'Minor Incursion' Russia Remark: History Proves It was a Mistake," *Heritage Foundation*, January 26, 2022. https://www.heritage.org/global-politics/commentary/joe-bidens-minor-incursion-russia-remark-history-proves-it-was-mistake

Chapter 16

1 Tom Norton, "The Year Putin Didn't Die," *Newsweek*, February 24, 2023. https://www.newsweek.com/putin-health-cancer-parkinsons-rumors-1783665.

2 Olena Harmash, "Ukrainian Refugees: How Will the Economy Recover with a Diminished Population?" *Reuters*, July 7, 2023. https://www.reuters.com/world/europe/however-war-ends-ukraines-diminished-population-will-hit-economy-years-2023-07-07/.

3 "Russia Claims Capture of Avdiivka After Ukraine Withdraws from Key City," *Al Jazeera*, February 17, 2024. https://www.aljazeera.com/news/2024/2/17/ukraine-troops-withdraw-from-frontline-city-of-avdiivka-army-chief-says.

4 Branko Marcetic, "Did the West Deliberately Prolong the Ukraine War?" *Responsible Statecraft*, December 4,2023. https://responsiblestatecraft.org/ukraine-russia-talks/.

5 James Marson and Oksana Grytsenko, "Ukraine's War Effort is Stuck. This Heroic Battlefield Failure Shows Why," *Wall Street Journal*, January 10, 2024. https://www.wsj.com/world/europe/ukraine-russia-war-counteroffensive-5b309595.

6 Charu Sudan Kasturi, "Food Security: One Area Where Putin's Plans Are Bearing Fruit," *G Zero*, April 19, 2022. https://www.gzeromedia.com/climate/food-security-one-area-where-putins-plans-are-bearing-fruit.

7 Anne E. Krueger, "Why the Russia Sanctions are Failing," *Project Syndicate*, January 18, 2024. https://www.project-syndicate.org/commentary/how-russia-circumvented-western-sanctions-by-anne-o-krueger-2024-01.

8   Dan De Luce, "China Helps Russia Evade Sanctions and Likely Most Supplies Tech Used in Ukraine, U.S. Report Says," NBC News, July 27, 2023. https://www.nbcnews.com/news/investigations/china-helps-russia-evade-sanctions-tech-used-ukraine-war-rcna96693.

9   Huileng Tan, "How Russia Has Avoided Bankrupting Itself After 2 Years of Waging War in Ukraine," *Business Insider*, February 18, 2024. https://www.businessinsider.com/russia-economy-how-moscow-pays-war-economy-afloat-sanctions-ukraine-2024-2.

10 Emerald Robinson and Brandon J. Weichert, "Is Zelensky About to Be Overthrown?" *The Absolute Truth with Emerald Robinson*, February 1, 2024, *Rumble*, 40:58-49:00, https://rumble.com/v4as3ai-the-absolute-truth-with-emerald-robinson-february-1-2024.html

11 Stephen Bryen, "Regime Change is Coming – To Kiev," *Asia Times*, February 20, 2024. https://asiatimes.com/2024/02/regime-change-is-coming-to-kiev/.

12 Holly Ellyatt, "Russia is Risking All-Out War to Prevent Ukraine from Joining NATO," CNBC, January 12, 2022. https://www.cnbc.com/2022/01/12/russia-is-risking-all-out-war-to-prevent-ukraine-from-joining-nato.html.

13 David Meyer, "Trump Has Long Wanted to Kill a Russia-Germany Natural Gas Pipeline. Navalny's Poisoning Could Do It for Him," *Fortune*, September 8, 2020. https://fortune.com/2020/09/08/trump-pipeline-russia-germany-natural-gas-merkel-navalny-poisoned-nord-stream-2/

14 Thane Gustafson, *The Bridge: Natural Gas in a Redivided Europe* (Cambridge, MA: Harvard University Press, 2020), pp. 215-22.

15 Anthony Faiola, "Germany Got Rich on Exports and Cheap Russian Gas. Now, It's in Trouble," *Washington Post*, October 14, 2022. https://www.washingtonpost.com/world/2022/10/14/germany-economy-recession-energy-exports/.

16 Statista Research Department, "Arms Imports Into Ukraine from 2018-2022, By Country," *Statista*. https://www.statista.com/statistics/1294196/ukraine-arms-imports-by-country/#:~:text=The%20United%20States%20was%20the,of%20arms%20imports%20into%20Ukraine.

17 Rob Picheta, "Germany is 'Wasting Time' on Sending Tanks to Ukraine, Its Allies Say. Here's Why the Leopard 2 is So Important," CNN, January 23, 2023. https://www.cnn.com/2023/01/20/europe/germany-leopard-2-tank-ukraine-explainer-intl/index.html.

18 Adam Durbin, "Ukraine War: Germany Sends Much-Awaited Leopard Tanks," BBC, March 28, 2023. https://www.bbc.com/news/world-europe-65095126#.

19 Michael Holden, "Britain to Send 14 of Its Main Battle Tanks to Ukraine," *Reuters*, January 15, 2023. https://www.reuters.com/world/europe/uk-has-ambition-send-tanks-ukraine-pm-sunak-tells-zelenskiy-2023-01-14/.

20 "'Thin-Armored' French Tanks Impractical for Attacks, Ukraine Commander," *France 24*, February 7, 2023. https://www.france24.com/en/live-news/20230702-thin-armoured-french-tanks-impractical-for-attacks-says-ukraine-commander.

21 Yasmeen Serhan, "Why Germany Agonized Over Sending Tanks to Ukraine," *Time*, January 24, 2023. https://time.com/6249710/germany-leopard-2-tanks-ukraine/.

22 "Former German Chancellor Gerhard Schroeder Becomes Chairman of Russian State-Controlled Nord Stream Pipeline Company Directly After Leaving Office," *Alliance for Defending Democracy*, November 2005. https://securingdemocracy.gmfus.org/incident/former-german-chancellor-gerhard-schra¶der-becomes-chairman-of-russian-state-controlled-nord-stream-pipeline-company-directly-after-leaving-office/.

23 Andrea Shalal, Andreas Rinke, and Jeff Mason, "Biden Pledges End to Nord Stream 2 if Russia Invades Ukraine," Reuters, February 8, 2022. https://www.reuters.com/world/biden-germanys-scholz-stress-unified-front-against-any-russian-aggression-toward-2022-02-07/.

24 Zack Colman and Ben Lefebvre, "'Everything is Pointing to Russia': U.S., EU Officials On Edge Over Pipeline Explosions," *Politico*, September 28, 2022. https://www.politico.com/news/2022/09/28/nord-stream-pipeline-explosions-eu-00059262.

25 Antony J. Blinken, "Secretary Antony J. Blinken and Canadian Foreign Minister Mélanie Joly at a Joint Press Availability," *U.S. Department of State*, September 30, 2022. https://www.state.gov/secretary-antony-j-blinken-and-canadian-foreign-minister-melanie-joly-at-a-joint-press-availability/#:~:text=It's%20a%20tremendous,years%20to%20come.

26 Forbes Breaking News, "JUST IN: Ted Cruz Confronts Top Biden Official Over Nord Stream 2 Decision," YouTube, January 26, 2023, 0:57-1:07. https://www.youtube.com/watch?v=VJdbMj8fStA.

27 Al Maydeen English, "Polish EU Lawmaker Deletes 'Thank You, USA' Over Nord Stream Tweet," *Al Maydeen*, September 29, 2022. https://english.almayadeen.net/news/politics/polish-eu-lawmaker-deletes-thank-you-usa-over-nord-stream-tw.

28 Johan Ahlander and Anna Ringstrom, "Sweden Ends Nord Stream Sabotage Probe, Hands Evidence to Germany," Reuters, February 7, 2024. https://www.reuters.com/world/europe/sweden-ends-investigation-into-nord-stream-pipeline-blasts-2024-02-07/#:~:text=The%20multi%2Dbillion%20dollar%20Nord,of%20methane%20into%20the%20air.

29 Gavin Maguire, "U.S. LNG Exports Both a Lifeline and a Drain for Europe in 2023," Reuters, December 21, 2022. https://www.reuters.com/business/energy/us-lng-exports-both-lifeline-drain-europe-2023-maguire-2022-12-20/

30 Tia Goldenberg, "Former Israeli PM: Putin Promised Not to Kill Zelenskyy," Associated Press, February 5, 2023. https://apnews.com/article/russia-ukraine-putin-politics-government-4ea6bd21cb2ac96dae731ce0e8ac2f22.

31 Nebi Qena and Yuras Karmanau, "Russia Says It Will Reduce Military Operations Near Kyiv as Peace Talks Continue," PBS *News Hour,* March 29, 2022. https://www.pbs.org/newshour/world/russia-says-it-will-reduce-military-operations-near-kyiv-as-peace-talks-continue.

32 Brandon J. Weichert, "Has America Almost Depleted Its Supply of Essential Weapons for Ukraine?" *The Washington Times,* May 3, 2022. https://www.washingtontimes.com/news/2022/may/3/has-america-almost-depleted-its-supply-of-essentia/

33 Brandon J. Weichert, "Breaking Russia? More Like Breaking Ourselves," *Asia Times,* February 11, 2023. https://asiatimes.com/2023/02/breaking-russia-more-like-breaking-ourselves/

34 Jim Heintz, "Russian Mercenary Boss Yevgeny Prigozhin Challenged the Kremlin in a Brief Mutiny," Associated Press, August 23, 2023. https://apnews.com/article/yevgeny-prigozhin-wagner-group-russia-crash-9982e25668efbf2863a4793fde65c03f

35 Lolita C. Baldor and Tara Copp, "Pentagon Accounting Error Provides Extra $6.2 Billion for Ukraine Military Aid," Associated Press, June 20, 2023. https://apnews.com/article/ukraine-russia-war-weapons-surplus-funding-72eeb6119439146f1939d5b1973a44ef.

36 Ellen Nakashima and Shane Harris, "U.S. Spies Learned in Mid-June was Planning Armed Action in Russia," *Washington Post,* June 24, 2023. https://www.washingtonpost.com/national-security/2023/06/24/us-intelligence-prigozhin-putin/.

37 Nic Robertson, "Why Prigozhin's Short-Lived Russian Rebellion Failed," CNN, June 27, 2023. https://www.cnn.com/2023/06/26/europe/prigozhin-putin-wagner-rebellion-analysis-intl/index.html.

38 Andrew Roth, "Prigozhin Calls Off March on Moscow to Avert 'Russian Bloodshed,'" *The Guardian*, June 24, 2023. https://www.theguardian.com/world/2023/jun/24/wagner-troops-may-reach-moscow-by-evening-as-kremlin-hurries-to-intercept.

39 Reuters, "Russia's Prigozhin Posts First Video Since Mutiny, Hints He is In Africa," Associated Press, August 22, 2023. https://www.reuters.com/world/africa/russias-prigozhin-posts-first-video-since-mutiny-hints-hes-africa-2023-08-21/.

40 Gabrielle Gavin, Douglas Busvine, Nahal Toosi, Eva Hartog, Lili Bayer, and Zoya Sheftolivch, "Wagner Boss Prigozhin Killed in Jet Crash in Russia," *Politico EU*, August 23, 2023. https://www.politico.eu/article/jet-believed-to-be-carrying-wagner-boss-prigozhin-crashes-in-russia/.

41 Danielle Ryan, "Dictator vs. Democrat? Not Quite: Russian Opposition Leader Alexey Navalny is No Progressive Hero," *Salon*, April 2, 2017. https://www.salon.com/2017/04/02/dictator-vs-democrat-not-quite-russian-opposition-leader-alexey-navalny-is-no-progressive-hero/

42 Bradley Devlin, "The Distressing Death of Alexei Navalny," *The American Conservative*, February 16, 2024. https://www.theamericanconservative.com/the-distressing-death-of-alexei-navalny/.

Chapter 17

1 Stephen Bryen, "Zaluzhny Out, Oleksandr Syrsky In, to What Purpose?" *Asia Times*, February 9. 2024. https://asiatimes.com/2024/02/zaluzhny-out-oleksandr-syrsky-in-to-what-purpose/

2 "Senior US Official in Ukraine Confident Congress Will Back Aid Package," Reuters, January 31, 2024. https://www.reuters.com/world/us/senior-us-official-ukraine-talks-amid-uncertainty-over-aid-2024-01-31/#:~:text=Nuland%20said%20she%20was%20leaving,nice%20surprises%20on%20the%20battlefield%22.

3 Mika Brzezinski and Chuck Schumer, "Sen. Schumer to Speaker Johnson: Do the Right Thing on the Border Bill," MSNBC, February 5, 2024. 0:51-0:59, https://www.youtube.com/watch?v=QFt6Rhccg6s

4 Steven Nelson, "Biden Tells US Troops They'll Be in Ukraine in War Gaffe," *New York Post*, March 25, 2022. https://nypost.com/2022/03/25/joe-biden-says-us-troops-will-be-in-ukraine-in-apparent-gaffe/

5 Christopher McCallion, "Russian Disintegration is a Dangerously Dumb Delusion," *The Hill*, February 3, 2023. https://thehill.com/opinion/national-security/3837672-russian-disintegration-is-a-dangerously-dumb-delusion/.

6   Stephen Bryen, "Biden's Emerging New Ukraine Policy," *Asia Times*, February 5, 2024. https://asiatimes.com/2024/02/bidens-emerging-new-ukraine-policy/

7   Susan Milligan, "Biden: Help Ukraine Now or Send Americans to Fight Russia with NATO Later," *U.S. News & World Report,* December 6, 2023. https://www.usnews.com/news/national-news/articles/2023-12-06/biden-help-ukraine-now-or-send-americans-to-fight-russia-with-nato-later

8   Euractiv Network, "Poland 'Key' in Western Weapons Supplies to Ukraine," *Euractiv,* March 1, 2022. https://www.euractiv.com/section/politics/news/poland-key-in-western-weapons-supplies-to-ukraine/

9   "The Ukrainian-Russian War: Which Countries are Fighting Side by Side with Ukraine?" *Visit Ukraine,* June 22, 2023. https://visitukraine.today/blog/2122/the-ukrainian-russian-war-which-countries-are-fighting-side-by-side-with-ukraine

10 Tim Lister, Tara John, Antonia Mortensen, Anna Chernova, Emmett Lyons, and Rhea Mogul, "World Leaders Hold Emergency Meeting as 'Russian-Made' Missile Kills Two in Poland," CNN, Nomber 16, 2022. https://www.cnn.com/2022/11/15/europe/poland-missile-rocket-nato-prze-wodow-ukraine-intl/index.html

11 Jon Henley, "Missile That Hit Poland Likely Came from Ukraine Defences, Say Warsaw and NATO," *The Guardian,* November 16, 2022. https://www.theguardian.com/world/2022/nov/16/poland-president-missile-strike-prob-ably-ukrainian-stray

12 Bogdan Kochubey, "Ukraine's Zelenskiy Blames Russian Missiles for Deadly Poland Explosion," Reuters, November 15, 2022. https://www.reuters.com/world/europe/ukraines-zelenskiy-says-russian-missiles-hit-poland-signif-icant-escalation-2022-11-15/#:~:text=Ukraine%27s%20Zelenskiy%20blames%20Russian%20missiles%20for%20deadly%20Poland%20explo-sion,-By%20Bogdan%20Kochubey&text=KYIV%2C%20Nov%2015%20(Reuters),significant%20escalation%22%20of%20the%20conflict.

13 Vanessa Gera, "Poland is Done Sending Arms to Ukraine, Polish Leaders Says as Trade Dispute Escalates," Associated Press, September 21, 2023. https://apnews.com/article/poland-ukraine-weapons-russia-war-trade-dispute-5e2e-7a194b5238b86c160f0f4848b4f3#

14 Vanessa Gera and Monika Scislowska, "Poland's New Prime Minister Vows to Press the West to Continue Helping Neighboring Ukraine," Associated Press, October 12, 2023. https://apnews.com/article/poland-new-govern-ment-tusk-d4c7cd71e983440b5a71e08236eaf4fc

15 Reuters, "Poland Says Russian Rocket Entered Its Airspace, Summons Diplomat," Reuters, December 29, 2023. https://www.reuters.com/world/europe/unidentified-object-entered-poland-direction-ukraine-says-polish-army-2023-12-29/

16 "Poland's New PM Promises to Push for Full Western Support of Ukraine," *Al Jazeera*, December 12, 2023. https://www.aljazeera.com/news/2023/12/12/polands-donald-tusk-says-hell-push-for-western-support-for-ukraine

17 Katie Bo Lillis, Jim Sciutto, Kristin Fisher, and Natasha Bertrand, "Exclusive: Russia Attempting to Develop Nuclear Space Weapon to Destroy Satellites with Massive Energy Wave, Sources Familiar with Intel Say," CNN, February 17, 2024. https://www.cnn.com/2024/02/16/politics/russia-nuclear-space-weapon-intelligence/index.html

18 Christian Davenport, Ellen Nakashima, Abigail Hauslohner, and Shane Harris, "With a Dire Warning, Concerns Rise About Conflict in Space with Russia," *Washington Post*, February 15, 2024. https://www.washingtonpost.com/technology/2024/02/15/space-weapons-russia-china-starlink/

19 Robert Hart, "Russia Rejects US Fears Over Russian Nuclear Weapons in Space as 'Malicious Fabrication,'" *Forbes*, February 15, 2024. https://www.forbes.com/sites/roberthart/2024/02/15/russia-rejects-us-fears-over-russian-nuclear-weapons-in-space-as-malicious-fabrication/?sh=450904e77ac3

20 William Noah Glucroft, "NATO: Why Russia Has a Problem with Its Eastward Expansion," *DW*, February 23, 2022. https://www.dw.com/en/nato-why-russia-has-a-problem-with-its-eastward-expansion/a-60891681

21 Sumantra Maitra, "Policy Brief: Pivoting the US Away from Europe to a Dormant NATO," *Center for Renewing America*, February 16, 2023. https://americarenewing.com/issues/policy-brief-pivoting-the-us-away-from-europe-to-a-dormant-nato/

INDEX